Displacements and Transformations in Caribbean Cultures

UNIVERSITY PRESS OF FLORIDA

Florida A&M University, Tallahassee
Florida Atlantic University, Boca Raton
Florida Gulf Coast University, Ft. Myers
Florida International University, Miami
Florida State University, Tallahassee
New College of Florida, Sarasota
University of Central Florida, Orlando
University of Florida, Gainesville
University of North Florida, Jacksonville
University of South Florida, Tampa
University of West Florida, Pensacola

Displacements and Transformations in Caribbean Cultures

EDITED BY

Lizabeth Paravisini-Gebert

AND

Ivette Romero-Cesareo

UNIVERSITY PRESS OF FLORIDA

Gainesville/Tallahassee/Tampa/Boca Raton/Pensacola

Orlando/Miami/Jacksonville/Ft. Myers/Sarasota

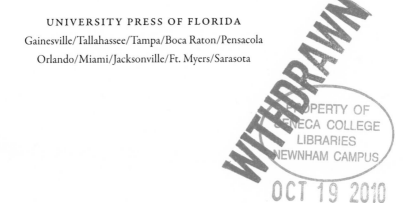

13 12 11 10 09 08   6 5 4 3 2 1

Library of Congress Cataloging-in-Publication Data
Displacements and transformations in Caribbean cultures/
edited by Lizabeth Paravisini-Gebert and Ivette Romero-Cesareo.
p. cm.
Includes bibliographical references and index.
ISBN 978-0-8130-3218-4 (alk. paper)
1. Caribbean Area--Civilization. 2. Caribbean Area--Relations--Foreign countries.
I. Paravisini-Gebert, Lizabeth. II. Romero-Cesareo, Ivette.
F2169.D57   2008
303.48'27299–dc22   2007044702

The University Press of Florida is the scholarly publishing agency for the State University System
of Florida, comprising Florida A&M University, Florida Atlantic University, Florida Gulf Coast
University, Florida International University, Florida State University, New College of Florida,
University of Central Florida, University of Florida, University of North Florida, University
of South Florida, and University of West Florida.

University Press of Florida
15 Northwest 15th Street
Gainesville, FL 32611–2079
http://www.upf.com

To Antonio Benítez Rojo,
in memoriam

Contents

Figures

Acknowledgments

My heartfelt thanks go to the scholars and artists who have so generously joined us in this project. Thanks are also due Bill Bollendorf of Galerie Macondo, Janet Feldman (and the Janet Feldman Collection at the Waterloo Center for the Arts in Iowa), historian Marcus Rediker, and Pebo Voss (curator of the Jonathan Demme collection of Haitian paintings) for their encouragement and assistance with securing images and permissions. The help of my research assistant, Christopher Freimuth, was invaluable throughout the several years involved in bringing this project to its conclusion. During one of those seemingly catastrophic computer crashes that too often plague scholars who don't always make back-up copies, the staff of Vassar's Computing and Information Services—particularly Lee Dinnebeil, Martin Sorensen, Tami Emerson, and most especially Marjorie Gluck—came to the rescue in their characteristic exemplary fashion. Vassar College's Research Committee awarded me a timely grant to help finalize research and secure rights to images, for which the members have my thanks. Finally my husband, Gordon, and our son, Gordon Jr., have been models of encouragement and patience. To them both, my love.

L. P.-G.

I want to thank the scholars and artists included in this collection for their interest and fruitful participation, especially the late Antonio Benítez Rojo, the traveler-intellectual who, while following the rhythms of a wandering circumnavigation, remained firmly anchored in our Caribbean archipelago.

I would like to convey my gratitude to Pebo Voss (curator of the Jonathan Demme Collection), Sarah H. Paulson (at the Ronald Feldman Fine Arts Gallery), José Roa (at the Galería Botello), and artists Teo Freytes, Antonio

Martorell, and María de Mater O'Neill for providing me with indispensable material and information. At Marist College, I am indebted to Artin Arslanian (dean of faculty and academic vice-president) and Thomas Wermuth (dean of the School of Liberal Arts) for securing the summer research grants and additional travel funds that facilitated my research trips for this project, and to Alexander Podmaniczky (director of the Digital Publications Center) for his invaluable technical assistance.

I am profoundly grateful to Mary Ann Gosser Esquilín for her constant encouragement and for allowing me the use of her Caribbean library/retreat, to Ian Anthony Bethell Bennett for graciously providing me with a home away from home during my many research expeditions, and to my coeditor, mentor, and *comadre*, Lizabeth Paravisini-Gebert, for her boundless enthusiasm for and joy of exploring new territories. To each of you, thanks for your friendship. My deepest appreciation goes to Al Desetta for being an island of strength and love. I send all my love to my son, Mario Sur Cesareo, the explorer par excellence, who will be mapping out future geographies.

I. R.-C.

Introduction

IVETTE ROMERO-CESAREO AND LIZABETH PARAVISINI-GEBERT

Insularity has always been a privileged and, by the same token, an ambiguous place,
the edge of every hospitality as well as every violence. Insularity [. . .] outlines a place
in which the edges [shores, sides, banks] do not share any terrestrial frontier, either
natural or artificial, with the other, such that this habitat, naturally protected on its
borders, also sees its body disarmed, open, othered on all its borderlines, given over
to everything that, on its shores, can happen [*arriver*] ("arrive," "happen,"
in the sense of coming as well as of the event).

Jacques Derrida, "Faxitexture"

My acquaintance with my mother in this house is from the schoolbooks stored
in boxes underneath. Worms have tunneled the pages, the covers are crossed with
mold—making the books appear ancient. She has left me to find her here, under this
house: I seek identity in a childish hand and obsolete geography.

Michelle Cliff, "Obsolete Geography"

Geography—literally "writing about the earth"—seeks to understand the
global stage where our lives unfold through the exploration and representation of space and location. Geographies, or the multiple discourses that
define our surroundings, are never wholly obsolete, but rather, through the
continual transformations they have suffered throughout the ages, have become palimpsests—multilayered texts affording an infinite number of readings leading to countless points of departure, trajectories, and sites of arrival.
Our conceptual texts—the cartography employed to map the Caribbean's
shifting sands, wandering mangroves, transnational multiethnic populations
and their cultural production—are oftentimes flawed or incomplete. Many
a struggle has been sparked by adherence to obsolete or faulty discourses,
documents, or maps.

The contours of the Caribbean—borne of geo-catastrophic upheaval, or oceanic violence, as Edward Kamau Brathwaite has recently reminded us (2005)—have changed throughout the centuries. Politically, Amerindian chiefdoms have given way to European colonies, which in turn have given way to nations of various political flavors, some of them remaining under the flags of European or North American nations and being classified by diverse and sometimes confusing nomenclatures: territories, protectorates, overseas departments, free-associated states, or commonwealths. The array of languages—by nature in a perpetual state of becoming—and the countless accents and timbres that may render communication from island to island difficult, have earned the Caribbean the reputation of being a tropical Babel. Inter-island travel itself has presented challenges through the centuries, dependent as it has often been on the mercantilist forces at play, the flow of labor in and out of the pan-Caribbean plantation, and the vagaries of the prevailing political situations. Movement from island to island has often been fraught with danger, especially when the traveling subjects—Taínos fleeing warfare, Caribs seeking shelter from encroaching plantations, slaves escaping the brutality of the sugar cane fields, revolutionaries forced into exile, boat people and *balseros* attempting to reach Florida—are caught in the crossfire of contending perceptions of national interests and political opinion.

After centuries of exploration and cross-discoveries, layers upon layers of transcultural encounters—indigenous cultures overlapping with African, European, North and Latin American, and Asian diasporas—and diverse economic and political routes, the Caribbean continues to present or invent itself as an arena of kaleidoscopic possibilities, regardless of whether or not the region's realistic potential for growth and development—political, economic, or cultural—can in fact do justice to the richness of the metaphors it engenders. No sooner has one thinker baptized the region with a seemingly fitting definition than a newer and more evocative term springs up to take its place in the sun. Myriad viewpoints project the Caribbean through multifaceted lenses: it has been described as a little Mediterranean Sea, a repeating island, the New Frontier, and it has elicited a confluence of categoric possibilities for pan-Caribbean expression such as negritude, creolization, *métissage* or *mestizaje,* and notions of hybridity, and for inserting the region in a wider framework of inquiry such as Joseph Roach's exploration of the circum-Atlantic as a busy intersection where "cultural transmission may be detoured, deflected, or displaced" (4). The terms themselves are amended, altered, and reconstructed in an attempt to capture a process of re-creation and restoration of boundaries, where territories, texts, and performances are continuously revised and reinterpreted. These amendments, alterations, and constructions sometimes connect only tangentially with the *real* Caribbean of eroding beaches, deteriorating infrastructures, or remittance-driven economies; at other times they serve to help us approach the elusive ideal of a region *meant* by its geography to be apprehended as a totality even though it is fractured by history and dispersed by language and discourse, its peoples barred from using its sea as the *mare nostrum* of free movement and exchange.

The dynamics of the constant shifting of the nomenclature and paradigms of study mirror the mutability of a region whose history is characterized by complex waves of flux and reflux, in and out of the unity prescribed by geography. As Antonio Benítez Rojo points out in *The Repeating Island*, the main impediments to any global study of the Caribbean are exactly those characteristics that scholars bring forward to define the area: "its fragmentation; its instability, its reciprocal isolation; its uprootedness; its cultural heterogeneity; its lack of historiography and historical continuity; its contingency and impermanence; its syncretism . . ." (1996, 1). There is in academic approaches to the Caribbean a recognized tension between the complexities of the specificities of local history, culture, and everyday life in the various islands that form the Caribbean region and the impulse to understand the region as a totality, to speak of the Caribbean as an entity and know precisely what we mean by the term. As *the Caribbean* develops as a field of study, the perceived need to speak regionally has often clashed against the specificities of local histories and cultures.

These tensions between notions of the global Caribbean and the complexities of national and territorial histories and cultures are the point of departure for the essays collected in this volume. Our combined project, as we have conceived and developed our separate studies, has been to take as our starting point the detailed analysis of a specific phenomenon in this regional complexity and explore through it what it means to our understanding of the broader Caribbean region. Beginning with the seemingly most specific and local, we have sought, somewhat paradoxically, to shed some light on the issues and phenomena that connect the Caribbean regionally. The essays offer us windows into the region's history and culture from Columbus's arrival in 1492 to the use of the American base at Guantánamo to hold prisoners of the Afghanistan and Iraq wars in the present day. Their fundamental methodology is that of narrative; through a wealth of detail, the product in many cases of exhaustive archival research, these essays tell the stories of significant moments of ethnic, creative, political, migratory, or literary history and show how their specificity can help us understand the forces at play in the broader Caribbean.

The paradigm we have selected as the shared basis of our studies is that of movement, displacement, and dislocation within the pan-Caribbean region. Precisely because the colonial history of the islands since the Columbian encounter fixed them into patterns of travel, movement, and exchange that were fiercely controlled by the metropolitan colonial powers through the imposition of an artificial geography, we have sought to explore here instances of resistance to those parameters, of attempts to fix new geographical configurations through migration, illegal patterns of exchange, new discourses, and art. In doing so, we have sought also to examine the usefulness of new approaches (ecocriticism, the critique of postcolonialism, comparative art history, North-South American studies, Caribbean-American diaspora studies, for example) to our understanding of what we mean by *the Caribbean*. As a group, these essays explore the various ways in which we can, through the study of specific moments in Caribbean history and culture, break away from the categories of study imposed by European colonialism (and the centrality they maintain through postcolonial studies) and get closer to the ways in which Caribbean peoples have themselves sought to resist and redefine their realities.

Our approach to these displacements and transformations—as illustrative of the responses of colonial representations and practices as specific to particular social, political, and geographical circumstances—follows Nicholas Thomas' *Colonialism's Cultures*, which argues for an understanding of a "pluralized field of colonial narratives, which are seen less as signs than as practices, or as signifying practices rather than elements of a code" (8–9). Thomas has based his notions on Pierre Bourdieu's analytic strategy, "which situates colonial representations and narratives in terms of agents, locations and periods" conducive to a vision of colonialisms rather than colonialism (9). These essays demonstrate, through their analysis of the specificities of colonial and postcolonial histories in the Caribbean, how the hierarchies of colonial control were never fixed and static but remained malleable and flexible as they adjusted to local conditions. The perennial struggle for control between colonial and local forces manifested itself through myriad compromises and uneasy pacts that reflected the fluidity of colonial relations in islands whose importance to their colonial metropolises ebbed and flowed according to the vagaries of markets and international politics. As colonies transformed themselves into island nations after independence, their paths to political and cultural definition have been marked as much by a redefinition of colonial configurations as by a rearticulation of their relationships with neighboring islands and a reassessment of their place in the dynamics of the archipelago.

The collection opens with two essays that address the lasting legacy of the momentous encounter between Europe and the islands of the Caribbean. Lizabeth Paravisini-Gebert's "Endangered Species: Ecology and the Discourse of the Nation" explores how Caribbean writers have addressed the ecological revolution brought about by colonization, the sugar plantation, and, beginning in the twentieth century, the dependence on the tourist economy. The deforestation, depletion of resources, and permanent alteration of pre-encounter topographies that followed in the wake of the colonial encounter, she argues, initiated a process whose consequences have brought the island nations of the Caribbean to desperate ecological straits.

Jalil Sued-Badillo shifts the focal point from natural resources to human resources. He traces the origins of the slave trade from the Middle Ages to the present and the global mercantilist trajectories of Christopher Columbus and others who reconfigured and transplanted ancient models of slavery to the Caribbean and manipulated the contradictions implicit in the trafficking of diverse bodies as merchandise. His historical essay broadens the study of slavery in the Caribbean and delineates how the region entered into the parameters of modern capitalism and a new world order.

This discursive reconfiguration of the Caribbean historical landscape is further explored in the two essays that follow, which continue to analyze the ways in which concepts and narratives shift, evolve, and are repositioned or manipulated to transform social realities. Peter Hulme studies how narratives of national sovereignty, personal freedom, and pro-indigenous movements were appropriated and deployed for the benefit of the U.S. imperialist thrust and assurance of strategic positioning on Cuba's shores and beyond. He investigates the relevance of "adventure stories" set in Cuba and published in the late nineteenth century in the midst of the cultural changes the Caribbean was undergoing at that historical juncture. By doing so he demonstrates how the literary works' focus on indigeneity and their engagement with political themes of the moment interlock with the language of "legitimacy" and myths of "survival" to justify the military interventions that would transform the trajectory of Caribbean economic and political life. Kevin Meehan outlines the path of philosophical and political thought moving from the Caribbean to the United States, Latin America, Africa, and back. He follows the interplay between C. L. R. James' intellectual growth and his radical fieldwork as he transited through various social spheres, showing how his analyses of African American social and political circumstances belonged to a discursive, diasporic continuum linking the history of slavery in the United States to the Caribbean experience of colonialism and the plantation.

Ivette Romero-Cesareo focuses on how the repercussions of traumatic moments in global history are manifested through Caribbean cultural production. She examines literature and the visual arts to illustrate how the devastating irruption of the AIDS/HIV pandemic in the Caribbean transformed the horizons and viewpoints of insular artists, forcing them to look outward to the global stage. Her essay explores how certain tropes of illness and loss coincide or diverge from island to island, and how these tropes are deployed to reflect the complex psychological, social, and political changes surrounding this trauma as the pandemic evolves. Focusing on another type of trauma, Martha Daisy Kelehan joins Paravisini-Gebert in uncovering multiple meanings and alternative historical accounts implicit in paintings and literature depicting the ordeals of the Haitian "boat people" in their trans-Caribbean crossings. They investigate how Haitian painters have developed an iconography to create history paintings that seek to synthesize onto canvas one of the salient experiences of Haitian history and how these images are echoed in Caribbean literature. They demonstrate that by creating a literary and visual language to narrate this tragic episode, Caribbean artists reconstruct traumatic experiences, forcing the spectators to remember and to re-examine a crucial historical moment.

The next group of essays broadens the discussion on diverse modes of cultural production in the last three decades of the twentieth century in the Caribbean. Michael Aronna focuses on the construction of the subject in Caribbean testimonial narratives of the early years of the Cuban Revolution and on the way in which their internal contradictions and dissonances operate to coincide with and resist conventional notions of nation building. He explores how this type of documentary narrative in the Hispanic Caribbean, both as an instrument for social change and as a constructed object in itself, constitutes a vehicle of self-identification and definition of people in an ongoing historical process. Yolanda Martínez San Miguel examines the intricate processes and problematic lenses through which different Caribbean groups are represented. Framing her study of Dominican *merengue* and Cuban *nueva trova* within Stuart Hall's theories on the reconfiguration of identities in a global and migratory age, Martínez San Miguel focuses on how contemporary Hispanic Caribbean music and its representations of migration, exile, and ideas of race, class, and nationality inform the Caribbean cultural and demographic scenario to produce myriad interpretations of the other. She rethinks the notions of globalization and migration as they are applied to the most recent massive displacements taking place in Cuba, the Dominican Republic, and Puerto Rico.

Antonio Benítez Rojo's "The New Atlantis" serves as an epilogue to this collection. Written before the arrival of the twenty-first century (and now reproduced after his death on January 5, 2005) this essay uncannily forecasts the present-day Caribbean and its position within repeating networks of global transactions, exchanges, and intercourse. He imagines and reconstructs the horizons of the islands, delineating a Caribbean meta-archipelago—a geographic "location" without a center or definite boundaries. He envisions the reverberation of these islands as they gaze beyond their shores and—communicating through the constant movement of ocean currents—establish links to other islands and shores.

Endangered Species

Caribbean Ecology and the Discourse of the Nation

LIZABETH PARAVISINI-GEBERT

Decimation from the aruac downwards is the blasted root of Antillean history,
and the benign blight that is tourism can infect all those island nations, not gradually,
but with imperceptible speed, until each rock is whitened by the guano
of white-winged hotels, the arc and descent of progress.

Derek Walcott, "The Antilles: Fragments of Epic Memory"

A line in Puerto Rican novelist Edgardo Rodríguez Juliá's recent book of cantankerous nostalgia, *San Juan, ciudad soñada, (San Juan, dreamed city)* provides the point of departure for this essay. "All the landscapes of my child-hood have disappeared," he writes, lamenting how familiar landscapes—both rural and urban—have vanished before his eyes in a rapidly developing, over-populated, resort-intensive Puerto Rico (3). He mourns, for example, the disappearance of the old road from Aguas Buenas to Caguas, "one of the most beautiful on the island, shadowed from one town to the other by a dense canopy of flame trees and jacarandas" (3). "The wound on my child-hood landscape," he concludes, "sends shivers down my spine" (4). His la-ment prompts a question about the impact of disappearing landscapes on our perception of our personal and national histories, one that Derek Wal-cott addressed with poignant urgency in his Nobel Prize acceptance speech, fearing the loss of those beloved spaces of St. Lucia that are neither hal-lowed nor invested with any significance, not even that of memory: "How quickly it could all disappear! And how it is beginning to drive us further into where we hope are impenetrable places, green secrets at the end of bad roads, headlands where the next view is not of a hotel but of some long beach without a figure and the hanging question of some fisherman's smoke at its far end" (1998, 83).

From the earliest days of the European conquest and colonization of the Caribbean region, the identification with nature—with the deeply green hills shooting out of the sea, the lofty mountains draped with lush vegetation, the translucent azure seas—has played a salient role in the development of nationhood and nationalism. From poem to national anthem, singing to the beauty of the landscape and celebrating the most distinctive geographical features of the various islands have helped to foment an emotional link between the land and the people who inhabit it, thus helping to create and preserve the idea of "the nation" in the collective imagination. The people of Dominica sing in their national anthem to their "isle of beauty . . . the isle of splendor . . . so sweet and fair" that "all must surely gaze in wonder at thy gifts so rich and rare." St. Lucians, in turn, sing to their "land of beaches, hills and valleys, fairest isle of all the earth," celebrating the end of the days "when nations battled for this Helen of the West."

Recent ecological studies, such as Richard Grove's *Green Imperialism* (1995) and Polly Pattullo's *Last Resorts* (1996/2004), have underscored the environmental revolution that was the result of conquest and colonization. The history of environmental degradation, from the deforestation needed for the development of the plantation economy in the seventeenth century to the destruction of fragile marine habitats for the construction of all-inclusive resorts and cruise ship ports in the twenty-first, has brought the relationship between natural landscape and nationhood to a crisis point. As Pattullo writes of the Caribbean at the beginning of the twenty-first century, "In a generation, land and seascapes have been transformed: the bays where once local fishermen pulled in their seine nets, where villagers went for a sea bath or where colonies of birds nested in mangrove stands now provide for the very different needs of tourists" (2004, 131). Given the ecological degradation demanded by rapidly accelerating tourism development, can a sense of nationhood and a national culture built partly on the celebration of unparalleled natural beauty emerge unscathed from the destruction of the landscape that served as their foundation?

I would like here to trace the impact of the discourse of environmentalism and ecological conservation on the changing interpretation of the links between nature and nationhood as seen through some examples of Caribbean literature. I look briefly at how profound and often vertiginous changes in the environment brought about by industrialization and tourism-related development have turned the geographies of the Antilles into unrecognizable landscapes, creating voids where the symbols of nationhood used to stand. In *A Small Place*, Jamaica Kincaid bemoans how a "big new hotel . . . with its own port of entry" has been built on a bay that "used to have the best wilks in the world, but where did they all go?" (57). It is the same hotel on whose beaches the locals are not allowed, and she fears that "soon the best beaches in Antigua will be closed to Antiguans" (58). Her concerns are echoed by Patrick Chamoiseau, Raphaël Confiant, and Jean Bernabé of the Créolité movement in Martinique and Guadeloupe, who in the documentary *Landscape and Memory* deplore the "cementification" of their islands (Gosson and Faden) and the disappearance of what Chamoiseau has described as the Creole neighborhoods that traditionally limited "the damage caused by sudden periods of massive urbanization" and tourism development and perpetuated "the environmentally friendly cultural practices of Martinique's rural past" (Prieto 242). The growing efforts of Caribbean writers to link imperialism and political chaos to environmental degradation, to mark the absence of formerly recognizable geographical spaces, to chronicle how and why they have disappeared, or to engage audiences about the need to preserve endangered species speak both to a continuation of the tradition of linking nature to nationhood and to a recognition that that link is not sustainable without concerted political action to preserve our natural landscapes. Are local governments, in their rush to bring employment and modernization to their islands, destroying the very nature that brings tourists to visit, risking leaving the islands despoiled of their beauty and filled with the unmanageable garbage of tourist consumerism, their fragile landscapes unrecognizable? In an environmental conundrum in which "global has become the scale du jour" and national concerns are seen as "increasingly passé" (R. White, 980), how can the Caribbean islands struggle to protect their environments in the name of the nation?

In the Caribbean region, the relationship between man and nature was determined early in post-encounter history by the ecological trauma represented by the establishment of the sugar plantation. Pre-plantation Arawak culture—as described in Spanish chronicles and most vividly in Friar Ramón Pané's *Relación acerca de las antigüedades de los indios* (*An Account of the Antiquities of the Indians*, 1571)—was dependent on a simple economy of subsistence agriculture and fishing centered on "a harmonious relationship between religion, culture, politics, and patterns of work and exchange" (Paravisini-Gebert 2004, 670). Although the assumed sustainability of pre-Columbian civilizations is still subject to debate, Pané's collection of Arawak myths and legends articulates poignantly the symbiotic relationship between man, nature, and the gods that was the foundation of pre-Columbian Caribbean cultures: man worked along with nature to produce the crops and claim the fish needed for the welfare of the community, and this labor was accepted as a pleasing offering by their principal deity, Yocahú, the provider of yucca and fish.

This symbiotic relationship was shattered the very moment that nature became landscape in European eyes. The moment Columbus and his men set eyes on the Caribbean signaled the instant the landscape began an irrevocable and speedy decline. Their first gaze inspired both a celebration of its amazing, virginal loveliness (a posture that required the textual erasure of native peoples and their environmental cultures) and the earliest assessment of the richness to be exploited. In his letter to Luis de Santangel, Columbus's greedy eye scans the beautiful horizon, *maravedí* signs dancing before him. He saw rivers that would facilitate the transportation of the precious woods covering the tall mountains. He saw fruits aplenty to feed his men and others to come. He saw mines of the most diverse minerals, fertile lands to plant, deep and protected ports, good clean river water gleaming with gold:

In it, there are many havens on the sea-coast, incomparable with any others I know in Christendom; and plenty of rivers so good and great that it is a marvel. The lands thereof are high, and in it are very many ranges of hills, and most lofty mountains . . . and full of trees of a thousand kinds . . . since I saw them as green and as beautiful as they are in Spain during May. And some of them were in flower, some in fruit, some in another stage according to their kind. . . . There are wonderful pine-groves, and very large plains of verdure, and there is honey, and many kinds of birds, and many various fruits. In the earth there are many mines of metals; and there is a population of incalculable numbers. Española is a marvel; the mountains and hills, and plains, and fields, and the soil, so beautiful and rich for planting and sowing, for breeding cattle of all sorts, for building of towns and villages. There could be no believing, without seeing, such harbours as are here, as well as the many and great rivers, and excellent waters, most of which contain gold. (Columbus, 11)

The irony of Columbus's quick assessment of the profitability inherent in this beauty was not lost on his first biographer, Bartolomé de Las Casas, who would comment on how, from its inception, Spanish expansion was dependent on the economic, political, and cultural exploitation of the native populations and new environments.

Throughout the Caribbean, this exploitative expansion found its most efficient form in the economy of the plantation. Caribbean societies, Eric Williams has argued, "were both cause and effect of the emergence of the market economy; an emergence which marked a change of such world historical magnitude, that we all are, without exception still 'enchanted' imprisoned, deformed and schizophrenic in its bewitched reality" (paraphrased in Wynter, 95). This change was both demographic and ecological. Thousands of African slaves were brought to the new world with the sole aim of making it possible to produce a luxury crop for the international market in plantations that required the complete transformation of the Caribbean's tropical landscape. The sugar plantation grew at the expense of the dense and moist tropical forests that needed to be cleared to make way for the new profitable crop. This rapid deforestation led to soil depletion, landslides, erosion, and climatic changes that included significant decreases in levels of moisture and rainfall recorded as early as the seventeenth century (Grove, 64–70). The resulting environmental degradation was exacerbated in many areas of the Caribbean by ungulate irruptions—the introduction of domestic grazing animals alien to the pre-encounter Caribbean environment—that transformed the cultural and social landscape. Together, these rapid environmental changes brought about an ecological revolution, "an abrupt and qualitative break with the process of environmental and social change that had developed in situ" (Melville, 12). It is often said that Dominica, whose dizzying cliffs and difficult terrain made plantation development nearly impossible and which, therefore, remains covered in verdant rain forests, is the only island Columbus would recognize from his encounter. It is, significantly, the only one that still retains a substantial Carib population living in an autonomous territory.

The history of how the dramatic changes undergone by the Caribbean landscapes were recorded in memoirs and other proto-literary writings between Columbus's letter and the development of Caribbean literatures remains to be written. A brief example, taken from a foundational text from nineteenth-century Puerto Rican literature, however, can illustrate how intricately connected was the identification with nature to the process of national formation. In José Gautier Benítez's poem "Puerto Rico" (1846), the most lyrical and exalted of celebrations of the beauty and sweetness of the Puerto Rican land and landscape, required reading in every Puerto Rican classroom, the young poet writes from the vantage point of the ship that takes him away to Spain, describing the landscape as it disappears in the distance:

> There is . . . sugar cane on the fertile savannah,
> a lake of honey rippling in the breeze,
> while its spume, the gentle *guajana*
> sways in the air like white gossamer plumes,
> and on the broad slopes of your mountains
> crowned by cedar and mahogany,
> the coffee trees boast their tender garlands
> while their sturdy boughs bow to the earth,
> their bouquets of carmine and emerald. (6, my translation)

This landscape of identification, the invitation to celebrate—to lift to the category of national symbol—the glories of the *guajana*, the undoubtedly beautiful flower of the sugar cane plant, amounts to a celebration of the plantation, of a landscape that has already undergone an ecological revolution and is far from the virginal territory of Columbus's description. As a poem to "nature," it also begs the question of whether the cane field can be a landscape of national recognition for all Puerto Ricans; could a slave, or later an exploited peasant, wax lyrical about the beauties of the cane field? Or are these landscapes that echo a vision of the nation that does not include slaves or peasants?

I use the example of Gautier Benítez's "Puerto Rico," however briefly, because the poem is so closely linked to the Puerto Rican process of national formation, and because it maintains its relevance as a foundational text through its prescribed reading in the local school system and its never-ending recitations in school events. It stirs echoes of Jamaica Kincaid's bitterly narrated episodes of endless recitations of William Wordsworth's poem on daffodils in *Annie John* (1985) and *Lucy* (1990), except that unlike the British poet, Gautier Benítez was incontrovertibly a Creole. The problems of the text are exacerbated when subjected to a reading that asks questions about the role of the physical setting in a literary text, the consistency of the values expressed in the text with ecological wisdom, how the metaphors of the land reveal the way it has been treated, and, more fundamentally in this text, how the text articulates the people's relationship to the natural world. The text of "Puerto Rico" celebrates a landscape that can only be beautiful to a very small segment of the population and posits, not surprisingly, a defense of Spanish colonization and of the Creole elite and a reminder to the masses that they must be placid and tranquil, restful and bountiful like the island, if they are to be good Puerto Ricans.

Rosario Ferré, writing from a comparable vantage point in her novella *Sweet Diamond Dust* (1988), chooses the garden, not the cane field, as "a landscape of nostalgia for a declining Hispanic aristocracy" (Lynch, 112); but her conception of the people's relationship to the landscape is just as class-bound and plantation centered:

> Guamaní's main crop has always been sugarcane, and the townspeople lived from the bustling commerce produced around half a dozen small sugar mills that had sprung up around it during the nineteenth century. But cane sugar was not the only dry staple they traded in. From our orchards and vegetable patches at the time there grew ... exuberant profusions of fruits and vegetables ... the claret-red yautia as well as the paled, sherried golden one ... the tumultuous tom tom taro roots, brought by African slaves on the wailing ships of death ... the poisonous, treacherous cassava streaked with purple orchid's veins, which the Tainos and the African slaves used to drink when they were about to be tortured by the Spaniards. ... (Ferré, 5)

As Barbara Deutsch Lynch argues, "Ferré's baroque description captures in a detached and ironic way the garden's productivity, its sheer biodiversity, and the cultural diversity that went into its creation ... to produce a diverse array of pleasures for the self-made landed elite of the Spanish colony" (112). It is deeply ironic, then, that Ferré's privileged garden space is that of the provision grounds where slaves were allowed to produce food for their own consumption or to sell at market. What Lynch calls, in her discussion of *Sweet Diamond Dust*, Ferré's "environmental nationalism" echoes Gautier Benítez's celebration of the cane land and the *guajana* as the embodiments of the nation. They are both texts by writers who, although separated by a century, "lament the disappearance of the garden with the advance of industrial sugar production and their own marginalization as a [planter] class" (114). Ferré's Arcadia, "adorned" and "embellished" by the toil and labor of the black and mulatto masses, assumes as "natural" a relationship to the environment rooted in structures of class and race institutionalized by colonialism.

These institutions and their approach to the environment remain viable despite the collapse of the plantation economy in mid-twentieth-century Puerto Rico and the advent of tourism as one of the pillars that sustains the new urban-centered economy. *Felices días, tío Sergio* (1986; *Happy Days, Uncle Sergio*, 1994) by Magali García Ramis, that most urban of contemporary Puerto Rican novels, chronicles the violent deforestation and digging into the entrails of the land—into the blood-red mud of the fertile valley surrounding the "área metropolitana"—to build a modern San Juan in the 1960s. García Ramis had no intention of writing a novel of ecocritical dimensions, but her book is perhaps the most eloquent revelation of the destruction of natural landscapes necessary for the expansion of San Juan; her characters celebrate the digging into the land to build a new airport, the carving out of a water reservoir, the new *urbanizaciones*, roads, *autopistas*, hotels, and resorts—all developments that destroy Rodríguez Juliá's beloved landscapes, forcing him to seek refuge in landscapes of the mind that stand for the changing nation. The loss of natural and urban signposts pushes Puerto Ricans into a dynamic relationship with their geography, constantly threatened by anyone with a few cinder blocks and a bag of cement.

Felices días, tío Sergio chronicles but does not question the priority of modernization and urbanization over environmental conservation. Set against the historical background of Operation Bootstrap during the 1950s and 1960s, the novel, from its professional middle-class perspective, exults in the implicit modernity exemplified by the national project of Governor Luis Muñoz Marín and his Partido Popular Democrático. The project, which involved the building of extensive facilities for tourism, was accompanied by a broad program of infrastructure development that included extensive highway construction, the building of water reservoirs and hydroelectric plants, and the modernization of sewage systems. During the 1960s, the manufacturing sector would shift from clothing, tobacco, leather goods, and apparel to capital-intensive industries such as oil refineries, pharmaceuticals, and electronics. These are changes recorded by the young protagonist of the novel—whose Uncle Roberto works for the government-run Puerto Rico Development Corporation—as a background to the tale of the changes brought to her family by the arrival of a long-exiled uncle with a different notion of the nation.

The Uncle Sergio of the title brings with him a concept of the nation drawn from the independence-by-any-means stance of Pedro Albizu Campos, leader and president of the Puerto Rican Nationalist Party. Despite being denounced for its advocacy of violence against the United States, which included an attempt to assassinate President Harry Truman in 1950, the party drew support for its firm anti-colonial stance, its defense of national sovereignty and cultural independence for Puerto Rico, and its ideal of an economic restructuring built upon a decolonized relationship between the people and the land. The presence of Uncle Sergio in the text does not speak overtly to the environmental consequences of the alternative concept of the nation implied in the ideological stance he represents, but it alludes to its connection to the values of a pre-plantation agrarian society that repudiates the development agenda of the burgeoning Commonwealth. It points, through the character's ideological centrality, to the serious environmental ramifications of the debate over decolonization and national sovereignty represented in the text by Muñoz Marín and Albizu Campos.

The agrarian dimensions of this debate had been at the center of the development of the novel in Puerto Rico, from Manuel Zeno Gandía's *La charca* (The stagnant pond, 1894) to Enrique Laguerre's *La llamarada* (The burning cane fields, 1939), a masterpiece about American control of Puerto Rican sugar production. The latter, the tragic tale of a young agronomist torn between his personal ambition as the employee in charge of a U.S. *central* and his sympathy for the plight of the cane field workers whose exploitation he must maintain, struck a chord among Puerto Rican readers and intellectuals, who recognized in the character's dilemma a portrait of the national quandary. His protagonist's renunciation of ambition as a salve to his conscience and his feelings of impotence against colonial and corporate institutions reflect Laguerre's ideological opposition to continued foreign-controlled economic development, a position Laguerre embodied as he emerged as an advocate for the environment, becoming in the process the first Puerto Rican public figure to link nationalism to a commitment to ecological conservation (Paravisini-Gebert 2005a). As a self-described "ecological humanist," he argued incessantly that Puerto Rico had followed a very shortsighted vision of socioeconomic development that had sacrificed the environment to the pressures of urban sprawl and consumerism. He campaigned indefatigably against the destruction of forests and mangroves to make way for broader highways, luxury hotels, and middle-class housing developments, arguing that true nationalism had to be linked to a respect for the geographical spaces that were the nation's most valuable patrimony. He fought against the turning of the coastal areas into one long strip mall, and through his efforts became a hero to conservationists for his leadership role in the campaign to maintain Puerto Ricans' free access to the island's beaches.

Laguerre's ardent defense of what he termed "the nation's most valuable patrimony" was echoed by Derek Walcott in his vocal opposition to the building of the Hilton Jalousie Plantation resort in the valley sloping down to the sea between the Pitons, the two great volcanic cones on the west coast of St. Lucia—"one of the great landscapes of the Caribbean" (Pattullo, 1) and now a UNESCO World Heritage Site. The Pitons, undeniably a natural space of great national significance, was threatened by the construction of a hotel that would be, in Walcott's words, "aesthetically like a wound" (Handley, 129). In an interview with George B. Handley, he explained his opposition to the Jalousie scheme as having derived from his perception of the Pitons as a "sacred space," a "primal site" that emanates power and which, having become the object of the people's devotion, should have remained inviolable (128). The building of a resort in such a space was tantamount to a "blasphemy." Writing in a local paper, Walcott argued that "to sell any part of the Pitons is to sell the whole idea and body of the Pitons, to sell a metaphor, to make a fast buck off a shrine" (quoted in Pattullo, 4). He equated the economic arguments in favor of the resort—that it would provide extra income and jobs—to proposing to build "a casino in the Vatican" or a "take-away concession inside Stonehenge" (quoted in Pattullo, 4). The loss of such a pristine space was the loss of a place that could help people regain a feeling of "a beginning, a restituting of Adamic principles" (Handley, 131).

The development of the Jalousie resort—which opened in 1994—is emblematic of the tensions that arise when different notions of what constitutes the nation and of how to exploit its resources are pitted against each other. As a site of national significance that was also a prime locale for potential tourist development, the Pitons became the focus of struggle between foreign developers, a local government seeking to increase foreign investment and foster employment, and a large number of conservation-minded citizens who understood the significance of the space in myriad ways. The debate involved the Hilton Corporation, the Organization of American States (which supported an alternative proposal for a Jalousie National Park at the site), the St. Lucia development control authorities, and numerous members of the community—Walcott included—with differing views of the role of the "nation's most valuable patrimony" in the nation's development. The Jalousie resort was duly built, nestled in a "sacred" space from which St. Lucians are now banned, thereby separating the local population from its natural patrimony. Ironically, despite great initial interest, the Jalousie resort has met with questionable success. Although still managed by the Hilton Corporation, the resort is now primarily financed by the St. Lucian government, despite a dwindling tourist base and indifferent returns.

For Walcott, there is comfort in the notion of nature's capacity to obliterate "history" when it appears in the shape of buildings and monuments. Living in the still verdant St. Lucia, he holds to the hope that in time nature will swallow the ruins of the Jalousie complex. In his poems and essays, Walcott has often alluded to the Adamic idea, which for him means "the feeling that one can rechristen things, rename things" (Handley, 133). It is a notion that leads him to see "the grass that emerges from the ruins" as "the grass that says it's a beginning again" (133)—an idea that allows him to place the construction of the resort as one more event in a long line of historical events that have left no "ruins and mementos" on Caribbean landscapes. From this perspective, Walcott would trust that despite all the frenzy of tourist-resort development, nature may still prevail if St. Lucians succeed in taking control of their island's development before it moves from environmental vulnerability to ecological crisis, before its carrying capacity is breached and all hope is gone. It is a notion akin to that expressed by Jacques-Stephen Alexis in his novel *Les Arbres musiciens*, where he speaks of the trees of Haiti's embattled forests "as a great pipe organ that modulates with a multiple voice . . . each with its own timbre, each pine a pipe of this extraordinary instrument" (quoted in Benson, 108). Walcott's blade of grass emerging from the ruins is like the voice of Alexis's musician trees, which "collapse from time to time, but the voice of the forest is always as powerful as ever. Life begins" (quoted in Benson, 108). As Walcott writes in his most recent collection of poems, *The Prodigal*:

> What if our history is so rapidly enclosed
> in bush, devoured by green, that there are no signals
> left, since smoke, the smoke of encampments

by brigand and the plumes from muskets
are transitory memorials and our forests shut
their mouths, sworn to ancestral silence. (2005, 99)

In this, he trusts to two phenomena: the capacity of Caribbean nature to
turn everything in its path to bush if left to itself and the power of literature
to confer significance on spaces, making of them hallowed markers of nationhood that would behoove everyone to conserve. Walcott's proposal, outlined
in his Nobel Prize acceptance speech, speaks to the possibility of those places
made significant by our literature turning into the loci of Caribbean nationhood and identity:

> Our cities . . . dictate their own proportions, their own definitions in
> particular places and in a prose equal to that of their detractors, so that
> now it is not just St. James but the streets and yards that Naipaul com-
> memorates, its lanes as short and brilliant as his sentences; not just the
> noise and jostle of Tunapuna but the origins of C.L R. James's *Beyond
> the Boundary*, not just Felicity Village on the Caroni plain, but Sel-
> von Country, and that it's the way it goes up the islands now; the old
> Dominica of Jean Rhys still very much the way she wrote of it; and the
> Martinique of early Césaire; Perse's Guadeloupe, even without the pith
> helmets and the mules. . . . This is not a belligerent boast but a simple
> celebration of inevitability. . . . (73)

Walcott's Adamic idea, his faith in nature's ability to renew itself, and his
belief in the sacredness bestowed on places either by their intrinsic power
or by the power vested upon them by being the settings of classic texts of
Caribbean literature are the foundations of an ecological stance rooted in
a moral relationship to the landscape. He has argued, from this standpoint,
that ignoring the moral question of how we relate to the environment can
lead to incalculable damage. "So the person who is protecting the sacred piece
of earth," he concludes, "is doing more than the person who thinks that right
now concrete and steel are going to do more for some other generation coming" (Handley, 129).

The moral question of the preservation of the Caribbean's sacred spaces
emerges with urgent poignancy in Haiti, where ecological tragedy has led to
the erasure of locales hallowed by their connection to history and the spirits. If Walcott's St. Lucia is a still verdant tropical paradise—threatened by

development yet still substantially covered in "forests . . . sworn to ancestral silence"—Haiti is the despoiled terrain that stands as a warning of the direst consequences that could face Caribbean nations that do not make a concerted effort to put a stop to environmental degradation. In spaces as small as many Caribbean island-nations (Dominica, for example, is thirty miles long by fifteen miles wide), the ecological balance is fragile, the level of vulnerability too high. As a result, the viability of the nation itself and the survival of its people are marked by an urgency unimaginable in continental settings. Nowhere in the Caribbean is this revealed more heart-rendingly than in Haiti. The devastation brought upon the Haitian landscape by continued deforestation, desertification, failed tourism development, and the collapse of agro-business amid governmental corruption has become the country's most glaring socioeconomic and political problem. Haiti's forests, already depleted for lumber to be sold in the international market in the twentieth century, have in recent years been cut down in catastrophic numbers for the charcoal used everywhere for cooking. As Haiti entered the twenty-first century, the country's extreme deforestation and the concomitant soil erosion, droughts, and disastrous flash floods have ravaged the countryside and led it to the very edge of environmental despair. With only 1 percent of the land covered in forests, previously fertile fields are now desert-like. Most of the topsoil has been washed to the sea, where it has contributed to the destruction of breeding habitats for marine life. The resulting decreases in rainfall have significantly reduced agricultural production. The fishing industry has long been in crisis. It is a situation exacerbated by the devastating loss of the sustaining connection between the people and the *lwa* or spirits of Vodou who reside in the family's plot of land or *heritage*. The most frequent question prompted by Haiti's environmental crisis is whether something can still be done to help the land of Haiti regain its ability to sustain its people. In *Collapse*, Jared Diamond describes Haiti's ecological condition in succinct terms, putting into question the country's continued viability as a nation:

> Its perennially corrupt government offers minimal public services; much or most of its population lives chronically or periodically without public electricity, water, sewage, medical care, and schooling. There is extreme polarization between the masses of poor people living in rural areas or in the slums of the capital of Port-au-Prince and a tiny population of rich elite in the cooler mountain suburb of Pétionville. . . . Haiti's

rate of population growth, and its rate of infection with AIDS, tuber-
culosis, and malaria, are among the highest in the world. The question
that all visitors to Haiti ask themselves is whether there is any hope for
the country, and the usual answer is "no." (329–30)

At the root of these troubles is an unimaginable ecological catastrophe
that speaks eloquently to writers across the Caribbean. Haiti's symbolic position as the region's first republic and as a land whose history has been emblematic of the economic and political vicissitudes that have plagued other
islands in the area gives the embattled nation a central position in Caribbean
environmental discourse. Its ecological conundrum, in the hands of its writers, becomes the focal point for meditations on the region's environmental
options.

Haitian writers have made the nation's environmental crossroads a central leitmotif. Understanding the centrality of Haiti's environmental situation—both as a historical reality and as a metaphor for addressing this history in literature—they have made it a cornerstone of the development of
the national novel. Their vision of the nation is closely intertwined with the
acknowledgment that the nation itself is in peril if Haitians cannot find a way
to restore to the land its fertility and its forests, making it again a proper place
for the people and their *lwa* to inhabit. The literature of Haiti has bemoaned
the environmental calamity that has befallen its people, denounced the practices that led to this catastrophe, and offered inspiration and ideas for solving
the nation's most central problem. Can literature, then, in any way lead to the
saving of the Haitian land and nation?

In Jacques Roumain's *Masters of the Dew* (1944), a seminal text in the
development of the Haitian novel, the hero, Manuel, returns after years of
working on the Cuban sugar plantations to the village of Fonds Rouge (a
microcosm of the Haitian nation) only to find it parched and dying from
a drought caused by acute and persistent deforestation (see Paravisini-Gebert 2005b). Mired in a violent dispute over inheritance of the land, the villagers must come together if they are to find a solution to their ecological
(and by definition national) crisis. Led by their revered priest Papa Ogoun,
who counsels during a Vodou ceremony that the villagers must dig a canal to
bring water from the still-forested mountains—where "the vein is open, the
blood flows" (Roumain, 190)—Manuel realizes that a *coumbite*, a bringing
together of labor of all the villagers, will be necessary to accomplish the task.

Despite Manuel's untimely death, the villagers unite and "a thin thread of water advanced, flowing through the plain, and the peasants went along with it, shouting and singing" (190). Roumain's understanding of the desperate ecological situation faced by the villagers of Fonds Rouge as a metaphor for Haiti's national plight turns his fable of Christian sacrifice and communal action into a prescription for facing the potential demise of the nation. A concerted effort, a national *coumbite*, but perhaps also a messianic leader willing to undergo the ultimate sacrifice, are the chief elements in his proposal for national renewal, a proposal congruent with Roumain's political goals as founder of the Communist Party of Haiti and his fervent call to the poor of Haiti to come together to fight against exploitation, poverty, and environmental degradation.

Marie Chauvet develops the link between Haiti's environmental crisis and the survival of the nation one step further in *Amour, Colère et Folie* (1968) through her condemnation of the neocolonial (U.S.) forces complicit in Haiti's twentieth-century deforestation. In *Amour*, she dissects the forces that led to the ecological revolution produced by deforestation as a factor in Haiti's internal politics and international economic relationships, especially during the nineteen years of American occupation, which lasted from 1915 to 1934. Claire, the clear-sighted narrator of *Amour*, describes how the devastation caused by deforestation by U.S. corporations operating in Haiti threatens the peasantry's hold on their *heritage*, endangering their survival and severing their connection to their history and their sustaining spirits:

> It has been raining without check, and what is worst is that the rains came after the intensive clearing of the woods. Monsieur Long's electric saw has been buzzing without interruption for the last fifteen days. A tree falls every five minutes. Yesterday, I took a long walk down the length of the coast to take a look at the damage. I saw huge trees falling to the ground, making the most awful noise, as if they were roaring before letting out their last breath. . . . Avalanches of soil stream down the mountains, forming mounds below. There is no longer any coffee, except in our memories. Mr. Long is no longer interested in coffee. He now thinks of nothing but the export of lumber. When the lumber is gone, he'll go after something else. Maybe he'll start exporting men. He can have his pick from among the beggars and easily ship them out. (Chauvet, 132)

In Chauvet's incisive analysis of Haitian politics in *Amour, Colère et Folie*, the competing forces laying claim to representing the nation—the U.S. occupiers convinced that their civilizing mission in Haiti and investment in its infrastructure will help them foster a powerful and loyal ally, the small elite bent on establishing their fortunes through trade and corruption, and the exploited peasantry seen as one more cheap commodity to use or export as labor—all become, willingly or unwittingly, peons in the protracted game of ecological mismanagement that has resulted in Haiti's despoiled landscape. The Haitian national anthem encourages its people to work together joyfully for their country and for their ancestors on fertile fields with courage and strength:

> For our forebears,
> For our country
> Let us toil joyfully.
> May the fields be fertile
> And our souls take courage.

But in Haiti, environment and nation have declined at the same pace, placing the nation and its people at risk.

The ghost of Haiti haunts the Caribbean imaginary in myriad ways. Will its example, the loss of what Laguerre called an island's most valuable patrimony, the beauty and fertility of its land, lead the island nations into an increasingly protective stance vis-à-vis their own land? It is a question that increasingly troubles the relationships among Caribbean nations, their governments, their landscapes, and their peoples, as it troubles Walcott, who ponders the question of whether the destruction of the Caribbean landscapes could signal the loss of the people who inhabit them—the end of island nations and their peoples:

> The Caribbean is not a [tourist] idyll, not to its natives. They draw their working strength from it organically, like trees, like the sea almond or the spice laurel of the heights. Its peasantry and its fishermen are not there to be loved or even photographed; they are trees who sweat, and whose bark is filmed with salt, but every day on some island, rootless trees in suits are signing favorable tax breaks with entrepreneurs, poisoning the sea almond and the spice laurel of the mountains to their roots. A morning could come in which governments might ask what happened not merely to the forests and the bays but to a whole people. (1998, 83)

2

Christopher Columbus
and the Enslavement of the Amerindians

JALIL SUED-BADILLO

As soon as the last Duvalier had fled Haiti, an angry crowd toppled the statue of Christopher Columbus in Port-au-Prince and threw it into the sea. This Columbus, the object of their wrath, was not, clearly, the great explorer of Western myth. Hispaniola, the island of which Haiti is a part, was the first European colony in the New World and therefore the first to suffer the ravages of colonialism. The crowd knew Columbus as the first of a long line of despots leading to Duvalier. He was, indeed, the father of modern colonialism and all that it meant in the New World—the expropriation of the natural resources for the benefit of capital accumulation in the metropolitan center; despotic governments run by foreigners; the decimation of the native population and its replacement by millions of slaves from Africa; the institution of slavery as an international system; and the establishment of Europe as the hegemonic power in the new order of international capital. Christopher Columbus is the first great symbol of modern capitalism.

In the words of Samir Amin, "The recognition that the essential elements of capitalism crystallized in Europe during the Renaissance suggests 1492—the beginning of the conquest of America—as the date of the simultaneous birth of both capitalism and the world capitalist system, the two phenomena being inseparable" (354). The real meaning of Columbus, much of the mystery, the fantasy even, surrounding the man and his discovery, stems from the inability of the present order to make an explicit connection between the explorer's arrival in the Caribbean and the real event that occurred: the beginning of the first five hundred years of world capitalist domination. The truth that lurks just behind the statues of Columbus is the guilty conscience of what has been called the original sin of Europe. Put simply, the price of the massive wealth of the European center has for over five hundred years been the enormous underdevelopment of the periphery. It was that truth that drove the Haitians to topple Columbus' statue.

History must be revisited and rewritten if we, today, are to learn from what really happened and get a sense of direction for our future. And where better to start than with Christopher Columbus? First to be jettisoned must be all of the political fiction written about the age of exploration and the exaggerated image of Columbus the man, all products of Spanish and Italian chauvinism. Then we can begin to place him in the complex historical reality of the time. To do this I shall focus on how the development of the world capitalist economy was intertwined with the spread of the slave trade from the Mediterranean to the Atlantic. In the center of the emerging web of slavery we find the first European slave trader in the Americas, Christopher Columbus. He was in many ways a product of the Mediterranean-based trade, but more than that, he was the initiator of the slave trade in the Americas, personally supervising seven shipments of Amerindian slaves from the New World to the Old.[1] This—along with his obsessive pursuit of gold—is the key to his great "Enterprise of the Indies."

The Origins of the Mediterranean Slave Trade

During the Middle Ages the slave trade had a continuous but uneven development. In France and England it hardly existed, but it flourished in the Italian cities and on the islands of the Mediterranean. Principally the demand was for domestic servants and secondarily for a steady supply of labor for the other service sectors in the cities. Women were preferred over men, and until the fifteenth century they came mostly from Eastern Europe; there were Tartars, Greeks, Russians, Serbs, and Bulgarians, white and predominately Christian. Thus the difference of color and culture between master and slave was minimal. In the Iberian Peninsula the slaves were predominantly darker Moslems taken during ethnic and religious conflicts in the region. But in all other respects the pattern was the same.

The medieval world, then, reached a truce of sorts with its conscience. Slavery was accepted as part of the social order while at the same time there were attempts to adapt to the contradictions that went along with it. The underpinnings of the slave trade were always mired in violence, whether overt or covert. But slavery itself was not always regarded as a social problem. The abuses and arbitrariness were different in different periods. The same can be said for the public reactions and suggested cures. As long as the actual practice of Mediterranean slavery was within the limits set by its traditional justifications there was no significant opposition to the system itself. Notwithstanding the Laws of King Alfonso the Wise and his private appeals for the value of personal freedom or the well-known "conscientious doubts" of Queen Isabella regarding her right to enslave the Native Americans, few people doubted that the institution itself was inevitable, natural, and desirable.

The situation was similar in the Moslem world. The Mediterranean was often an arena of violent encounters and competition, not only between Moslems and Christians but within each community. But religious conflict has been overemphasized as a historical explanation. Of equal prominence were the political and economic rivalries of the period, such as those dominated by the struggles and alliances between Genoa and Venice, Catalonia and the Moslems from Venice, the Turks and Genoa, and so on. It is these political and economic rivalries, rather than religious differences, that are most crucial to an understanding of Mediterranean slavery (Fernández-Armesto).

Although the slave trade traversed all the commercial routes in the Mediterranean, it was not very efficient. It depended on improvised expeditions of pirates and smugglers and on local conflicts that either increased or decreased the supply of available slaves. The trade was important for medieval society in that it was a traditional and desirable activity, but it was not vital or indispensable for material or social development.

In the economic development of the medieval Mediterranean world the Italian towns and their efforts to control commerce played a central role. While Columbus' Genoese background has often been emphasized in the legend surrounding him since it seems to separate him from Spanish imperial designs, this background in fact makes his role as a slave trader more "understandable."

The first empire of Genoa and its commercial colonies dominated the eastern Mediterranean until the Turks expelled them from Byzantium. No less influential for centuries were the Venetians with their forts on the Adriatic and their formidable navy in the Mediterranean. Their privileged relationship with the Byzantine Empire allowed them to dominate vital trade routes. From the Turks the Genoese got slaves, many of them Christians, whom they later resold in their own country, where they were traded for arms, wheat, and spices. The relationship between Genoa and the Moorish Kingdom of Seville dates back to the eleventh century and its commercial relations with the Kingdom of Valencia to the thirteenth century. Mercantile ties have rarely been based on religious or ethnic loyalties. Besides being merchants, the Italians were moneylenders, naval consultants, mercenaries, pirates, and explorers. In this context Christopher Columbus was just another name in a long historical process.

The Italians should also be remembered for the formative role that they played with respect to two other important activities in the Mediterranean, two distinct pursuits that later merged into one: sugar production and agricultural slavery. It was to be expected that the luxury items from the East that were used by the privileged of Europe would at some point also be produced in Europe. Such was the case with sugar, the silkworm, and the plant needed for its growth. Sugar was important in the manufacture of medicine and for the preservation of food. From the twelfth century on, sugar cane plantations were found in Palestine, the Arabs having introduced them to the Mediterranean; but the Italians gradually took over and extended them to their colonies in Cyprus, Crete, Sicily, North Africa, and the Spanish peninsula. Stuart Schwartz states that "by the 15th century a flourishing industry provided enough surplus to permit Genoese merchants to carry on a brisk trade with Italy and northern Europe" (Schwartz, 8). In the beginning, the sugar plantations provided work for both wage laborers and some slaves, but soon the quest for profits gave way to plantations with great forces of slave labor (Amaral Ferlini). The development of these estates led to a new form of slavery, which we know as plantation slavery. Sugar cultivation is labor intensive.

Ample land, windmills, and many slaves were needed to process the cane. Such conditions existed in the Moslem world and in the Latin Orient. Before that sugar plantations existed in the Holy Land, near Tiro and Tripoli, where the Venetians had extensive possessions, and much later in southern Cyprus, in the rural areas of Lemura, Paphos, and Aschelia, in the diocese of Limassol, and also on the lands of the Catalonian family Ferrer and the Venetian family Cornaro near Piscopi. The introduction of the crop in Sicily, then in Calabria, and much later in Valencia, where a large German company from Ravensburg had vast possessions and sugar refineries near Gandía, and later still in the Algarve in the south of Portugal created a huge demand for slave labor (Heers, 130). It is therefore impossible to see the development of the sugar industry as occurring in only one place. Nevertheless, the Italians were clearly central to the entire process, and the Genoese played a pivotal role in the supply and demand of slaves for sugar plantations. In their role as pirates as much as in their role as merchants the sons of Liguria dominated the slave trade. For example, in the fourteenth century they provided 32 percent of the slaves for Cyprus.

Important geopolitical changes in the Mediterranean around the middle of the fifteenth century were to move commerce in other directions. The Turkish advance and the rising military and economic potential that it represented (symbolically associated with the capture of Constantinople in 1450) displaced commerce in the eastern Mediterranean and forced the opening to the Atlantic. These difficulties with eastern commerce led to the penetration of Africa by Portugal and Castile. This took place initially in Berberia and later along the African Atlantic coast. The new bases of mercantile capital became Cádiz, Seville, and Lisbon. Slowly, throughout the fifteenth century, the islands in the Atlantic were occupied—the Azores, the Canaries, the Cape Verdes—laying the groundwork for the journey to America. The Italians played an important part in this process. Looking for new areas for investment, they added to or established new colonies in Spain and Portugal, and owing to their vast military and commercial experience they influenced the course of events in those countries, which up until that time had played a rather passive role in the history of the Mediterranean. This strategy, successful for more than a century, is known as the period of "covert colonialism." By 1460, according to Heers, an Italian by the name of Antonio di Noli had established a sugar plantation on the Cape Verde Islands, off the coast of Senegal, and had a license from the king of Portugal to import as many slaves as he wanted from Africa. Black slaves, who up until that time had been regarded as luxury items for the very rich, were now being used as a labor-intensive workforce on the new plantations springing up along the Atlantic coast.

This new type of slavery grew up in response to the scarcity of labor in the south of Spain and Portugal. Moreover, the western Mediterranean had not recovered from plague, the demographic crisis of the fourteenth century, and thousands of Africans helped to repopulate the region (North and Thomas, 127). The islands off the coast of the Atlantic became, in effect, the experiment stations where slaves were incorporated into the new productive processes of mercantile capitalism.

The Italians were very resourceful about incorporating capital, technology, business, and exploration into the new system, and their role in the economic and political life of Spain and Portugal must not be underestimated. From 1475 on, it can be said that Genoa had its second commercial empire with Andalucía as its center. That year Ferdinand of Spain reconfirmed all the privileges traditionally given to Genoese merchants in Seville, and in 1493 he signed a document of the sort that we still refer to as a "most-favored nation" treaty. Along with this treaty the Genoese supplied the financial and logistical support to the kings of Castile and Aragon for their conquests of Grenada and the Canary Islands. Much the same can be said for the Portuguese. The Italians in Portugal and the Atlantic colonies were their principal source of financial and mercantile support, allowing them to sustain their colonies in North Africa and along the Atlantic coast.

Aside from the Azores, the most important Portuguese possessions in the Atlantic were the Madeira Islands, which had been colonized around 1425. When discovered the islands had no population or exportable resources, and wheat was planted for internal consumption. But by 1452, the first sugar refinery on Madeira with slaves from the Canary Islands was in operation. By 1460, sugar had replaced wheat as the principal crop (Braudel, 111). In 1493, the island had eighty mills that produced 100,000 twenty-five-pound bags of sugar (Schwartz, 6). The Genoese had been responsible for the introduction of the crop. From the beginning of the next century, the Canary Islanders were no longer available as slaves, and they were replaced by two thousand Africans (Phillips, 60). By the end of the century, according to Schwartz, Madeira had become the largest sugar producer in the Western world.

The economic dynamic of the Madeira experience is an excellent example of the fusion of two different mercantile enterprises in the early history of European colonization of the Atlantic. Both crops and slave labor were imported to the area of cultivation. The close proximity to Europe insured a wide, guaranteed market, and the proximity to Africa ensured an ample supply of slaves. This same formula was later applied in the development of black slavery in the colonization of the Americas.

The slave trade between West Africa and Portugal began in 1441, when Antam Gonzalves took the first cargo to Lisbon (Blake, 85). Initial explorations of the African coast had not yielded the gold and riches the Europeans dreamed of, so they turned to the hunting of slaves. At the end of the fifteenth century, the number of slaves in Portugal was so high that the surplus was exported to the rest of Europe, where from then on slavery "had penetrated into the middle class, the business world, and into small production and the crafts" (Heers, 127). But the destiny of the slave trade was linked to the success of the sugar islands and that was how the system spread. The islands off the Atlantic coast were the sites of the first experimental alternatives to non-slave agriculture in the European homelands. Slavery never developed in Europe the way it did in the colonial areas.

The double standard of Europe regarding who is a human and who an animal became a matter of controversy in the sixteenth century, when the European invaders immediately enslaved the natives they encountered in the New World, but antecedents were perfectly apparent in the Atlantic a century earlier. It was in relation to these slave colonies that the ideological contradictions first surfaced.

The new states of Castile and Portugal had neither the time nor the economic and political resources to exclude the private sector from the spoils of conquest, and the alliance between state and capital was frequently put to test in the latter half of the fifteenth century. The role of arbiter in these conflicts was played by the Vatican, not only because the clashes often brought into conflict the subjects of different sovereign states, but also because the excesses and scandals of the private sector collided with the ideological understandings of the church-state alliance. In the process of mediation the values and standards necessary to justify slavery in the newly conquered lands were defined. Rome, by issuing several papal bulls, began to create a new body of law, which despite its contradictions and changeability, provided guidelines for Catholic expansionism. These bulls were quite similar to today's international accords, in the sense that they could not be imposed on strong states and were always adapted to suit the interests of the most powerful of the moment. Although Rome lacked the material power to impose its rule on the new national states, its ideological hegemony allowed it both to promote its own interests and to perform a valuable mediating role in a European colonial expansion that would otherwise have been chaotic. For example, from 1434 on, with the papal bull *Creator Omnium*, Pope Eugenio IV excommunicated anyone who enslaved a native already converted to Christianity. That same year the Vatican also prohibited actions in the Canary Islands, denying the validity of certain forms of conquest ostensibly for the conversion of slaves. The conquest of the Canary Islands, because of the poverty of their resources, degenerated into a bloody and cruel hunting of slaves in the name of the gospel and forced the Vatican and the Catholic monarchs that came after the act to condemn it. One may, of course, look behind these restrictions to see the power politics of royalty and private interests at play. Backstage diplomacy at the time, as we know, was intense and complex. But that is of secondary interest. What is important is the gradual institution of a system of law that defined the parameters and structure of a new type of slavery for the new colonial order that was being born.

In 1436, for example, King Duarte of Portugal requested that *Creator Omnium* be suppressed, and he described the infidels of the Atlantic islands in very demeaning terms. This can be seen as an important ideological precedent for the enslavement of the natives of America (Pérez Fernández, 167). In 1472, Sixtus IV in *Pastoris Alterni* issued indulgences for the conversion of the natives of the Canary Islands in such ambiguous terms that King Ferdinand took them as carte blanche to repress the natives.

In 1476, Sixtus IV in *Regimini Gregis* supported the conversion of the natives of the Canary Islands and Guinea (the name by which Africa was known at the time) and issued instructions to excommunicate all captains or pirates who failed to comply with it. What had been established was a clear difference between converted natives and those who resisted conversion. A year later, Ferdinand and Isabella felt pressed to support the papal bull and ordered the seizure of the natives of La Gomera, who were taken as slaves to Andalucía in order to resolve their legal status. A while later they were freed and ordered to be returned to their place of origin. Religious belief became, then, the principle defining citizenship. One suspects that the Castilian crown, given a choice, was much more interested in the incorporation of the possessions into its empire than in any profit it might obtain from the sale of slaves. This issue caused a separation of interests between slave traders and the crown (Fernández-Armesto, 237).

A final aspect to consider is the straitened financial circumstances of these states at the time and their search for capital to finance their enterprises. During the Middle Ages the kingdoms of the Iberian Peninsula had distributed some of their properties and rents to the nobles as a means to insure their support. In this new centralist conjuncture the process needed to be reversed, the investment to be recouped, and new ways to be found to finance the state undertakings inside and outside the country. The reign of Ferdinand and Isabella is remembered for the steps it took in that direction. But the expansionist mood of the time left them with little to spend and they had two options to consider: the first was to go to private financiers, mainly Italian Jews, and the second was to use the money authorized by the papal bulls and other public collections for the conversion of the natives. In almost all cases the second option was chosen. The kings asked, Rome obliged, and both profited. Such was the case with the papal bulls supporting the conquest and colonization of America. But the requests were not always granted. In 1477, Ferdinand and Isabella reserved for themselves funds collected under *Regimini Gregis* for the conversion of the inhabitants of the Canary Islands and Africa. Apparently they tried to sidetrack those funds (Pérez Fernández, 167). Their action did not please the Vatican, which abolished the bull and stopped public collections. The effects of this measure were quick to appear, when in 1492 with the conquest of La Palma and Tenerife in the name of the monarchs the Spanish captured and sold two hundred natives. Pérez Fernández states, "This was the only capital available to support conquest since the Bull *Regimini Gregis* of 1476 was abolished" (172). It was evident that slavery, aside from being a source of profit for merchants, was also a way to resolve economic problems of the state.

The World of Columbus

Enter Columbus. We should not be surprised that this young man from Genoa, a converted Jew according to the most recent reliable studies from Spain, appeared in the western Mediterranean, the new colonial frontier of Europe, looking for a profitable future (Gil). In his country this was not possible or he would not have left it. But what is interesting to us is not his fantasies or his personal projects. We are concerned with the experiences that formed the way he thought. Columbus is interesting as a man of his time and as an exponent of the values of that period. The rest is myth.

Let us begin with the effects of his religious status, a converted Jew in a rigid Catholic country, to understand his early abandonment of Italy and his affinity for travel. Recent philological studies show that Columbus spoke a hybrid tongue reflecting not only a poor basic education but also a constant change of place during his long years of travel in the world of his day (Varela 1982, prologue). His writings demonstrate a knowledge of the Mediterranean and Italian outposts along the sugar route. He mentions Chios in the Aegean, as well as Sicily and Sardinia. Early in 1470, he was in Lisbon working for the commercial house of Centurion and Negro, well-known merchant families from Genoa involved in the sugar slave trade. From Lisbon he traveled the

North Atlantic, to Galway in Ireland and Bristol in England. There is some speculation that he reached as far as Iceland. In 1478, he was sent on a very important commercial mission to Madeira, the most important sugar plantation of the time. There he met and married the daughter of a Lombardian merchant named Perestrello and settled on the island. Thus he became a member of the colonial circles of the Atlantic. From Madeira he traveled to the Gulf of Guinea, visited La Mina, the great slave center of the time, and wrote some years later, "I have been in the castle of the King of Portugal, La Mina, located under the equinox, and I am a witness that it is not, as they say, uninhabited" (Columbus 11). Pérez Fernández places the Congo expedition of Columbus and his brother-in-law Diego Cao in 1485 and locates Columbus with Bartolomé Díaz at the Cape of Good Hope (186–87). There is no doubt that he was familiar with the forms of slave colonization in vogue at the time, models that his fellow countrymen helped to perfect as they amassed great fortunes and widened their spheres of influence and prestige. To Bartolomé de Las Casas, his first biographer, there was no doubt of the slave inclinations Columbus absorbed in the Atlantic with respect to "the practices that the Portuguese followed, and even today follow, in the negotiations and tyranny in Guinea" (436).

During this period Columbus must have entertained many projects for exploration but found no support in the Portuguese courts. He left for Castile, hoping for better luck. The story of the misunderstood dreamer, fighting alone against the world, is only a legend. Columbus had left Portugal with letters of recommendation from Genoese in Lisbon to his fellow countrymen in Seville. At all times, he was supported by Italian merchants in the courts of both countries. Let me mention just two names, Berardi and Pinelli. Juanoto Berardi knew him from the early years in Lisbon; he was a Florentine who represented the powerful house of Francesco de Medici. Berardi was a notorious figure in the slave trade. Consuelo Varela identifies the circle of Florentines who supported Columbus in Spain and of Berardi says that from 1486 on he showed "a perfect assimilation to the commercial trade, fundamentally of African slaves" (Varela, 37). His network included cities such as Málaga, Cádiz, Jaén, and Seville. Berardi also lent money to the Catholic monarchs and participated financially in the conquest of the Canary Islands. At the time, another Florentine named Amerigo Vespucci worked for him as a commercial agent. It was a small world. Varela tells us that between 1489 and 1499 Florentine merchants controlled the monopoly on African slaves in Spain and Portugal. It was also in that period that Columbus and Berardi became partners, setting the foundation for the American venture. According to all evidence, Berardi not only helped to finance the first trip of Columbus but was entrusted with his affairs during the voyages.

Francesco Pinelli was a Genoese and a converted Jew. When Columbus traveled to Spain, Pinelli was an advisor to King Ferdinand, and because he was a part of the powerful Centurion family, Columbus met with him almost immediately. Pinelli was well regarded in the courts of Castile for his administrative abilities and his contributions to planning the conquest of the Canary Islands. He was also a supplier and financier for the royal family. In 1490 Pinelli was a magistrate in Seville and together with Luis de Santangel, another Jewish convert, was a director of the treasury of the Sacred Brotherhood, the military political police of the crown. Pinelli advanced so far in the service of the crown that in 1503, when the gold from the Antilles began to flow into Seville, he was named as a first agent for the Casa de la Contratación (House of Trade). He was possibly the most influential of the Genoese in Castile, marrying into the nobility and working his way into the highest circles of power. Pinelli was a protector of Columbus. Fernández-Armesto puts it succinctly: "It was on political and financial backing, not informed assent, that the launching of Columbus' enterprise depended" (203).

The first voyages of Columbus were financed jointly by loans from the Sacred Brotherhood and the collections of the papal bull in the diocese of Badajoz. Columbus's friends, Pinelli and Santangel, administered those funds and must have suggested them to the king as a source for financing the trip to America. That is the reason that the first letter Columbus wrote upon returning from the Caribbean was addressed to Santangel.

The rest of the funds—actually loans—including the part that was supposed to be contributed by Columbus, came privately from Italian capitalists. That same group of Italians, converted Jewish merchants who were close to the court, including Pinelli, who financed Columbus' fourth trip, were involved from the beginning in the enterprise of the Indies. Fernand Braudel says of these Genoese businessmen, "This extraordinary financial aristocracy devouring the world is the greatest adventure of the sixteenth century" (quoted in Collado Villalta, 93).

Fernández-Armesto is correct when he states that one of the factors favoring royal support for Columbus was the exclusion of Castile from the African coasts. For centuries the Castilians had nursed rising expectations about the gold of Ethiopia. Those expectations were kept alive with the gold arriving from the Sudan, which was controlled by the Arabs and the Portuguese with their partners from Genoa. The expansionist policy of Ferdinand and Isabella in North Africa, and afterward along the Atlantic coast, had the result that they had inserted themselves prominently in the circle of metallic wealth. But with the end of the war between Castile and Portugal in 1479, Castile saw its access to the African gold closed (Fernández-Armesto 205). The capture of slaves became an unavoidable substitute for the principal objective of the exploration, the search for gold. This explains the repeated references to gold in Columbus' diary, even though the first samples were so poor.

Since many different motives have subsequently been attributed to Columbus's first voyage, it is important to note that the Capitulaciones of Santa Fé does not mention either the search for new routes across the Atlantic or any objective other than to discover and capture new territories. That these lands existed at a reasonable distance no one doubted. One only has to look at the map made by Andrea Bianco in 1436, and also one by Toscanelli in 1474 (Lucena, 23, 33). In both are islands identified as "Antilia" and "Brasil." The association of these unconquered lands with and their supposed proximity to the continent of Asia are not that important. The determination of the Spanish monarchs to promote the conquest of the Canary Islands and other new explorations implies that their real objective was the possession of new bases to compensate strategically for those lost to Portugal in the Treaty of Alcazovas. Understood in this context, Columbus' trip was organized for much the same purposes as similar undertakings by other adventurers: to occupy the islands that bordered Africa.

Judging from the resources and investment allocated, the expectations for the enterprise were not high. The risk for the private investors was also low, their costs easily covered by the capture of slaves and the other unscrupulous practices associated with the venture. The Andalusian mariners, in particular, had years of practice in smuggling and piracy, activities that were more or less legal during the war with Portugal. The Pinzón brothers, for example, had long experience as corsairs in Catalonia, which did not trouble the monarchs when they hired the brothers for the Columbus enterprise (Coll y Juliá). Decidedly, neither the investment, the crews, the ships, nor the documents could lead us to conclude that Columbus' trip had the goal that it reached. If the Spanish and Portuguese monarchs had been convinced that the voyage would open new routes to the East and new enterprises to their rich and powerful kingdoms, Columbus would have been given a powerful fleet, not three small ships and an undisciplined crew without a priest. On the contrary, the trip would have been organized along the lines of the second expedition: seventeen ships, twelve hundred well-armed men, and provisions for establishing commercial and diplomatic agreements (Ramos Pérez). And the intense diplomatic effort upon his return to obtain papal support and international recognition for the trip would have taken place beforehand, not afterward. Indeed, there was no mention of a religious mission in the Capitulaciones, even though the trip was financed with funds from the papal bull for the Cruzada. Of course, when all those involved were confronted with the real economic potential of the Antilles, the rush to cover all legal aspects was urgent.

The value of the Caribbean islands was judged in the context of the explorations in the Atlantic. From the Azores to the Cape of Good Hope, no territories comparable to the Antilles in size, population, vegetation, and gold had yet been discovered. The Canaries were the only islands hitherto found to have a native population, but they lacked exploitable resources. The Azores and Porto Santo, Madeira, Arguin, and the Cape Verde Islands were all unpopulated when they were discovered. Their only value was to serve as bases for slave raids on the African coast. But the Antilles were something else, and it did not take long for Columbus to recognize this. He accurately sized up their economic potential despite his tendency to exaggerate and immediately realized the importance of the discovery. The contrasts between these new lands and those already known were dramatic and exciting in themselves and help to explain what happened afterward, without resorting to the myths that were spun centuries later.

Direct Implications of the First Trip

Columbian historiography was confused from the beginning, owing to the language used by Columbus to cover the practical aspects of the enterprise. The best source for precise information is not the diary of the first trip but a letter Columbus wrote to Luis de Santangel, dated February 15, 1493, a short time after his return. In this letter the situation is summed up as follows: many populated islands were discovered and all were taken possession of in the name of the monarchs, "with flowing royal flags, proclamations, and no real opposition" (Columbus, 4). This is very important. Rivera-Pagán (1990) has shown that the terms "discover" and "take possession" were synonymous. The occupation of the islands was, first of all, a consummated act that Columbus presented to the monarchs for political validation. Second, the islands were largely populated: "there are people there in uncountable numbers" (4). Third, the Indians were not worshippers of idols and could be converted. This imposed upon the monarchs the moral responsibility for their conversion. Fourth, the lands were very fertile, "to plant and to sow, to raise cattle of different kinds, and for the construction of villages" (3). Also, "there are many metal mines" (4). These were lands of great economic possibility. And fifth, but of considerable import, their populations, in addition to being numerous, were easy to subjugate. They had no weapons of importance, were of a generous nature, "extremely fearful," not ignorant, and "of a subtle intelligence"; in other words easily ruled, unlike those whom they found in the Canary Islands (5). Military entanglement would be unnecessary.

In the diary Columbus added something he omitted in the letter: "These people are very simple in weapons, as you can see with the seven captured . . . if you want to take them all to Castile, or keep them on the island as captives . . . with fifty men they can be subjugated and they will do whatever we want."[2] In this passage, he was proposing immediate subduing of the natives. The Taínos were not worshippers of idols or infidels, and they had not yet opposed conversion; neither had they resisted with arms the presence of the conquerors. Therefore, the first recommendation of Columbus reflects his predisposition to the Portuguese practice of the plunder and enslavement of the natives along the coast of Africa. But this policy had already been questioned by Rome, and the monarchs would not have accepted it. For this reason, it is significant that Columbus did not propose it in the letter, but substituted it with the other option, the charge of cannibalism. He referred to the existence of another people (that he had not seen yet) just at the entrance of the Indies, who were very ferocious and cannibal. This is the beginning of the myth that the Caribbean was populated by people who were violators of the natural law. Consequently their enslavement needed no further justification.[3] Also, the degrading judgment passed on the natives as an argument for enslavement had close antecedents. Just decades before, Portuguese looters employed this argument and King Duarte of Portugal used it on Pope Eugenio IV during the Council of Basilea in 1436 (Pérez Fernández, 156).

Columbus reused this justification for slavery that over the years had become crystallized. This ideological argument was there from his first trip, and indeed its use was almost inevitable. The cannibals were at "the gateway to the Indies," in a position to threaten strategically the Christian enterprise where the rumor of gold deposits was strongest. During the first trip, cannibals and gold were thus indissolubly wedded. If the gold was to be obtained the natives had to be subdued. All arguments, specific and symbolic, marshaled by Columbus led to the conclusion that the natives must be enslaved. For that reason he recommended immediate enslavement and exportation: "and slaves as many as you want and they will be idol worshipers" (Columbus, 13). That option accomplished various purposes. One, in the absence of other, more immediate resources, slavery would help cover the costs of the expeditions. This same device, we should not forget, was used earlier for the Canary Islands. Two, it avoided conflicts with the Vatican that protected the converted natives and that forbade conquest as a way of spreading the gospel. In many ways it was a clever proposition, since it played well into European prejudices that had been spread for centuries—the anthropofagia, as Hulme (1986) relates, was used to support anti-Semitism. At the same time, it also excluded cannibals from the projects of conversion. Decades later, this interpretation was refuted by Las Casas and Francisco de Vitoria, the great jurist, who argued that violations of natural rights were not a cause for a just war.[4]

But still, that counterargument had little support. For that reason, Columbus set a very important precedent in favor of slavery, which, although it had historical antecedents, had not yet explicitly been incorporated into the judicial system of the time. The later resistance of the Native Americans to conquest, their custom of keeping human bones as war trophies, and the general degree of ignorance among the conquistadors gave a certain credibility to this justification of slavery that was unwarranted by the facts themselves. Archeological studies have not to this day been able to confirm cannibal practices anywhere in America.[5]

The legislation against those accused of cannibalism that was approved by the monarchs years later manifested a shift of emphasis from traditional policies. In the case of the natives of the Canary Islands the sequence was conquest-subjection-conversion-freedom; in the Caribbean after 1503 it was conquest-subjection-enslavement. Columbus was the architect of a new ideological model derived from practice during his voyages.

The Second Voyage

The support for the second trip was more an acknowledgment of Columbus' ability to sell his ideas than a reward for his real achievements. The material results of his first trip were meager; the investment in his second, however, was very impressive—seventeen ships and twelve hundred men. Everyone traveling was convinced of its economic potential. But reality did not meet expectations. The tropical islands defied easy conquest. There were rich gold deposits, but the thick forests made it difficult to extract. The natives were friendly but this too had its limits. The enthusiasm of the invaders was greatly diminished when the new colonies became the exclusive monopoly of the crown with Columbus as its only partner. The rest of the settlers were excluded from exploiting the resources. Moreover, free trade was prohibited, and this brought many to ruin, spreading desolation and frustration. The enterprise itself was called into question and dissension among the Castilians threatened to end the first colonial experiment in America. Columbus, afraid more than anything else that he would lose support from the crown before the project began to be profitable, chose the slave option. With the memorandum of 1494 that he sent to the monarchs with pilot Antonio de Torres, he also sent twenty-six prisoners clearly designated as cannibals and slaves (Gil and Varela, 143). Columbus was thus making it clear that he regarded cannibalism as sufficient cause for enslavement. Through the native envoys (or slave offerings), he was in effect inquiring into the position of the monarchs on the slavery question.

The answer from the courts was very cautious, accepting the action in principle, but recommending that conversion to the gospel be made in the islands. The modifications demanded by the crown were both religious and legal. But Columbus went further, and in another part of the memorandum he proposed another line of reasoning, more strictly economic.

> Item, you will say to the monarchs that for the benefit of the souls of the cannibals and those that are here, I think that the more that are taken there, the better the crown could be served. . . . If your Majesties can give orders and license to a number of ships to come here every year bringing cattle and other useful things to cultivate and to take advantage of the land and all these at a reasonable price which could be paid for with slaves made from these cannibals, fierce people, well proportioned and disposed of good understanding, and which, taking away their inhumanity, we believe will be better than other slaves; and if in each one of the ships your Majesties put someone of trust, who will defend and command the ships and who will not stop any other place but here, where all the merchandise will be, and the slaves to take

away, leaving it up to your Majesties to take care of their rights over there; then you will so reply, so that we can do our job here with more confidence, if your Majesties approve. (Gil and Varela, 149)

The answer of the royal council to this proposal that slavery cover the expenses of the enterprise was not favorable. Possibly the magnitude was shocking or the proposal was made too early. The twenty-six natives sent with Torres in 1494 ended up in the hands of Columbus' commercial agent, Juanoto Berardi, who described them arriving in Seville: "Item, they bring twenty-six Indians of diverse islands and tongues . . . and here in our home we have twelve Indians who will be sent to the King, three were castrated, three were cannibals, and six Indians" (Gil and Varela, 214).

Meanwhile in Hispaniola, the situation was changing; the capture of new slaves was accelerating with the resistance of the natives to the new abuses by the impoverished settlers. Though the native resistance was increasing it was never a serious threat, and it offered an argument for more enslavement, with "captured in war" as a reason. With this new allegation, the crown tolerated the subjection and sale of peoples who had initially accepted the government of the Christians but subsequently rebelled. With the bull of Pope Alejandro VI, *Intercoetera*, of June 28, 1493, which named the Catholic monarchs as natural lords and the natives their vassals, the rebelling natives could be accused of treason for resisting enslavement. It is not known whether these legalities were known in Hispaniola or whether they were only the court's interpretations. But subsequent shipments of natives to Castile during the time of Columbus were designated as rebelling natives, not cannibals, and accepted as "prisoners of war," legalizing this second justification for enslavement of the American natives.

With the arrival of a great contingent of slaves in 1495, Bishop Fonseca, who was in charge of colonial issues, informed the king and queen, who sent their response from Madrid on April 12: "The King and Queen: Reverend in Christ, Father Bishop . . . and about what you have written to us about the Indians that came in the ships, we think they can be sold better in Andalucía than in any other place, and you can sell them the best way you think. . . ." Giménez Fernández 2:460). But awhile later, the bishop received a different order, one that reflected the concerns of Queen Isabella, or one of her consultants, about the legality of selling Indians. In a letter dated in June of the same year, they had asked opinions of legal scholars about the selling of

Indians, in order to advise Columbus, but the response did not arrive. Giménez Fernández, the biographer of Las Casas, charges that King Ferdinand and Bishop Fonseca conspired to hide the queen's counterorder: "It was tolerated and everyone looked the other way five more years as successive arrivals in Seville brought new slaves, many by the defeated settlers returning to Castile" (Giménez Fernández, 2: 461). The truth is that from that point on the human traffic from Hispaniola reached very high numbers.

The Shipment of 1495

When Columbus returned to Hispaniola on his second trip, he was confronted by the terrible spectacle of the burned-out village of La Navidad and the thirty-nine dead Christians who had been living there. This was the answer given by the Taínos to the gross abuses of the mariners: the attacks on their women and the spiritual licentiousness prevalent after Columbus's departure. Andrés Bernáldez, the chronicler for the king and queen, gives us a description of what happened and the consequences:

> The Admiral [Columbus] didn't forget the thirty-nine dead men and made his own inquiry and found out from the natives themselves who did the killings. He went out and captured many and sent them on the second shipment, 500 Indians, men and women, all of good age, from twelve to thirty-five. All were delivered in Seville to Sr. Juan de Fonseca; and they came from their countries the way that they were there, naked as they were born, with very little to eat, so they were starved and were taken badly advantage of, most of them dying. (Mederas)

War had begun in Hispaniola. At first it was directed against the chiefs Caonabo and Maireni, who were accused of the attack on La Navidad. But the battles spread to other regions. Las Casas gives more information about the events behind the big shipment of slaves in 1495: "In those days the Admiral sent to make war on the chief Guatiguara because he had put out orders to kill Christians, in which the Christians . . . killed many and took some of them to Castile, more than 500 slaves in the four ships that brought Antonio de Torres on February 24, 1495" (Las Casas 1995, 405).

Under Columbus's direction that warlike day they took 1,600 prisoners. Approximately 550 were sent to Castile and the rest, as related by Las Casas, died in port during a storm (de Cuneo quoted in Gil y Valera, 235–60). As to what happened to the shipment, we have a description by Michel de Cuneo, a fellow countryman of Columbus who traveled with them:

> When we arrived near Spain about 200 of the Indians had died and we threw them into the sea; I think the cool air was too different for them . . . and soon we arrived at Cadiz. There, we unloaded all the sick slaves. For your knowledge let me tell you they are not strong, are afraid of the cold weather, and do not have a long life.
>
> More than a hundred slaves were crowded into each ship, all naked in the middle of winter! We also know what happened to some of the survivors. Fifty of them were sent to the galleys in the Mediterranean under the orders of Juan Lezcano, a captain in the Royal Armada. They were to stay there until their legal status was determined, but it never was. (Quoted in Saco, 238)

In the archives of the cities of Seville and Valencia there are bills of sale for some of those who entered the commercial circuit as slaves (Cortés, 138). In 1497, the first Taíno was taken to Venice by the then Spanish ambassador (Peña Vargas, 23). Regardless of the ambiguous legal condition of the Amerindians in Spain in those days, the reality was that between 1494 and 1500 there was unrestricted and unquestioned slavery for the natives of Hispaniola. The justifications that Columbus elaborated were legalized by practice.

The Shipment of 1496

On April 20, 1496, Columbus returned to Spain. But instead of taking the direct route from Hispaniola, he took the long route through the Lesser Antilles. On the island of Guadeloupe, he stayed for nine days preparing for his crossing of the Atlantic. According to the testimony of his son Fernando, there were thirty native slaves with him. In Guadeloupe, he kidnapped two women, one the wife of a chief and the other her daughter, alleging that they were coming of their own accord. On the island of Santa Cruz in November 1493, his sailors also kidnapped women. They justified the action by saying that the women were cannibals. But that did not stop Columbus from giving a chiefly woman to his countryman, Michel de Cuneo. Nor did it stop the latter from raping her, according to a very graphic description that he wrote months later (see Gil and Varela, 174–5). Eventually the unhappy woman chief was sent to Castile as a specimen of what a cannibal was like.

The first time Columbus was in Guadeloupe, days before the assault on Santa Cruz, he also took ten women, supposedly prisoners of the Carib natives. Alvarez Chanca, the doctor on board, said that they were from Puerto Rico. But some days later, when going past that island, the Spaniards did not free them.

Each of these incidents involves the kidnapping of women by Columbus, and while the justifications change the results remain the same. This pattern was repeated again along the coast of Paria in 1498. These gratuitous actions by Columbus explain the later so-called aggression by the natives better than their allegedly inherent warlike nature.

Some months after Columbus's departure for Spain, his brother, Bartolomé, who was in charge of affairs in Hispaniola, sent a new shipment of three hundred slaves. The three ships under the command of Pedro Alonso Niño arrived in Cádiz on October 29, 1496. From this lot, twenty-four were sent to Seville immediately, but ten died going up the river Guadalquivir. Las Casas relates the circumstances:

> Having received the letter from the Admiral and with them the ones that were being sent to the monarchs, his brother Bartolomé decided to send them immediately on the three ships swollen with slaves (about 300 innocent Indians), and with the reasons and justifications stated above, because the Admiral wrote to the monarchs that certain Indian chiefs from the island had killed some Christians (without saying how many of the Indians had been hacked to pieces); and the Kings responded that all of the ones he found guilty should be sent to Castile, I myself think as slaves, as captives of war. Considering the justification and counsel that the Admiral had given to the monarchs for war against these peaceful people who lived in these lands without offending anyone and in whom the Admiral, on his first trip, saw so many qualities of goodness, peacefulness, simplicity, and gentleness, at the very least it seems that we should question that justice or injustice; but only the Admiral was believed, and since nobody spoke for the Indians, their side of the justice or injustice was not considered. . . . They remained judged as delinquents from the beginning and were destroyed until they were all gone without anyone feeling for their deaths or taking it as a crime. (Las Casas, 439)

This wonderful defense of human rights shows that at the very time that slave colonies were begun in America, there was also, in Columbus' own time, a voice of repulsion and censure of his actions. But from the very first, Las Casas, who was hardly an enemy of Columbus, was always cautious to widen the circle of responsibility for the practices that he criticized. Of Columbus' slave policy he said: "As for his errors, blindness, and ignorance . . . there is no excuse . . . but that the Admiral, not being a learned man, was ignorant of the injustice by the monarchs and the Courts is no great surprise" (Las Casas, 440).

In other words, it was the advisors to the court who should be condemned for tolerating slavery, and what could be expected from someone like Columbus who was not educated? Las Casas used Columbus' poor education and intelligence many times in attempting to exonerate him, and shifted the responsibility to those who had the power and authority to avert what was happening.

The Shipment of 1498

In 1498 the slave enterprise of Columbus reached its pinnacle. If the Indian chiefs would pay the tributes imposed on them and produce enough food, the settlers would survive. But the land did not spontaneously yield its fruits and the settlers did not have an efficient administration. The colonies under the Columbus brothers were a caricature of what an enterprise was supposed to be, and only the terrible human costs prevent us from calling the whole enterprise a comedy. The inefficient administration, the severe bureaucracy, the envy for little favors, the deep resentment against Columbus for being a foreigner, and the effects of the high cost of living induced the Castilians to insubordination and conspiracy. These factors helped the natives intensify their resistance. Ironically, when the native insurgency started, the anxiety and tension of the Castilians toward each other dropped and they united in the face of war, with its prospects of booty, plunder, and the capture of new slaves. Las Casas stated: "Those taken alive will become slaves, and that was the principal crop of the Admiral, with which he expected to cover the expenses that the monarchs exacted for supporting the Spanish in the islands to the advantage of the monarchs, in order to tempt merchants and people to live there without expecting a salary from the monarchs, and without any necessity of giving one" (Las Casas, 71).

Columbus administered Hispaniola as a Guinean trading post. Peasants, who could have changed the nature of the whole undertaking, were excluded.

The royal monopoly of all the benefits raised the cost to levels that were insupportable. Florentine friends of Columbus pressed for an opening of business just as Berardi, Columbus' partner and agent, had done. But the crown was not ready to share with anyone else the fruits of the looting and exploitation, being still resentful of Columbus' participation in the benefits. In 1498, Columbus proposed an increase of the slave trade to attract merchants who would supply the island, paying them with slaves. And he did not wait for a reply. On October 18 of that year, five ships left Hispaniola carrying eight hundred Taíno slaves. Of these, six hundred were to be sold and the rest were payment to the sailors to cover the cost of the fleet. Columbus had converted the Indians to merchandise, and they became the principal means of paying for the enterprise.

The increase in the sale of slaves from America began to become politically difficult for the monarchs. According to Herrera, the official chronicler, Columbus proposed that "the monarchs profit from the natives the way the Portuguese monarchs profited from the blacks of Guinea" (Las Casas, 436); but Castile did not have the sugar colonies into which Portugal had invested a vast number of slaves. Furthermore, the Taínos were not highly regarded for domestic purposes because of their high death rate. For one reason or another, Columbus' policies opened the way for a confrontation. In his correspondence with the monarchs, Columbus admitted that without doubt the slave trade would continue to move forward, the prose being less rhetorical and more calculated. When, for example, he brought up the mortality rate during travel, his attitude was naked and stripped of any pretense: "It is alright that they die now, it will not be always that way; such was the case with the blacks and those from the Canary Islands, and despite that we profited from them." Las Casas recognized that out of one hundred slaves, a year later, only ten were alive, and he asked: "How enormous and blind is this insensitivity?" (Las Casas, 438).

The Last Shipment of 1499

In that year, the seditious Castilians under the order of Juan Roldán, who had been causing Columbus so much trouble as he sought to establish control over the new colonies, returned to Spain with three hundred natives given to them by Columbus to win them over. The sharing of slaves among individual settlers with permits to take them out to Spain was for Columbus a serious abuse of his power. The queen, who was in Seville when the shipment arrived, gave the order of confiscation and freed all of the slaves. This action taken on June 20, 1500, has been blown completely out of proportion by conservative Castilian historians and used to support the notion of the queen's anti-slavery position. Taken out of context, it leaves Christopher Columbus as the only guilty party in the slave traffic of the Antilles. The truth is that what the queen was protesting was the introduction of private interests into participation in the slave trade. Columbus had not been given authority for this. As long as Columbus was acting within the limits set by the crown, the crown did not have many scruples. And even the order for confiscation had arrived too late. The natives had been sold in Andalucía. They could find only twenty-one; two stayed of their own free will, so out of three hundred they returned only nineteen.

Since 1494, about two thousand slaves had been brought to Castile. Ferdinand and Isabella allowed this because they were considered prisoners of war. In 1492, using the same argument, the monarchs acceded to the sale of the Guanches. In 1503, Isabella authorized the unrestricted seizure of the Caribs, opening the door to the vicious hunting that would last for centuries. Then the cover was the incentive for exploration, because private initiatives were easily made palatable. And it was also Queen Isabella who had legalized the distribution of the natives through the ominous system of the *encomiendas,* which in practice became responsible for the disappearance of the Taínos. Decidedly, Isabella has passed into history as a pious woman, and no doubt she may have been; but that is one of the reasons for the popular Spanish saying that the road to hell is paved with good intentions. After her death in 1504, Ferdinand openly supported all the slave projects that the *encomenderos* and merchants on the islands asked for. Decades later most of the islands were "unpopulated." The mining companies now in full operation were the incentive. Seen in perspective, Columbus becomes only a factor in a historical process moved by a complex interplay of interests.

With the arrival in Hispaniola of Knight Commander Francisco de Bobadilla, the administrative regime of Columbus was over. Licenses for exploration were given to other entrepreneurs, taking away his exclusive control. Moreover, Columbus was prohibited from setting foot in Hispaniola. With the arrival of Bobadilla, the settlers, relieved after years of Columbus' chaotic administration, did not forget their resentments. From all over the island they came to complain about Columbus, who, according to them, was only interested in pursuing an unjust war against the natives "in order to send slaves to Castile." That slave policy seems to have affected the settlers, who would have preferred to keep the natives on the islands working for them. Columbus had touched too many interests on and off the islands. He was personally blamed for delays of the enterprise and also for what the enterprise could never have achieved. Giménez Fernández, for example, states: "During the period from 1493 to 1500, Hispaniola was nothing more than a military base and a merchant trading post, without ever becoming a colonial settlement much less a missionary post" (Giménez Fernández, 2: 574).

But Giménez Fernández mistakenly assumes that the latter reasons were the ones that took Christopher Columbus to America in the first place. The statement thus has an ideological subtext. In reality it was the gold that kept Columbus in the Antilles and gold that attracted the invaders in the first place. The Antilles were the first enterprises of this type overseas. The error, if we can call it that, was in not being able to survive the initial stage. Curiously the church, and doubtlessly for religious reasons, was the most critical of the Hispaniola adventure. Father Juan de Robles, in a letter to Cardinal Cisneros, the queen's confessor and the leading representative of the Castilian interests in court, wrote: "If he [Columbus] came back everything will be destroyed and in this nothing will remain alive, neither Christian nor religious"; Father Juan de Trasiera, another priest on the island, wrote: "Dear Reverend Sir: For the love of God, so much good was done when Pharaoh [the name given to Columbus] left this place, make sure that he or any of his countrymen never return to these islands." The criticism was extended to the people of Genoa in general. The Franciscans also sent an accusatory memorandum: "Item, that your Majesty never send Genoese here again, because they rob and destroy, because of their greed for gold . . . they will take the money to other lands, and the island would be laid to waste, at much too high a price" (Giménez Fernández, 2: 574).

In the final part of the story, capitalist merchants, who had been promoting the "Indies Enterprise" from the beginning, appeared beside Columbus. They were his accomplices. History is not made by individuals after all. Columbus and the coterie of Italian and Spanish merchants that were behind the early conquest of America were only the forerunners of a new international order that was crystallizing as the new hegemonic power. Implicit in this structure was a new division of labor that now, with the new wealth from America, would be imposed as a worldwide order. The Caribbean was its first manifestation on the American stage. In the bill of indictment of that long and terrible history of servility and slavery in the capitalist world system, Columbus has the distinction of being the first to introduce that new order to America.

Notes

1. Beginning in 1493, Columbus was directly responsible for the enslavement and sale in Spain of some 2,000 Amerindians. In 1493, Columbus brought 12 slaves back to the Old World from Cuba and Hispaniola. In 1494, he sent 26 from the Lesser Antilles and Puerto Rico. In 1495, he sent 550 from Hispaniola. In 1496, he himself carried off 32 from Hispaniola and Guadeloupe while his brother shipped on a separate trip 300 additional slaves also from Hispaniola. In 1498, he sent 800 slaves, and again in 1499 another lot of 300 Taínos left the island colony for the Mediterranean slave markets.

2. Varela 1982. All of Columbus's writings are reproduced here.

3. On the Caribs' and cannibalism, see Sued-Badillo 1978, Hulme 1986, and Myers 1986.

4. Las Casas discusses the subject in his *Historia de las Indias* and his *Apologética*.

5. For a recent discussion, see Whitehead 1984 and Davis and Goodwin 1990.

Under the Cuban Flag

Notions of Indigeneity at the End of the Nineteenth Century

PETER HULME

Until the Indian marches again, America will limp.

José Martí, *Our America*

Why, in a popular novel of 1897 set in Cuba, about United States involvement in the movement for Cuban independence, is there to be found an indigenous community that has survived untouched since the early sixteenth century, when all historical accounts have Caribbean indigenous communities as virtually extinct from soon after the European invasion?

In Frederick Ober's novel *Under the Cuban Flag, or The Cacique's Treasure* (1897), three U.S. citizens are landed on the northeast Cuban coast in the bay of Nipe by a boat delivering arms to Cuban rebels. The captain of the boat describes them to the rebel leader as a "harmless" professor "who only wants permission to study the natural history of the island"; a military instructor who has a letter from the Cuban junta in the States recommending him to General Maceo but whom the captain thinks "is sent down here on secret service by the president of the United States, to report on the exact situation"; and a "light-headed Yankee . . . prospecting for cash" (Ober 1897, 15–16). They are, respectively, Professor Brown, Major Carrolton, and Doctor Johnson.[1]

This is an adventure story, so there is much spying, suspicion of spying, melodrama, and lifesaving. It is also a romance, so the Cuban rebel leader, Santos Gomez, has a sister-in-law, Hortensia, with whom the Major and the Professor both immediately fall in love. By this time, the action has moved to the rebel camp on top of El Yunque. Here the Professor finds a cave that has been used as a burial place for indigenous caciques. They also meet a young boy from Boston, Archie Goodwin, the son of a banana merchant, who, in return for saving the life of another infamous rebel, Carlos Lopez, had been sent a gold figurine made by Indians. Lopez eventually shows the Professor the full extent of the treasure from which this piece was drawn:

> Don Carlos thrust his hand in underneath a rock, and drew out an earthen vessel shaped like an ancient amphora . . . . He inverted the amphora, and out rolled a stream of golden trinkets, falling with mellow music upon the shelf of semi-translucent limestone. There were objects like grinning satyrs, beetles, tortoises, little gods with arms extended, heads of men and women, some with crowns, and others with coils of golden hair . . . spear and arrow heads, some as broad as the palm of one's hand, and all of gold! Reaching in again, he drew out another earthen amphora, and out of this tumbled figures of golden parrots, fern-leaves, monkeys—all nature seemed to be duplicated in this collection cunningly wrought out by the ancient aboriginal artists. When he had done, there lay before the astonished spectators two shining heaps of almost priceless treasures. (Ober 1897, 104)

When they emerge from the cave, they see in the distance "the white walls of the port of Baracoa" (79), from which all this "treasure" is destined to leave the island.

The rebels are tricked into believing that the Major is a Spanish spy. He is condemned to death but is rescued by Hortensia, who thereby declares her love for him. The embattled group flees into the mountains of the Sierra del Cristal, guided by the maid, Juanita, who is a *mestiza* descendant of the aboriginal inhabitants and who still speaks the Indian language. Eventually, they enter a deep ravine and are ambushed and captured by Indians carrying bows and arrows, wearing only breechcloths and feathers, and dressing their hair in scalp locks—in other words conforming fully to North American depictions of American Indians at this time. There are signs in the mountains of ancient cannons and arquebuses.

> The chief saw that the Major's attention was attracted by these antiquities . . . and in good but archaic Spanish briefly told him their history. It seems that a Spanish general, some time in the fifteenth century, learn-

ing that the Indians had fled to this retreat in the mountains, invaded the forest with a force of men and artillery. He never went back, nor were any of his men ever seen again by their countrymen. Led astray by false guides at first, then hemmed in and ambuscaded, the last of the Spaniards perished at the very verge of the Indian valley. "But," explained the chief, with a shrewd twinkle in his black eyes, "we did not kill the horses that drew the cannon, and we lured them on and on, until very near the spot you saw them; then we fell upon the remnant of soldiers and put the last one to death. That was the last time our country was invaded; no white man has ever been here since. Long ago we used the last pinch of powder—long since fired the last arquebuse. Now we depend upon our arrows, spears and lances; but we kill not much game, for our gardens and the fields and forests give us enough for our wants."

"But I thought—all the world believes—that the last of the Indians were killed by the Spaniards many, many years ago," said the Major.

"Yes? That is good; that is why we have been preserved, instead of being hunted like beasts as our ancestors were. It was in Cacique Hauetey's [*sic*] time that, believing the end was near, our fathers assembled together and took counsel of wisdom. They fled to these mountains, and the Spaniards believed they had all committed suicide, as, indeed, many of the Indians had. Ever since we have lived here, shut in from the world, knowing nothing of what the world has done for more than three hundred years. You are the first invaders; it was predicted long, long ago that you and the beautiful woman by your side should come; that you should arrive on the eve of an important festival; so we went down to meet you, and lo, here you are! You will never return, neither you nor your lovely companion, but you will not be prisoners; no, as free as the air around us, you shall be, until—." (205–6)

Drawing on a knowledge of Indian psychology gained from his long campaigns against the Apache and Plains Indians, the Major fears they are going to be sacrificed and that he will need all his cunning to insinuate a different course of action into the chief's mind. The Indians expect a message from the divine Hortensia, which the Major concocts "to the effect that, if the Indians wished to preserve themselves from extermination, they should remain concealed in their stronghold yet another decade, or until another message should acquaint them with the Cacique's wishes. Meanwhile, they should still pursue the paths of peace, carefully refrain from committing bloodshed, and endeavour to improve their material and moral condition" (225).

In a flurry of incidents toward the end of the novel, the Major and Hortensia are married in Key West; the Doctor returns on a filibuster and is captured by the forces of General Weyler, the Spanish commandant; and Carlos brings news of the death of General Maceo, one of the Cuban leaders, betrayed under a flag of truce. The Doctor spells out the novel's message: "If I had the means, I'd fit out a filibuster every month for the assistance of those gallant insurgents fighting over there, in the island we have just left behind. In other words, if our Government hasn't the backbone to assist those people struggling for freedom, right on our very coast, then let our own people take a hand in the game!" (314–15).

In broad terms *Under the Cuban Flag* is clearly an adventure story for boys in the nineteenth-century tradition of Jules Verne, G. A. Henty, and Mayne Reid, all of whom were popular in the United States and whose work features the same panoply of treasure, old maps, bones, and heroic young westerners; but Ober's detailed topographies, contemporary settings, and historical characters separate his novels from the classic adventures that usually take place in a vague or entirely fictional geography and are usually set back in time. Two features of *Under the Cuban Flag* are therefore particularly worthy of note: its fictional engagement with political themes of the moment—the insurgent war in Cuba, the persistent filibustering from the United States, the death of Maceo; and, second, its highlighting of the indigenous theme—the treasure of the caciques and the discovery of an aboriginal community that has survived untouched in the mountains since the end of the sixteenth century. I'll deal with the two aspects separately, focusing on the key year of 1897, when the novel was published, before finally moving out from the novel itself to some broader questions.

The year 1897 saw the strengthening of the influential group of U.S. imperialists led by Theodore Roosevelt. On January 2, 1897, Roosevelt wrote to his sister Anna:

I am a quietly rampant "Cuba Libre" man. I doubt whether the Cubans would do very well in the line of self-government; but anything would be better than continuance of Spanish rule. I believe that Cleveland ought now to recognize Cuba's independence and interfere; sending our fleet promptly to Havana. There would not in my opinion be very serious fighting; and what loss we encountered would be thrice over repaid by the ultimate results of our action. (Roosevelt 1951, 573–74)

In May, naval historian Alfred Thayer Mahan published the latest in his series of analyses of sea power, providing the intellectual foundation for Roosevelt's strengthening of the U.S. Navy: "In the cluster of island fortresses of the Caribbean is one of the greatest of the nerve centers of the whole body of European civilization; and it is to be regretted that so serious a portion of them now is in hands which not only never have given, but to all appearances never can give, the development which is required by the general interest" (261). In response, on May 3, 1897 Roosevelt wrote a revealing and confidential letter, which was studded with the prophetic phrase, "if I had my way": Hawaii would be annexed, Spain would be turned out of the Caribbean, the Danish islands would be acquired (607–8). On November 19, 1897, now as Assistant Secretary to the Navy, and with growing self-assurance, he wrote to another correspondent:

> I would regard a war with Spain from two standpoints: first, the advisability on the grounds both of humanity and self-interest of interfering on behalf of the Cubans, and of taking one more step toward the complete freeing of America from European dominion; second, the benefit done our people by giving them something to think of which isn't material gain, and especially the benefit done our military forces by trying both the Navy and the Army in actual practice. (717)

While there were obvious limits as to what Roosevelt could say in public, the death of José Martí in 1895, followed by the military successes of Máximo Gómez and Antonio Maceo, and then by Maceo's own death in December 1896, had already galvanized popular U.S. interest in events in Cuba. By 1897 there was widespread public support for filibustering, which encountered sporadic official opposition in U.S. ports. One contemporary observer compiled a list of thirty-six vessels that made seventy-one expeditions to Cuba between March 1895 and April 1898 (Olivart). Archie Goodwin's father in *Under the Cuban Flag* is said to have run a banana-exporting business from Baracoa to Boston, which suggests the career of Capt. John S. Hart, of Philadelphia, one of the largest importers of bananas into the United States. Hart had substantial investments in such a business and, finding it destroyed by the outbreak of the revolution, promptly turned his ships into filibusters. He was eventually tried and convicted in a U.S. court and imprisoned in Philadelphia (R. T. Hill, 214; and Wisan, 231–32, 291).

The U.S. press—especially the Hearst newspapers—spent much of 1897 looking for a symbol of Cuba to further its campaign for U.S. intervention. It had one false start in February when Hearst's leading reporter, Richard Harding Davis, filed a story about Clemencia Arango, a woman being expelled from Cuba for carrying dispatches to her brother's rebel forces; she had been undressed and searched by the Spanish authorities on the boat taking her to Florida. Frederic Remington, safely back in New York, illustrated this story with an imaginative sketch under the headline: "Does Our Flag Shield Women? . . . Refined Young Women Stripped and Searched by Brutal Spaniards While Under Our Flag on the *Olivette*" (*New York Journal*, February 12, 1897). Massive indignation followed until the *New York World*, the *Journal*'s chief rival, interviewed Arango on the quay at Tampa and discovered that she *had* been searched, but by a woman, and with no men present in the room.

Hearst did better with the story of Evangelina Cisneros, the young Cuban woman imprisoned in the Recojidas gaol in Havana after resisting the attentions of a Spanish officer whom she had petitioned for the release of her father, a political prisoner on the Isle of Pines. Evangelina Cisneros became the very symbol of Cuba: "The unspeakable fate to which Weyler has doomed an innocent girl whose only crime is that she defended her honor against a beast in uniform has sent a shudder of horror through the American people" said the *Journal* (August 19). That "beast in uniform" "held her father's life and liberty in his hands, and demanded of her the sacrifice of all a true woman holds dear as the price of her father's safety" (August 30).[2]

Evangelina was described, in various *Journal* articles over the next month or so, as "young, beautiful, cultured, guilty of no crime save that of having in her veins the best blood in Cuba" (August 17); "a girl of sensational beauty and great refinement . . . ," possessing "excellence of character, high social position, refinement and exceeding beauty . . ." (August 18). These descriptions can be compared to those of Ober's Cuban heroine: "blue-black hair in a massive coil at the crown of a daintily-poised head; deep-gazing, liquid eyes, with long, curled lashes; a mouth like a heart of a red rose, teeth white as milk, and a complexion of cream and strawberries" (Ober 1897, 47). Together Evangelina and Hortensia offered an image of "acceptable"

Latinity: dark-haired and dark-eyed, but light of complexion and of good breeding.

Dramatically rescued by Karl Decker, the *Journal's* own reporter, Evangelina arrived in New York on October 13. Two days later there was a reception at Delmonico's followed by a rally in Madison Square that was attended by one hundred thousand people: "Karl Decker, tall, stalwart, even ferocious looking, with his six feet two of brawn and muscle, formed a fitting foil to her spirituelle loveliness" (October 17). She was sent off to Washington to meet the president, undertook a tour of the United States to rally support for Cuba, and was then swiftly forgotten. The *Journal* brought out a small book in which she and Decker told their stories, introduced and embellished by Julian Hawthorne:

> The desirable component elements are all present. A tropic island, embosomed in azure seas . . . a cruel war, waged by the minions of despotism against the spirit of patriotism and liberty; a beautiful maiden, risking all for her country, captured, insulted, persecuted, and cast into a loathsome dungeon. None could be more innocent, constant and adorable than she; none more wicked, detestable and craven than her enemies. All is right and lovable on the one side, all ugly and hateful on the other. As in the old Romances, there is no uncertainty as to which way our sympathies should turn. (Cosío y Cisneros, 15)

The hero, Decker, is described as "a young American of the best and oldest strain, with the Constitution in his backbone and the Declaration of Independence in his eyes. . . . Beyond his frank and simple bearing was conveyed the impression that here was one who could keep his own counsel: could hide a purpose in the depths of his soul, as a torpedo is hidden in the sea, and explode it at the proper moment in the vitals of his adversary" (Cosío y Cisneros 1898, 17–19, 23–24). This was clearly intended to be read as a national self-image, a portrait of the United States in its young manhood, before it had yet exploded any torpedoes in the vitals of any adversaries, but at a moment when it was beginning to realize that it was capable of doing so. The country's nationhood, disembodied from the manifest destiny of continental expansion, was redefining itself through an identification with the prowess of the individual male body. It is ironic then, tragic even, that the "torpedo" would soon explode not in its adversary's vitals but in its own, with the destruction of the *Maine,* which was to follow in February 1898.

Under the Cuban Flag, aimed at an adolescent readership, can be usefully set alongside one of the best-sellers of 1897, Richard Harding Davis's *Soldiers of Fortune*, an adventure story firmly grounded in the actual relationships between U.S. industry and Cuba in the 1890s. The hero of *Soldiers of Fortune*, Richard Clay, is working for a mining company after discovering masses of red hematite ore lying exposed on the side of a mountain in the fictional country of Olancho. As he explains, "The people know it is there, but have no knowledge of its value, and are too lazy to ever work it themselves" (R. Davis, 30). The value of the ore lies in its high iron content, making it perfect for the Bessemer process that had recently revolutionized steel making and therefore the twin industries of railways and armaments.

The setting for *Soldiers of Fortune* is very closely modeled on the development of the U.S. mining interests on the south coast of Cuba where, in the 1880s, Frederick Wood, an agent to the Pennsylvania Steel Company and one the country's top mining engineers, found what would prove to be 15 million tons of hematite rock with 62 percent iron content, making him an almost exact forerunner of his fictional counterpart, Robert Clay. Within six months Wood was back with engineers and plans for a railroad to carry the ore to Santiago. Mineral rights were secured free of charge. Mining began in 1884. By 1898 the Juraguá Iron Company owned eleven of the seventeen mines in the region and was called "a powerful, progressive, and well-managed American corporation, which has done more to develop the mining industries of Cuba than all the other interests combined" (Clark, 409). Its output averaged a quarter of a million tons in the ten years up to 1897. All told, the U.S. iron-mining companies in Cuba represented an investment of U.S. capital of about $8 million, and in the fourteen years of operation prior to 1898 they had paid $2 million in import duties on iron ore into the U.S. Treasury (Porter, 323).[3] Davis's Olancho, the setting for *Soldiers of Fortune*, is a northern South American country bordering on Ecuador and Venezuela, but it is not Colombia; in other words Davis deliberately rules out a direct correlation with any single country. However, Olancho's capital city, Valencia, is very clearly based on Santiago de Cuba. When he was twenty-two Davis, who was born in Philadelphia, had visited Santiago and its surroundings in the company of an old friend of his who was president of the Bethlehem Iron Company. He saw how the ore was taken down on a narrow-gauge railway across the river Juraguá to Siboney, where it was loaded onto trains running to the docks of Las Cruces on the eastern side of Santiago harbor. This exact topography appears in *Soldiers of Fortune* (Lubow, 28; see Javis, 35–36; and Foner, 2: 482). A few years later U.S. historian Irene Wright was sailing toward Santiago:

> We stretched our eyes towards Daiquirí and Siboney, where the American invaders landed in 1898. Commercial-minded that I am, I was more interested in the approximate situation of the iron mines of Juragua,— camp of another and more important American invasion. I desired to know just where it is that the land thrusts that closed fist into the sea which Richard Harding Davis's 'Soldier of Fortune' was intent to make let go its riches at his will. The geography of this vicinity is that of the novel. (353)

Clay's association with Cuba is emphasized when a young girl asks about his father: "'My father, Miss Hope,' he said, 'was a filibuster, and went out on the *Virginius* to help free Cuba, and was shot, against a stone wall. We never knew where he was buried'" (R. Davis, 175). The reference is to the summary execution of fifty-three U.S. citizens in 1873 for running guns onto the south coast of Cuba, an incident that came close to causing an earlier war between Spain and the United States. The filibusters were killed in Santiago, Davis's Valencia, close to where this fictional conversation takes place (see R. Bradford).

Frederick Albion Ober (1849–1913) was a travel writer, journalist, novelist, naturalist, public lecturer, children's writer, biographer, and historian, successful enough in his day, though without the public profile of Richard Harding Davis. In the last three decades of the nineteenth century he was an almost constant traveler, principally in the Caribbean. Ober initially saw himself as a scientist, but after the commercial success of his travel book, *Camps in the Caribbees: The Adventures of a Naturalist in the Lesser Antilles* (1879), he broadened his horizons and made a career for himself as a writer. Since his death nobody has taken much interest in Frederick Albion Ober, but during the last decade of the nineteenth century he probably knew as much about the Caribbean as anyone in the United States. He had traveled widely in the region, especially in the more remote parts rarely visited by other travelers, met with many of the statesmen and leading figures, and read broadly in the area's history. In one sense, though, this made Ober an atypical figure: after 1898, when the stream of writing about the Spanish-speaking Caribbean became a torrent, he would seem like a minor voice, an amateur drowned by the instant expertise of economists, sociologists, and other analysts of the backward islands that had fallen into U.S. hands.

Like Davis, Ober had previous knowledge of Cuba to draw on. In his case, the success of his travel book about the Caribbean and his connections at the Smithsonian Institution had led to his appointment as Special Commissioner to the West Indies for the 1893 Chicago Columbian Exposition, charged with arranging loans of Columbus-related material: he took the opportunity to write a book about his journey through the islands, modestly entitled *In the Wake of Columbus*. Ober headed from Massachusetts to Washington, D.C. , to receive his instructions on December 31, 1890 (Ober 1893, 121–22), therefore passing through New York just as Martí's essay "Nuestra América" was published and as more extensive accounts filtered through of the massacre at Wounded Knee, which had taken place on December 29. After visiting Havana, he traveled east by steamer to Gibara, then past the Bay of Nipe to Baracoa, taking the opportunity of recounting the story of the Indian genocide: "Nothing remains now of the native population, and the only reminders of them are the rude implements of warfare and agriculture sometimes discovered" (165); and noting how Spanish soldiers "are devastating the land like a curse of grasshoppers and locusts" (162).

Setting, date, and genre all therefore link *Under the Cuban Flag* with *Soldiers of Fortune*. More important, both novels deal with what they see as the kind of relationship that should pertain between the United States and Cuba. The connection between indigeneity and mining will emerge more slowly.

Under the Cuban Flag ties the political moment of 1897 to a notion of Cuban indigeneity. In the United States, the invasion of Cuba in 1898 was seen in some sense as a continuation of its own Indian wars, so the Indian-Cuban link might not in any case seem so strange. Many of the military personnel involved in the invasion had fought, like the fictional Major Carrolton, against the Apache and the Lakota during the 1870s and 1880s: Generals Shafter and Wood were both renowned Indian fighters. Roosevelt, the leading proponent of intervention, had written a long book, *The Winning of the West* (1900), in praise of westward expansion over Indian lands, and the unit he commanded in Cuba was known as the Rough Riders, named after Buffalo Bill Cody's Congress of Rough Riders. To confirm the connection, Buffalo Bill's show soon included a version of the so-called Battle of San Juan Hill taken from

Roosevelt's description in *The Rough Riders* (1902), displacing the show's previous representation of Custer's Last Stand. More ambiguously, one of Roosevelt's horses was given the name Rain-in-the-Face by his black body-servant, a name that had become famous as the name of the Sioux warrior popularly supposed to have killed Custer, cut his heart out, and eaten it: this story seems not to have been true, despite Longfellow's eloquent poem on the subject (Utley, 126–31). Ironically, the horse was drowned off Daiquirí.

From within Cuba, a factor in the political relevance of indigeneity is clearly the development in the Caribbean in the early nineteenth century of the use by Creole intellectuals of the symbols of a pre-Hispanic past to provide an alternative to Spanish identity. The terms *borincanos* (from Borinquen, the indigenous name for Puerto Rico) and *quisquellanos* (from Quisquella, Hispaniola's indigenous name) came into use at this time, although no Cuban equivalent is necessary since the island had managed—like Jamaica—to retain its indigenous name. From these years, the most resonant event is the naming of Haiti, a black republic surprisingly taking an indigenous name (Geggus). Associated with Creole consciousness is the development of literary movements that explored indigenous themes and vocabulary. The Cuban variant, *ciboneyismo,* has frequently been seen as insignificant and artificial, even by distinguished Cuban critics (Vitier, 159–60; Arrom; Pérez Firmat, 95–111; but cf. Schulman). At its best, *ciboneyista* poetry can summon the image of the lost utopia of an Indian world, an invocation that has always had a strong political charge. As José Fornaris wrote, in the 1888 edition of his *Cantos del Siboney* (1855), drawing out the political implications of *ciboneyista* writing:

> Only in a symbolic way could a poet express his love for his country and protest against the unjust and insolent manner in which it was governed. The word *patria* was heard by those governors as an insurrectionary shout.... I know full well that this corresponded to the idea contained in the verses. In them could be seen a symbolism in which the Ciboney Indians represented the oppressed Cubans, and the Carib Indians represented the unjust oppressors. (quoted in Vitier, 158)

By the 1890s the ideological battle against Spain, waged by Cubans and others, often turned on *Spanish* treatment of the aboriginal population of the Caribbean (rather than, as with Fornaris, on *Carib* attacks on native Cubans). In *Under the Cuban Flag* this criticism comes from the mouth of a beautiful, upper-class Cuban woman, Emilia Del Monte, whom Carlos Lopez eventually marries:

> Spain was recreant to her high trust; she not only neglected the great opportunity given her of God, to save the souls of the heathen millions but she sent them rather into perdition. We all know, for Spain's own priests and bishops have left it on record, that their country plundered and murdered the innocent, inoffensive people of this island; and, within the century that it was discovered, she had nearly exterminated them all, to the number of hundreds of thousands. (Ober 1897, 270)

A letter by Antonio Maceo from early 1897 sets the Cuban struggle within the context of Spanish cruelties dating back to the early sixteenth century, a connection made more compelling by General Weyler's policy of *reconcentración*. Maceo himself was often compared to the sixteenth-century Taíno leader Guamá, with Máximo Gómez as the Haitian Hatuey (Morote Creus, 369–70; García Arévalo, 24; Ortiz Fernández, 10). So, from both the United States and Cuban sides, there were Indian reference points for the rebellion of the 1890s and therefore a possible logic to the plot of *Under the Cuban Flag*.

At the end of the novel, the cacique's treasure is sold for $80,000 to a U.S. museum, and with this money a filibuster fund is established at Indian Key. The very last paragraph of the novel reads:

> At all events, the papers of late have been full of the doings of a trim little schooner, filled with arms, ammunition, and medical stores, which has repeatedly run the blockade off the Cuban coast, and cheered the hearts of the insurgents mightily. It was their own venture, and as it was fitted out with funds furnished by the Cacique's treasure: thus had time at last avenged the poor Indians of Cuba! (Ober 1897, 316)[4]

There are certain ironies here. The United States—in the novel still providing filibusters rather than full-scale invaders—"avenge[s] the poor Indians of Cuba" against the Spaniards who exterminated them just seven years after one key event, the massacre at Wounded Knee, during which the United States attempted to exterminate part of its own Indian population. Meanwhile, within the fiction, the "poor Indians" can only be thought of as "avenged" through the occlusion of their fictional survival in the Sierra del Cristal, which provides the novel with a dramatic encounter, but one whose narrative consequences are then ignored. The survival of an Indian community is *ideologically* important (for reasons that will soon emerge), but it turns out to be a narrative cul-de-sac. As a result of all this, the genocide of the Cuban Indians can be "avenged" by military assistance purchased with the sale of indigenous "treasure" whose ownership is never even questioned—it simply belongs to its finder, not to the descendants of those who made it. The Indians here have survived against the odds, helped by the mountainous terrain but also by the lack of development of the Cuban economy under Spanish rule. The Indians have only survived, the novel suggests, because Cuba has been inadequately modernized by Spain. That situation will change once the United States becomes fully involved with the island—a process of modernization that would inevitably lead, as the novel does not point out, to the disappearance of those Indians.

Despite widespread U.S. sympathy for the Cuban cause, it was always clear that, for the *usanos* (those from the United States) there were significant differences between the two peoples, usually ones that demonstrated how much the Cubans would need U.S. help to win a military victory. In the first few pages of *Under the Cuban Flag* the Major has to teach the rebels how to use their new rifles. The three visitors are then drawn into a fight. The rebels could, Ober writes, have stood their ground and shot the advancing Spaniards—this would have been the properly rational approach: "But the fiery Cuban nature would not allow them to pursue this safe plan; they could not stand still and merely pump bullets into an enemy when he was hardly an arm's length away. '*Al machete! Al machete!*' shouted their Colonel, waving his sword in the air and setting the example by charging into the face of the coming column" (Ober 1897, 29). The Major and the Doctor stick with Gomez when his men fall back after the failure of this charge (31). The unworldly Professor shoots the Spanish commander as he is about to kill Gomez; and "The Major and Doctor . . . formed a rallying point for the encouraged Cubans, who followed wherever they led, charging madly upon the now retreating foe, and pursuing them so long as a vestige of opposition remained" (32).

This language of "rescue" dominates U.S. accounts of the invasion of Cuba, as Andrew Draper's title of 1899 has it: *The Rescue of Cuba: An Episode in the Growth of Free Government*. According to this motif, the United States is a modern knight in shining armor and Cuba should be a beautiful but helpless maiden, just like Evangelina Cisneros or Hortensia in *Under the Cuban Flag*, a fitting wife for her chivalrous rescuer. The U.S. descriptions of Cubans in 1898 are deeply revealing of the disappointment felt when this proved not to be the case. Some recall Spanish descriptions of native Cubans in 1492: "a collection of real tropic savages," in Stephen Crane's words; with another writer complaining more bluntly that the Cubans were happy to "go around half-naked." However, the Cuban soldiers were clearly not Indians: "They are nearly all half-naked and a large proportion are of negro blood" reported the *New York Evening Post*. Winston Spencer Churchill saw volunteer service with the Spanish army and reported: "If the Revolution triumphs, Cuba will be a black Republic. . . . Their army, consisting to a large extent of coloured men, is an undisciplined rabble"; "the Cuban soldiers were almost all blacks and mulattos," said Roosevelt.[5]

One description of "the Cuban" is especially revealing. It comes from John Parker, who commanded the Gatling Gun detachment of the Fifth Army:

He is a treacherous, lying, cowardly, thieving, worthless, half-breed mongrel; born of a mongrel spawn of Europe, crossed upon the fetiches of darkest Africa and aboriginal America. He is no more capable of self-government than the Hottentots that roam the wilds of Africa or the Bushmen of Australia. He can not be trusted like the Indian, will not work like the negro, and will not fight like the Spaniard; but he will lie like a Castilian with polished suavity, and he will stab you in the dark or in the back with all the dexterity of a renegade graduate of Carlisle. (Parker, 76)

If quality of insult is a sign of disavowed admiration, then Parker was deeply impressed by Cubans. The first sentence is an extraordinarily dense combination of everything that is frightening to *usanos* of "the best and oldest strain" about miscegenation, more deeply horrid for being a mixture of the European, the African, *and the Indian*. Indeed, the indigenous component seems, rhetorically at least, the most important of the three. Other indigenous societies—the Hottentot and Bushmen—provide the comparisons for governmental incapacity; and the essentially *treacherous* nature of the Cuban can only be conveyed by reference to Carlisle, the famous school for turning Indians into good U.S. citizens, which, when it failed, produced the ultimate nightmare of an educated and vengeful savage.

Parker's description is deeply offensive. Yet if we recast it slightly and bear in mind the much more positive current connotations attaching to the word "mongrel," it could almost operate as a definition of a transculturated Cuban national identity. It could, for example, be set alongside Fernando Ortiz's famous invocation of the *ajiaco*, its name a trope of its substance, an indigenous dish promiscuously mixed with African and European ingredients (5–6; cf. Pérez Firmat, 24–33). Ortiz's notion of transculturation and its culinary metaphor date from 1940 but clearly has its roots in Martí and his development of the idea of "our América" as "a mestizo people" (Martí 1992, 2: 110). Ortiz provides an important link back to the 1890s in his story of how, in 1895, when he was fourteen and had recently returned to Cuba, he had been instructed by his grandfather that all Cuban separatists were either black or mulatto. When the young Ortiz came up with the name of the recently dead Martí, his grandfather's response was "he was a mulatto on the inside" (1993, 111).

A similarly uncomplimentary U.S. comment on Cuban soldiers in 1898 — "They were of another race and the greater part of them were unable to understand the steady nerve and the businesslike habits of their American rescuers" (quoted in Louis Pérez, 200)—is interestingly foreshadowed in a description of the U.S. boy, Archie Goodwin, in *Under the Cuban Flag*: "As he was a sturdy young fellow, with a smile and a greeting for all, and a brisk air of business quite at variance with the bearing of the native boys, he made friends wherever he went" (Ober 1897, 80–81). By "native," Ober here means "Cuban." And Ober's description of the *aboriginal* community in the mountains is very different from that of his *native* Cubans: "They were beautiful examples of vigorous youth and manhood; every one lithe of limb and shapely, their frank, open faces wreathed in smiles, their speech soft and gestures amiable" (204). These are not the terms by which either North American Indians or Cuban soldiers could or would be described by U.S. journalists or fiction writers at this period. But the vocabulary does recall both the description of Archie in the novel and of Karl Decker in Hawthorne's encomium. Vigor, frankness, amiability—this was the white, male, U.S. self-image recognizing itself in the aboriginal population of Cuba.

There is a logic to this unexpected identification, though it takes a little disentangling. Anthropology emerged as a professional discipline in the 1890s, with American Indians as its primary object of study, an object in the process of "disappearing"—or more accurately, being swept away by the forces of capitalist modernity (Dippie 1982). Underlying the language of "disappearance" is a theory in which cultures begin as full or plenary and are drained of their essence until extinct. Under Darwin's influence, indigenous peoples were seen as analogous to animal species and watched with morbid fascination as their numbers decreased to single figures before the "last man" and "last woman" died, their remains ghoulishly fought over by western scientists (see Ryan, Brantlinger, and Stafford). According to this model, initial contact in the Caribbean had been between well-defined groups (usually Ciboney, Taíno, Carib, European, and African), which then got larger or smaller during the colonial period—and of course the native Caribbean groups were seen as getting smaller as African and European groups got larger.

As Frederick Putnam put it in 1893, when organizing the anthropology exhibits at the Chicago Columbian exposition:

> We know well that four hundred years has brought the last generation upon the stage of action, when it will be possible to bring together the remnants of the native tribes . . . in anything approaching purity of stock, or with a precise knowledge of the ways of their ancestors. These peoples, as great nations, have about vanished into history, and now is the last opportunity for the world to see them and to realize what their condition, their life, their customs, their arts were four centuries ago. The great object lesson then will not be completed without their being present. Without them, the Exposition will have no base. (quoted in Hinsley)

The anthropological interest in American Indians was in what they were four centuries ago, because that provided the base line against which white progress could be measured. But all over the continent, Indians weren't what they used to be. In the Caribbean, according to Ober's own account of his visits to Dominica and St. Vincent, the Caribs were *different* from what they had once been, the clearest marks of which were the loss of their language, of their fierce behavior, and of their physical features: more and more of them had interbred with blacks.

Sanctified by the undisputed aboriginal claims to the land, the Indians in *Under the Cuban Flag* respond to the anthropological ideal of the Indian untouched by outside presence. In order to conform to that ideal, they have to be removed from the perceived reality of Amerindian identity in the Caribbean at this time as an aboriginal nation tainted through its association with Africans. The isolation of the Cuban Indian community has served to protect it as much from miscegenation with Africans as it has from extermination by Spaniards.

In narrative terms, the political novel, rooted in the events of the 1890s, has to be linked with the purity of aboriginal survival in the Sierra del Cristal. That link is provided by the brother and sister, Juanita and Felipe, described respectively as *mestiza* and "half-breed" (Ober 1897, 253). Juanita leads Hortensia and the Major to safety among the Indians when the Cuban rebels are ungrateful enough to condemn him to death. Felipe is left to represent the "unconscious of the text," the unmotivated evil force who tries to kill the Spanish prisoner Archie has taken, attacks Archie, betrays the Major, sets fearsome bloodhounds on his trail, and wishes his own sister dead. Felipe is not on any particular side; rather, he is antagonistic to everyone (and thus useful in moving the plot along). Not accidentally, the female mixed-blood is assimilated and the male mixed-blood is a renegade. The suspicion is that, ideologically if not physically, Juanita is a white/Indian mix, Felipe a black/Indian half-breed.

Soldiers of Fortune offers the best clue as to what the Indians of *Under the Cuban Flag* actually represent. There was something in Cuba that was, like Evangelina Cisneros and the Indians of the Sierra del Cristal, genuinely hidden, passive, helpless, and in need of rescue—the iron ore of the province of Santiago, which when extracted by U.S. mining companies and turned to steel in the mills of Maryland and Pennsylvania, would provide the guns and ammunition for the filibusters and, more important, the ships and the torpedoes to protect the commercial and strategic interests of the United States, as Roosevelt's and Mahan's ideas were put into practice. Clay makes the point to Mendoza, the rebellious villain of the book: "The mines have always been there, before this Government came in, before the Spaniards were here, before there was any government at all" (R. Davis, 52). In other words, both novels rescue what is primordial, authentic, natural, and pre-Spanish, about Cuba: the natural resources and the indigenous inhabitants—or rather, their treasures. Both novels operate a separation: in *Soldiers of Fortune* the separation is between the mineral resources and the Spaniards and Cubans who "own" them but who are incapable of exploiting them; in *Under the Cuban Flag* it is between the pure but unworldly Indians and the treasure of their ancestors of which they know nothing and to which they are assumed to have no claim. The U.S. "recognition" of similar moral qualities to their own among the indigenous population acts as a claim that the rescuers are the *proper* protectors and rightful inheritors of the island's resources. Ober's novel works ultimately as a claim to *rightful* possession of the island. However, since it is the cacique's treasure that avenges the Indians, U.S. agency in the matter is itself underplayed: the United States is seen as carrying out the vengeance of history rather than being—as it in fact was—a modern state acting out of self-interest.

Both novels employ frontier rhetoric: beyond the frontier, which is where Cuba was situated in U.S. eyes, "exists a world of naturally abundant and un-appropriated resources" (Slotkin, 41). Adventure, exploration, geology, science, treasure: this is an old Caribbean combination. An interest in natural history—such as first took Ober to the region (1879a and b)—is rarely innocent. The transformation of Europe began with Caribbean gold and silver, a process not unconnected with the initial genocide of the indigenous population; and Cuba suffered many centuries of extraction from what Eduardo Galeano memorably called the "open veins" of the continent (Galeano).

According to histories of the U.S. invasion of Cuba, the landing of the military forces on the south coast of the island was a haphazard affair, its sites decided only at the last minute (see Cosmas; Trask; J. Bradford; and United States Adjutant-General's Office). That may be so, in which case it was only of symbolic interest that one part of the U.S. army landed at Siboney, securing the interests of the Juraguá Iron Company, which was controlled from Pennsylvania, while the Fifth Army landed at Daiquirí, securing the interests of the Spanish-American Mining Company, Juraguá's main rival, controlled by John D. Rockefeller. What's for sure is that both operations made a swift return to mining after the capitulation of Santiago.[6] Claims at Juraguá and Daiquirí were set to expire in 1903: General Wood extended them indefinitely and for good measure exempted all future mining claims from Cuban property taxes or mining royalties in an addendum that was not published with the original ruling (Reutter 76). In that sense the indigenous ore of the island was successfully rescued.

In a peculiar way, anthropology then proceeded to imitate fiction, cementing the relationship between indigeneity and mining interests. After 1898, engineers from Philadelphia working for U.S. mining companies reported coming across "wild Indians" in the Sierra Maestra, and Stewart Culin, from the Free Museum of Science and Art at the University of Pennsylvania, came haring down to investigate this dramatic survival.

Culin carried a letter of introduction dated May 16, 1901, from Josiah Monroe of the Juraguá Iron Company, Philadelphia, addressed to Louis V. Placé, Havana, stating that Culin "is especially interested to get all the information possible on the subject of the original Indian inhabitants of the Island, of which some are said to still live somewhere near the centre of the eastern end" (Culin n.d.); and Culin mentions *Soldiers of Fortune* early in his account, confirming that the crucial nexus for these years is the one that runs from Santiago to Philadelphia. Culin's short work (1902) is important because of its clear demonstration of the distinction between the myth of cultural survival—which brought him to Cuba—and the reality of the transcultural process he literally faced and that was of no interest to him.[7] After this article Culin never wrote another word about the Caribbean.

The year 1898 brought into view, in the title of José de Olivares' huge photographic survey (1899), "*our* islands and *their* people": new territories for anthropological practice and for collecting the items to stock *our* new museums. The natives of the Caribbean held a special position as the first Americans encountered by Columbus and had therefore been favored with some attention, especially in connection with the quatercentenary in 1892, but it was only after 1898 that any serious anthropological and archaeological work was undertaken in the islands by U.S. scientists. Before the end of 1898, Daniel Brinton was already suggesting "promising localities for research" (256) and W. H. Holmes and Otis Mason had visited from the Smithsonian Institution. In 1904, encouraging Jesse Fewkes to pursue a thorough ethnological research of the Caribbean, Mason remarked that the region would open "a new and rich field as a relief from the overthrashed straw of our own native tribes" (quoted in Hinsley, 116). The Heye Foundation—and its associated Museum of the American Indian—took an immediate interest. Of its first set of nine "contributions" to scholarship on the American Indian, seven related to the Caribbean.

Then in 1915 the Heye Foundation sent to Cuba the young anthropologist Mark Harrington. Harrington spent nearly a year in Cuba, traveling extensively in the area around Baracoa, collecting materials, and taking notes. He was in many respects a transitional figure of great interest. He represented the latest in anthropological training in the United States (at Columbia University) at a moment when anthropology was becoming established as a discipline. Unlike many of his successors, he had read extensively in the locally produced literature and both learned from and engaged with it. His work was also warmly welcomed by Cuban scientists, prompting for example Fernando Ortiz's *Historia de arqueología indocubana* (1922), which is at once a summary, an appreciation, a critique, and an extension of Harrington's work.

At the same time, despite the substantial nature of his *Cuba Before Columbus*, what Harrington published was supposed to be merely a preliminary to the major study of indigenous social structure he promised, but which was never completed. In several respects, then, Harrington's *unpublished* work set an unfortunate precedent. He was not the last U.S. anthropologist to use one of the Caribbean islands as a stepping stone to professional advancement into more prestigious areas. Neither was he the last foreign archeologist to leave the Caribbean with materials—physical or informative—that were not only never returned, but which have never entered the public realm at all. And his failure to address indigenous social structure has set a pattern only recently challenged by a Latin American social archeology in which Cuban scientists have played an increasingly important role (see Dacal Moure and Rivero de la Calle, 30–39).

Harrington was employed by George Heye, who was infamously more interested in collecting objects than he was in developing the science of anthropology and, in this respect, Harrington follows in the thoughtlessly acquisitive footsteps of Ober's Professor Brown. Take, for example, the stunning petroglyph Harrington found in the Cueva Zemi, in La Patana:

> The removal of the image, or *zemi*, seemed impossible at first, for it weighed 800 or 900 pounds; but the problem was finally solved by sawing it into five pieces with the aid of a two-man lumber saw (which had to be sharpened frequently), carrying these pieces by hand out of the cave and up out of the pit, loading them on mules and thus transporting them to Maisi, where they were packed in boxes made of wide cedar boards sawed out by hand from the trees of the forest, and loaded on a little schooner which touched occasionally to bring provisions to the lighthouse when the weather was good. This in turn took them to Baracoa, where they were shipped on board a Norwegian fruiter to New York. (Harrington, 2: 270–71)

And that is where, as Ortiz rather sharply puts it, "we Cubans will have to go to admire it and to study it, if we want to do work on national archaeology" (1922, 87). This is exactly the route that the cacique's treasure takes in

Under the Cuban Flag. So much for "harmless" professors. Harrington was later to work undercover for the U.S. intelligence services (Patterson, 60).

That archeological treasure remains in New York. But Harrington's booty also contained the human remains of seven Cuban Indians excavated from cave burials. After extensive discussions those remains were repatriated to Cuba by the Smithsonian Institution's National Museum of the American Indian in June 2002 and then received in January 2003 by Cacique Panchito Ramirez and the Taíno descendant population of Caridad de los Indios from the eastern mountains of Cuba, where they were reburied with due ceremony.

Harrington's removal of this petroglyph in 1915 is probably the factual incident most closely related to Professor Brown's removal of the cacique's treasure in *Under the Cuban Flag* eighteen years earlier, and it therefore brings to a close any proper extrapolation from the fictional text as indicative of ideological attitudes that would be put into practice after 1898. But what connections can be made between this material and the questions that face us today? In conclusion, I'll suggest a number of present imperatives that might be illuminated by this rather insistent attention on events of more than one hundred years ago.

According to the account of Caribbean anthropology established in the English-speaking world, the subject effectively began with the setting-up of the Caribbean Anthropological Program at Yale in 1933, with the first *proper* archeological work in Cuba carried out by Cornelius Osgood in Pinar del Río and Irving Rouse in Holguín in the early 1940s and published in 1942. In this picture, Harrington counts as a precursor but doesn't belong to the full history: Rouse calls him, rather dismissively, an "excavator" (forthcoming, 6).

A revisionist history of the kind that has begun to emerge in recent years would cast its net rather wider. The origins of the Caribbean Anthropological Program would themselves be traced back to 1898. When U.S. anthropology followed the course of empire, it was the archeologists and collectors who were put to work in Cuba and the other islands, not the ethnographers: the seminal articles from the early years of the century are entitled "*Prehistoric* Puerto Rico" and "*Prehistoric* Culture of Cuba" (Fewkes 1902 and 1904), thus sealing the indigenous populations of the islands into the dark world of "prehistory," not only exiled into another time, but put outside history altogether. Eventually followed by those working under the aegis of the hegemonic patterns of U.S. anthropology, which in this case means the typological study pioneered in the 1930s (Patterson, 76), this path has been well-financed, fully professionalized, and supported by major institutions and universities. According to this paradigm, the indigenous cultures of the Caribbean, belonging to "prehistory," must be studied through burial sites, dwelling places, and ceramic sequences. Cultural materials are severed from living populations, becoming objective evidence, which must be under the control of the scientific disciplines. Under this account the Yale Program marks a professionalization of anthropological study but not a fundamental shift from the paradigm effectively established by Fewkes, Culin, and Harrington in the twenty years after 1898.

However valuable the Yale and Yale-inspired work has been in providing materials toward an understanding of population movements and cultural processes in the Caribbean before 1492, interpretations of the social and political dimensions of those materials have usually reproduced the stereotypes that served the European colonial powers so well during the sixteenth and seventeenth centuries. Work pursued under the Yale paradigm has had almost nothing to say about the Caribbean after 1492. For the "plenary" model of culture, the indigenous Caribbean was never properly *itself* after 1492 and therefore scientific inquiry has to end at that date.

Revisionist work—which might properly be described as postcolonial—has various overlapping strands: the work of intellectual critique carried out by cultural historians (for example Sued Badillo 1992, 1995; Whitehead 1995); the work of social and economic analysis, often employing a Marxist perspective (Moscoso; Tabío and Rey); and the social archeology that has its roots in Venezuela, but that is beginning to influence Latin American practices more widely (Vargas-Arenas). This work tends to be multidisciplinary, ethnohistorical, attuned to national imperatives, and skeptical both about colonial sources and about the interpretation of archeological evidence, especially where social groups have been invented on the basis of ceramic innovation: it is postcolonial work in the true sense, serving to question, challenge, and replace the deeply embedded colonialist assumptions through which the history and present of the Caribbean have so often been viewed. Particularly important aspects of the revisionist paradigm are its rewriting of the history of Caribbean anthropology; its insistence on giving equal weight to the colonial period; and its concern with the social dimensions of questions of identity.

In one sense, the revisionist model is just that: it contests the assumptions, protocols, and tropes of the hegemonic model. However, it also has a history that would allow us to see it running in tandem with what it would—in the 1980s—eventually contest. That history can hardly be rehearsed in detail here, but it is important to acknowledge the centrality of the concept of "transculturation" for this revisionist paradigm. Fernando Ortiz's work has a long and complex development, but several of his key essays, including "The Social Phenomenon of Transculturation," were published precisely when Osgood and Rouse were undertaking their archeological work in Cuba; and transculturation clearly has its origins in the notion of cultural *mestizaje* elaborated in the 1890s by José Martí, at the very moment when the "plenary" model of identity was becoming enshrined as the anthropological norm in the United States. So, in at least two respects, the histories share key moments, allowing illuminating comparisons to be made.

When Ortiz put forward his concept of transculturation in his great work, *Cuban Counterpoint* in 1940, he famously had the support, in an introduction, of Bronislaw Malinowski, the distinguished Polish anthropologist, who agreed that the term was preferable to the more common "acculturation" (see Coronil). At this very moment, in 1941, Irving Rouse, the first of the Yale archeologists to work in Cuba, was preparing for his visit. Rouse was well aware of the historical literature on the survival of Cuban Indians and had this to say about Culin's report of 1902:

> Governor Mazariegos was shocked by their condition when he inspected the interior of the island in 1556. He ordered all Indians to be gathered together into towns near the principal Spanish settlements. . . . The Indians survived well into the nineteenth century. . . . It is unfortunate for the anthropologist that these towns were not isolated like the Indian reservations in the United States, thus preserving the aboriginal culture for modern study. In Cuba the aborigines gradually intermarried with their white neighbors and adopted the Spanish language and culture. . . . The process of acculturation is well illustrated by the archeological data to be described below. . . . In 1901, Stewart Culin . . . searched for descendants of the aborigines in the mountains of the province of Oriente. . . . Everywhere the Indians were halfbreeds, who spoke Spanish and differed little from their Cuban neighbors. Only two aboriginal customs (besides those prevalent among the white population of Cuba) still survived. . . . (Rouse 1942, 29–30)

The text within the parentheses implicitly suggests that within this paradigm only that which is *different* from what has survived to become part of normal social or economic practice is of interest to anthropologists: the term "acculturation" simply serves to cloak what has survived *and been widely adopted*. That aboriginal customs should have survived and "become prevalent among the white population of Cuba" is irrelevant to Rouse—although it would be deeply important to a student of transculturation.

Felipe Pichardo Moya put it exactly in 1945 when he wrote that the indigenous absence from Cuban history owed most to historian's *attitudes* that "prevented them from seeing the properly vernacular content of our past, of which indigenous survivals formed a part" (6). The failure is often a failure of vision, of not seeing properly: it is a matter of ideology and therefore of language and interpretation. "Survival" itself is the key term here, itself a survival from the earliest anthropological theory (Tylor 1871), rich in theoretical connotations but also full of emotional resonance. Most historical sources say that the region's indigenous population had disappeared by the middle of the sixteenth century. In the sense that indigenous social formations as they had existed before 1492 were no longer functioning in the same way by 1550, that assertion has an element of truth, and yet it may also be deeply misleading.

Let me offer a few tentative distinctions. That what was once thought "lost" has in fact survived is a powerful myth—most recently exploited in Spielberg's dinosaur films, which themselves draw on Arthur Conan Doyle's novel, *The Lost World* (1912). The "survival" of indigenous Caribbean communities into the nineteenth or twentieth centuries is a myth that has its versions on almost all Caribbean islands. It is a powerful and consoling myth, but one whose temptations need to be resisted. Only if the *myth* of survival is resisted can the historical and attested presence of indigenous communities be properly understood. One of the potent ironies that all indigenous communities face is that the myth of "survival" can only gain its power when peddled against the supposed "historical reality" of complete indigenous disappearance: "survival" in its plenary sense is simply the other side of the coin of "extinction" or "extermination." However, inadequate as this language might be to deal with the complexities of cultural change, we need to remember that it is the chosen textual model of the victims of genocide and therefore intrinsically worthy of attention. It is also important to recognize that there is a record of "survival" in the unmodulated sense of that word still properly to be registered in most parts of the Caribbean, where recognizably indigenous communities certainly survived much later than almost all historiographic accounts allow.

How to discuss the survival of indigenous elements in the larger process of transculturation is a problem of a different order. Clearly there is a massive amount of work to be done—anthropological, archeological, historical, linguistic; and a massive amount already done but largely unknown (or ignored) outside Cuba.[8] In 1944, Pedro Henríquez Ureña noted with reference to the Caribbean that "at the important and visible level the European model was imposed; at the domestic and everyday level many autochthonous traditions were maintained" (quoted by García Arévalo, 11). It is precisely the domestic and everyday that produces—to use related distinctions—the vernacular and the subaltern as opposed to the elite ostentation of official languages and monumental architecture. Attention to that vernacular world has begun to reveal its indigenous components: in adaptation to peasant life under Spanish control, possibly within such forms as the *guajiro* and *jíbaro* traditions of Cuba and Puerto Rico; in indigenous participation in unofficial Creole communities on the margins of authorized areas of settlement; in guerrilla warfare, sometimes, especially in the eighteenth century, in conjunction with African maroons; and in a process of ethnic reconstruction and identity reformulation.

We need to know much more, though, about the modalities of the term "survival." There is, in fact, a theoretical dimension to the discussion, perhaps illuminated in a small way by the intermittent dissension over the "survival" of Cuban Indians in the area around Baracoa, close to the setting of *Under the Cuban Flag*. In an article in *Granma* a few years ago, Dr. Estrella Rey—seemingly responding to the work of Oscar Tejedor Alvarez (see Gutiérrez)—was quoted as saying that, because of the history of mixing, "there are no absolutely legitimate Indians left in our country" (Blanco). The introduction of the law into these matters always leads to trouble. Does this statement imply that there are "illegitimate" Indians left? Who gets to decide? When the term "legitimate" is employed, it usually means that the state has taken an interest. According to this understanding, there is such a thing as a "true Indian," much as imagined by Ober locked in the fastnesses of the Sierra del Cristal; and any actual twentieth-first-century Indian will by definition appear inadequate to the fullness of that example. Often, as in the U.S. case, the state arrogates the power to define who is and who is not a "legitimate" Indian, a definition that is not easily challenged and which anyway serves to define those who seek to challenge it. Too often, historians seeking to count Indian populations, in the Caribbean and elsewhere, have relied on censuses in which state officials have taken decisions based purely on the presence or absence of what they take to be significant markers of "Indianness," often long, black hair.

The language of "legitimacy" can be challenged in two ways. The dangerous route goes into the language of science to demonstrate that those deemed "illegitimate" are *really, authentically* on some level Indians. There are twin dangers here. Scientific observation has not progressed beyond the deeply subjective analyses offered by Culin and Harrington, again rooted in the presence or absence of certain features. For example, Gates' 1954 study of the area is based purely on physical features, with a pseudo-scientific codification of skin color and a set of tabular remarks such as "Indian features," "Looks Indian," or "Nose depressed (Negro)" (80–81). It is also marked by a tendency to read off the supposed inheritance of psychological characteristics ("in all these mixed families where there is considerable Indian ancestry the quiet temperament of the Indian makes itself apparent" [93]). Pospíšil's account of a 1964 expedition to central Oriente concludes that the group studied—in Felicidad de Yateras and Caridad de los Indios—"can be considered as Indian" on the basis of a schema put forward in 1910 by Giuffrida Ruggeri that is deeply embedded within the racist discourse of its moment. The subjective nature of these exercises is not disguised by the tables of measurement. Identity is a social category. Its somatic component is undeniable, but we should not imagine that the complexities of identity are resolvable by any form of quantification. In these circumstances, a more significant yardstick may well be self-perception, what José Barreiro, in a felicitous phrase, calls quite simply "a casual sense of Indian identity" (58). The historical irony here is that just as more sophisticated notions of identity seem to offer the prospect of a break with the blood quantum obsession that has been the constant companion and weapon of colonial categorization, there appears on the horizon, in the shape of the Human Genome Diversity Project, the "promise" (better "illusion") of a supposedly conclusive and scientifically objective index of ethnic identity through genetic analysis (Wilkie; J. Moore). The real problem with all such measurement, whether of skull size or genetic make-up, is that it relies upon a notion of race. There are temptations in this game: if the one-drop rule that raised the black population of the United States were applied to Indians, indigenous numbers in that country would increase a hundred-fold overnight. But such fantasies only demonstrate in the long run the *reductio ad absurdum* involved in all racial calculus—a point that José Martí understood better than anyone at the end of the nineteenth century, and that Fernando Ortiz franked in his 1934 homage to Martí, words with which I conclude, not least because they speak a truth that the rest of the world still struggles to recognize:

> At the end of the day it's clear that there are no pure races and that all of us, as human beings, are the mixed product of innumerable crossings. The Cuban José Martí, like everybody else, was just a drop of blood, one of those always spilt when loving couples cleave together in their eternal humanity. And, like all geniuses, he carried in his mind the essential outcome of all that mixing of ideas that occurs when the cultures of the world embrace each other. (1993, 135)

Notes

An earlier version of this essay was read at the "Indigenous Legacies of the Caribbean" conference in Baracoa, Cuba (November 16–23, 1997). I would like to thank José Barreiro and the participants in that memorable conference for their responses and encouragement.

1. For a general account of Ober's work, see Hulme 2000, 37–96. A kind of companion piece to this essay (Hulme 1997) analyses another of his novels, *The Last of the Arawaks* (1901).

2. For longer analyses, see Hulme 1996; Campbell; and Prados-Torreira, 137–46.

3. The iron ore supplemented U.S. supplies; but the eastern half of Cuba also had extensive deposits of manganese, an essential raw material in the manufacture of Bessemer steel, for which U.S. demand greatly exceeded supply. The Cuban deposits were the nearest available (Porter, 323). See also Lisandro Pérez; and Iglesias.

4. In his eighteenth-century history of the West Indies, Bryan Edwards had presented the rebel atrocities in St. Domingue as retribution for the sixteenth-century genocide of the indigenous population—"as if the blacks were punishing the cruelties of the conquistadors, not those of the planters" (Geggus 129). This was part of common anti-Spanish rhetoric employed by the English (a continuation of the Black Legend), which conveniently forgot that the English were at that time (the 1790s) fighting one of the remaining parts of the Caribbean's indigenous population into virtual extermination in St. Vincent.

5. All quoted from Louis Pérez, 199–204, except Churchill, which is from a newspaper article of 1896 quoted in H. Thomas, 326.

6. Reutter 1988, 73–74; and cf. Lisandro Pérez. The iron mining of Santiago features prominently in Leonard Wood's first report on insular affairs (United States Army 1899), and in Robert Porter's specially commissioned report (1899), as it had in William J. Clark's well-timed *Commercial Cuba: A Book for Business Men* (1898).

7. Culin begins his article with the story, heard from an Englishman he meets on the steamer, that survivors of the original Lucayans are still living "in primitive savagery" on the island of Little Abaco in the Bahamas (1902, 185). That such a possibility could be mooted for so small an island suggests the depth of the psychic investment in the *idea* of indigenous survival.

8. See, for example, Pichardo Moya; Rivero de la Calle 1973 and 1978; Barreiro; Yaremko; and cf. D. Davis.

4

"To Shake This Nation
as Nothing before Has Shaken It"

C.L.R. James, Radical Fieldwork,
and African American Popular Culture

KEVIN MEEHAN

Prelude: Existential Density

In his essay of 1948, "The Revolutionary Answer to the Negro Problem in the United States," the Trinidadian journalist, social theorist, and writer C.L.R. James concludes with a well-known rhetorical flourish:

> Let us not forget that in the Negro people, there sleep and are now awakening passions of a violence exceeding, perhaps, as far as these things can be compared, anything among the tremendous forces that capitalism has created. Anyone who knows them, who knows their history, is able to talk to them intimately, watches them at their own theaters, watches them at their dances, watches them in their churches, reads their press with a discerning eye, must recognize that although their social force may not be able to compare with the social force of a corresponding number of workers, the hatred of bourgeois society and the readiness to destroy it when the opportunity should present itself, rests among them to a degree greater than in any other section of the population in the United States. (1996c, 147)

James touches here on several key themes associated with his legacy as a Caribbean Marxist thinker from the anti-Stalinist left. First, "The Revolutionary Answer" voices confidence about the ability of everyday people to organize themselves spontaneously, and (because James casts the African American freedom struggle as an autonomous social force) it expresses a measure of skepticism about vanguard leadership. Second, while his view of black activism as independent might seem to imply a separatist brand of nationalism, James emphatically locates black culture and politics inside the larger national collective, not apart from it. We see this in the passage when he rates African American anti-bourgeois sentiments as strongest in the United States, thereby presenting black life as quintessentially national in character. Third, the comments about dances, churches, and the black press offer a condensed version of something James frequently argued, namely that popular cultural activity is crucially important as a base of political organizing and articulation.[1] Fourth, his view of African American social and political oppression as belonging to a diasporic continuum linking the history of slavery in the United States to the Caribbean experience of colonialism and the plantation signals a new direction in Caribbean thought, away from the parameters dictated by the colonial metropolis and toward a collaborative and integrative Caribbean–North American approach to solving the problems of race and class oppression faced by black people across the Americas.

Also implicit in the final sentence is a claim on James' part to know African American culture, history, and politics not simply as historical and theoretical objects but also as lived experience. This claim is important not so much for what it adds to the historical or theoretical content of "The Revolutionary Answer" but rather for the light it sheds on James' method as a Caribbean activist and writer. When James refers to churches, dances, and the black press, this suggests immersion in grass-roots networks, yet, intriguingly, there are no anecdotes to flesh out James' confident assertion of his intimacy with black life in the United States. Indeed, the lack of autobiographical detail in "The Revolutionary Answer" contrasts sharply with the following passage, written much later in life, describing events from earlier in James' U.S. sojourn. Because it comes from an unfinished and unpublished autobiography, I quote at length from this description of performances at Harlem's Apollo Theater, which James frequented beginning in the late 1930s. He writes:

> I was always ready to listen. I would go to their theatres, that is to say to the Apollo and other places where they were having a show; I would go there to listen to the music, listen to the black performer and would watch the people around to get to know them as I knew the people in

the Caribbean—in fact even more than I knew the people in the Caribbean because now I had some historical background. . . . And they opened at 11 in the morning and the first show was half price and lots of the black boys and one or two black girls in Harlem, they had no work to do, they were idling around, they would pay their half price and go into the Apollo and once you had gone in you needn't come out, they would let you stay there, at least if you didn't go out you [could] stay in, and some of them would go and listen to one or two performances. And I would go there, whenever I went to the Apollo I would hear Louis Armstrong, Artie Shaw, Ella Fitzgerald, Benny Goodman, Jimmy Lunsford [sic]—a whole bunch of magnificent performers used to come and perform at the Apollo for the Harlem population and some people who used to come up from town to hear them. . . . And what struck me was this: a period when the music or the singer got so very much carried away, he would carry with him those people in the back seats where I was sitting, the young people in Harlem for the most part, and they would start to beat their feet and clap their hands and sometimes say some words, or make some sounds in harmony with the music that was being played on the stage or the song that was being sung. And time and again I noticed the extraordinary power that came from them. I had never seen and never was to see or hear an audience anywhere, or a section of the audience, that was giving out so much power in response to a public performer. They made no distinctions about whites—Artie Shaw, Benny Goodman, and these others would get the same reception for when the music moved as Duke Ellington or Louis Armstrong or Jimmy Lunsford or the others would. They had no racial prejudice inside there, they were responding to the music and the response was such that I know I said on one or two occasions, all the power is hidden in them there, it's waiting to come out, and the day when it comes out and it takes a political form, it is going to shake this nation as nothing before has shaken it. I know I came to that conclusion before I finally came to what I came to on the black question. (CLRJI 797)[2]

This autobiography was composed in the 1970s and 1980s with James dictating into a cassette recorder and others transcribing.[3] In such retrospective writing, there is always potential for projecting a later stage of consciousness back onto earlier events, but arguably this passage transcends such concerns.

The rich detail and existential density of the autobiographical document are undeniable and make it worth considering more closely regardless of whether or not James had, based on his interactions at the Apollo and elsewhere, already in 1938 formed the conclusions expressed in "The Revolutionary Answer." The relative paucity of such detail in "The Revolutionary Answer" calls attention to a feature of James' writing on African American popular culture that changes over time and that, accordingly, we can track and analyze with interesting results. The argument I want to explore in this essay is that living through and writing about fieldwork experience is a crucial component of James' method, and radical fieldwork is something he practiced consistently from the very beginning of his intellectual life in Trinidad.[4] By immersing himself directly in a popular milieu, whether it be a tenement yard or a cricket match in the Caribbean, or a nightclub, church service, or clandestine strike meeting in the United States, James has a chance to test ideas, to face reality, to push what is abstract toward concretization; also, whether he is writing fiction, history, political theory, cultural criticism, or memoir, the combination of radical fieldwork and fieldwork notes allow James to record the words and deeds of everyday people typically erased from history (even radical history). Together with archival research and political theorizing, it is this commitment to fieldwork that defines a consistent anti-imperialist praxis linking blacks in the Americas, even in James' earliest, pre-Marxist work in Trinidad. Yet, when it comes to James' treatment of African American popular culture, firsthand experience is something that only accrues over time. A sense of direct contact is missing from his earliest statements about the black freedom struggle in the United States, and if we contrast *A History of Negro Revolt*—written before James' arrival in the United States—with subsequent statements from the late 1930s on, a correlation appears between how much fieldwork experience James has logged, how much his writing on African American issues is marked by existential density, and how optimistic he is about the potential for African American self-organization and liberation.

Book Learning

James first lived in the United States beginning in 1938, when he came to help shape Trotskyite policy on the Negro Question (as it was known at the time). He was subsequently deported in 1953 after several months of internment at Ellis Island. Because James's most direct contact with African American people came during this stretch of fifteen years, any effort to understand and assess his view of African American popular culture—and the role of radical fieldwork in forming this view—will rightly focus on this period. During this time, he was immersed in a full spectrum of black cultural life, meeting with intellectuals such as Richard Wright and Ralph Ellison, working with striking sharecroppers in Missouri, and interacting with rank and file workers through the anti-Stalinist Workers Party, the Socialist Workers Party, and the Johnson-Forrest Tendency.[5] One of James' closest collaborators during this period, Grace Lee Boggs, played a leading role in the Johnson-Forrest Tendency and has published several pieces of memoir that offer invaluable commentary on James' modus operandi. In Boggs's account, Johnsonites developed a distinct approach to Americanizing Bolshevism. Aware of a need to rethink the basics of Marxism in a North American context, they created an activist method characterized by sharp theoretical debate (emphasis on Hegel via Lenin) and radical labor history. "We were extremely conscious," she writes, "that without a notion of the philosophical and historical basis of what you are doing, you don't understand anything. Some of us were philosophically trained, but the workers among us had also developed this habit. In the other tendencies this was not true" (Boggs 1995, 42). While theoretical and historical discussions doubtless found James in his element, he also reveled, according to Boggs, in a third aspect of Johnsonite practice, namely close contact with rank and file workers: "What he liked even better than reading was sitting down with members of the organization (usually at 629 Hudson St., the home of Freddy and Lyman Paine) and listening to them talk about their lives and their work. These rank-and-file workers, women, blacks, and young people inside the organization were his transmission belt to reality" (39–40).

In Boggs's view, James became less effective as a revolutionist after his deportation, in part because he lost the grass-roots contact that "had provided him with a method of knowing reality and a way to become part of the process of changing it" (1995, 43). Boggs's lasting impression of James is of "the intellectual whose ideas came mostly from books" (1998, 109). I will come back later in this essay to the claim that James lost his "method for knowing reality," but first I want to consider more seriously the question of book learning. In Trinidad and England prior to 1938, what sort of ideas about African American culture, history, and politics did James glean from books and periodicals, and how does James characterize the African American story in *A History of Negro Revolt* (which was published in England just prior to his departure for North America)?

Though one has to read somewhat between the lines to find its traces in colonial Trinidad, African American culture and politics do register in a nineteenth-century intellectual legacy that encompasses Jean-Baptiste Philippe's *Free Mulatto* (1824), which pled the case of North American slaves liberated during the War of 1812 (Cudjoe 2003, 23–24), and J. J. Thomas's *Froudacity* (1889), with its invocation of "extra-Africans: ten millions in the Western hemisphere" poised to join in "grand racial combination" (quoted in James 1980a, 242). While James was aware of this intellectual history and considered himself a proud product of it, most discussions of his intellectual and literary formation focus on the absorption of British Victorian culture, dislocated in time and place by the vectors of colonialism to early twentieth century Trinidad.[6] Here, critics are following James' lead in *Beyond a Boundary*, "Discovering Literature in Trinidad: The 1930s," and other sources that privilege the shaping influence of classical Greek and Roman sources and canonical British writing by Shakespeare, Milton, Hazlitt, Dickens, Arnold, and Thackeray. At least one critic, Helen Pyne-Timothy, makes the point that references to African American writing are conspicuously absent from James' account of his literary origins, despite the fact that he and his collaborators in Trinidadian salons of the 1920s and 1930s were making breakthroughs analogous to those of Harlem Renaissance writers Langston Hughes, Zora Neale Hurston, Jean Toomer, and others (52–53, 58–59; see also Carby).

In the margins of his autobiographical discourse, however, there are indications that James, while still in Trinidad, read, heard, and knew more about African American issues than is typically understood to be the case. Worcester (11–14) and Buhle (1998, 26) note in their biographies that James read Marcus Garvey's *Negro World* on a weekly basis, and this is amplified in a late interview by Larvester Gaither in which James claims he also subscribed to *The Crisis*, edited by W.E.B. Du Bois (Gaither, 10). In an interesting supplement to the published accounts of his childhood home in *Beyond a Boundary*, James reveals in an unpublished autobiographical note that Booker T. Washington's *Up from Slavery* was one of two books permanently on the dinner table in his grandmother's house in Tunapuna (the other was the Bible) (CLRJI 770).

While it takes us out of the realm of book learning, strictly construed, and closer to the terrain of fieldwork, it is also worth mentioning that James enjoyed a network of human contacts through which he further developed an early awareness of African American issues and perspectives. Albert Gomes, the Portuguese Creole firebrand from Trinidad who co-edited *The Beacon* (in which James's early fiction was featured), spent three years in the United States and returned to pen militant editorials. One, titled "Black Man," carries extensive commentary on U.S. race politics and calls for the "Black man" to "bare your fangs as the white man does" in response to the fact that "your children are being slain by the dozens in America, in Africa, in the Indies" (Gomes, 223; see also Worcester, 16; and Buhle 1998, 27). Foremost among James's personal links was a close friendship with Malcolm Nurse, better known by his pseudonym, George Padmore. Padmore's father, James Hubert Alfonso Nurse, a schoolteacher like James' father, was a family friend and James's memory of the elder Nurse's abode is vividly drawn:

> It is one of the few rooms I have seen in the Caribbean which was covered all round with books. . . . He was a man who had defied the government, he lived in an atmosphere of books and he declared himself a Moslem. He said he had left the Christian church—he would have nothing to do with Christianity, he was a Mohammedan—and I did not understand what that meant—nobody knew anything about Black Moslems then. I believe he had been reading a book by a famous Barbadian (what was the name? Blyden), *Christianity, Islam, and the Negro Race*, and that book was talked about a great deal. (James, 1984c, 252)

According to James, Nurse's son, Malcolm, "continued the tradition that his father had left," intensifying race politics in an intellectual milieu that included black periodicals from North America: "I was wrapped up in English literature, European literature, English history, Greek history, but I was interested in the Black question and I used to read THE NEGRO WORLD, Marcus Garvey's magazine, and THE CRISIS by Du Bois. I used to read them to be a part of the Black struggle but I never was in it to the extent that Padmore was" (Gaither, 10).

Malcolm Nurse departed for the United States in the mid-1920s and the two friends did not meet again until James moved to England in 1932 and encountered Nurse operating as a prominent Communist agitator under the name George Padmore. Along with his insider knowledge of revolutionary politics and personalities in the United States, Russia, and Western Europe,

Padmore brought further anecdotes and firsthand knowledge of black life in the United States gained while studying at Columbia University, Fisk University, and finally at Howard University Law School. London is also the place where James befriended and collaborated with Paul Robeson, thereby deepening an emerging pan-African consciousness through cross-cultural links to North America.[7]

James' first written treatment of African American mass movements comes in *A History of Negro Revolt.* A previous essay refuting the application of U.S.-based pseudo-science research to Trinidadian social reality had led James on the one hand to generalize that "the negro child in America . . . inevitably suffers in spirit" while referencing on the other hand a string of great men—James Weldon Johnson, Du Bois, and Washington among others—who disproved allegations of racial inferiority (James 1978, 232, 235). In *A History of Negro Revolt,* except when discussing the Civil War, which in James's reading was precipitated by fugitive slaves through their alliance with white abolitionists, and during which black soldiers created a decisive military edge for northern forces, the history of organized black resistance in the United States is presented as uniformly tragic. James characterizes slave revolts in the colonial era and early republic as "ill-organized uprisings which are always crushed with comparative ease" (1969b, 21). Closer to the present moment (1938), Garveyism shows organizational numbers that hint at "the fires that smoulder in the Negro world" (71) but U.N.I.A. ideas and programs amount to "pitiable rubbish" (69). In his lengthiest evocation of an African American ethos, James summons up the image of a suffering, beaten-down people: "Thus, the American Negro, literate, Westernized, an American almost from the foundation of America, suffers from his humiliations and discriminations to a degree that few whites and even many non-American Negroes can ever understand. The jazz and gaiety of the American Negro are a semi-conscious reaction to the fundamental sorrow of the race" (66).

In contrast, Caribbean and African peoples receive much better notice as historical and contemporary contributors to pan-African revolt. James includes long commentaries on the Haitian Revolution, earlier anti-colonial struggles in western and southern Africa, and the militant labor flare-ups that had just occurred in Trinidad and Jamaica in the late 1930s. In writing about contemporary uprisings in Africa he focuses on the role of Jehovah's Witness propaganda—*The Watch Tower*—in forging anti-colonial consciousness (1969b, 80–85).

Why is there a difference in how James depicts black struggles and black people in North America versus Africa and the Caribbean? Outlining one possible answer will allow me to sum up this discussion of book learning and direct the focus back upon fieldwork and its place within James' "method of knowing reality." As I suggested above, reading and personal networks provided James with more early exposure to African American issues than is normally alleged. And even though, admittedly, the man who said about *The Negro World* and *The Crisis* "I used to read them to be a part of the Black struggle" seems the very embodiment of Grace Lee Boggs's "intellectual whose ideas came mostly from books," James had a solid basis in source material for writing African American history. By the time he wrote *A History of Negro Revolt*, moreover, James had progressed far beyond his younger, magazine reading self to become a superb historian and theorist of revolution. If, however, we read *A History of Negro Revolt* while keeping in mind the Johnsonite method outlined by Boggs, we see that James was able to apply all three critical approaches—history, theory, and fieldwork—to Caribbean and African issues, but his writing about African American revolt only utilizes the first two—history and theory—as conceptual levers. Ultimately, unenriched by fieldwork connections, his book learning resulted in a vision of African American victimization that differs markedly from the interpretations he soon was to formulate.

Radical Fieldwork

James became involved with a wide range of African American people immediately upon his arrival in the United States, and almost as quickly his writing begins to emphasize revolutionary rather than victimized status in his characterizations of black life. A music lover who was already a fan of American jazz (Buhle 1992, 59), he naturally gravitated to dance halls and nightclubs. Conversing with black intellectuals who knew of his books on the Haitian and Russian revolutions, James delved more deeply into African American political ideas, trying to understand why Trotskyist organizations were failing to connect in Harlem and discovering in particular that the left's *idée fixe* of a black state in the south was "opposed by all the intellectuals and more literate among the Negroes" (James 1939, 22).[8] James visited a black church with two white Trotskyists and saw that the "white comrades evoked great hostility," but concerning the church members he concluded that "of their revolutionary ardor there was no doubt." James also comments critically on the flow of call and response exchanges between pastor and congregation: "A similar passion was also obvious in the church service, and there, the weeping, the shaking of hands, the response to the preacher's references to oppression were no doubt a sublimation of revolutionary emotion. The greatest response was made to the passage on oppression and suffering" (1939, 21).

After receiving rave reviews for his initial lectures in New York, James quickly embarked on a national speaking tour through the Northeast, the Midwest, and the West Coast that lasted from December 1938 through April 1939, when he traveled from southern California to Coyoacan, Mexico for a summit conference with Trotsky. Throughout the tour, James spoke not only to predominantly white audiences such as the one at Mandel Hall in Chicago, where he won a public debate against the famed British philosopher Bertrand Russell; as well, James appeared at black churches, men's clubs, and community centers, sometimes to crowds numbering over a thousand (Lopez 1983, 96–103). That James was reworking his concept of black life as suffering and victimization is evident in the notes he prepared for the meeting with Trotsky and in the transcripts of their discussions. In these documents, James theorizes African Americans as "potentially the most revolutionary section of the population" (James 1996b, 4). He strategizes for Trotskyites a bold departure on the Negro question by arguing for "self-determination" but against the idea of a separate black state in the south (James 1996b, 8–10; and James 1984b, 31–39). Self-determination for James means creating a semi-autonomous Negro organization, affiliated with but independent of existing Trotskyite institutions and modeled on the London-based International African Service Bureau as a primary means of furthering the African American freedom struggle through education and political work (James 1984b, 39–51).[9] One striking comment underscores the importance of direct contact as a methodological issue for James in formulating revolutionary strategy. Speaking with Trotsky and several other Fourth International leaders, James declares:

> The Negro must be won for socialism. There is no other way out for him in America or elsewhere. But he must be won on the basis of his own experience and his own activity. There is no other way for him to learn, nor for that matter, for any other group of toilers. *If he wanted self-determination*, then however reactionary it might be in every other respect, it would be the business of the revolutionary party to raise that slogan. (James 1996b, 8, original emphasis)

Though James' reservoir of grass-roots contact—what I am referring to as radical fieldwork—was growing every day throughout his first six months in the United States, the documents associated with the Coyoacan summit of 1939 are political and theoretical in nature and leave little room for anecdotal testimony. As such, the Coyoacan documents show a dramatic change in James' assessment of the black freedom struggle, but they do not register the daily encounters that formed a basis for his paradigm shift.[10] James' radical fieldwork did not, at this point, find a ready outlet in fieldwork notes, and indeed, one could argue in hindsight that the most provocative writing James produced about African American popular culture—that is, about African American life as an active, vibrant experience shared by millions—remains private and unpublished.

One important exception to this pattern is a series of reports James wrote for the Workers' Party bi-weekly journal, *Labor Action,* detailing a series of collective actions taken by black sharecroppers who farmed cotton in southeastern Missouri. The nature and extent of James' involvement in Missouri is subject to debate, but we know for certain that his work with the sharecroppers was concentrated in and around the town of Lilbourn, and that it occurred during two episodes, the first coming at the end of the 1941 growing season, and the second in the spring and summer of 1942. In an initial set of articles for *Labor Action*, published in September and October 1941, James traces the history of mobilization during the mid- to late 1930s, including the formation of a loosely organized chapter of the Southern Tenant Farmers Union, and then the more structured Local 313 of the United Cannery, Agricultural, Packing, and Allied Workers of America. Characteristically, James casts this activity as *self*-mobilization, claiming that "there were no organizers, but sharecroppers and day hands heard of the new organization through a grapevine and joined" (1996e, 24). The high point of mass movement prior to James' involvement was a lengthy sit-down action in which as many as five thousand people blocked the main highway leading to St. Louis. What leaders there were—a minister named Whitfield and a Stalinist CIO official named John Moore—urged the militants to back down, but instead they armed themselves and refused to vacate the highway in the face of demands from local and state authorities. The impact of this mass action was still intensely felt when James appeared on the scene, leading him to conclude that

everything now starts from the demonstration. They think in terms of it. A careful account of it should be written, the good points emphasized and the mistakes and weakness pointed out. The action has given them a sense of power and a consciousness of solidarity. Naturally with their dispersal and the passing of time, this cohesion may seem to have dissipated. It is not so. It is there, as can be seen from conversations with any half dozen separate individuals. It forms a practical and psychological basis for the organization of the sharecroppers to take industrial and political action. The masses learn best from the examination and analysis of their own common experience. (26)

This assessment comes as part of a composite portrait of the black sharecropper that makes up the bulk of James' second dispatch. In the third installment from Missouri, James analyzes interracial dynamics in the area. Despite the fact that the black population is outnumbered numerically, according to James, "at present it is the Negro workers who are active" and "the union, such as it is, is overwhelmingly black" (1996e, 32–33). While black and white sharecroppers were divided by the landlords' racist propaganda, as well as unequal distribution of relief benefits, James reported on black expressions of solidarity toward the white croppers, some of whom participated in the black-led highway sit-down of 1939, and more of whom again seemed ready to strike with the black workers in the present. Overall, the black workers' "attitude to these white workers is revolutionary, to the highest degree. The white worker, many of them say, is stupid. He is fooled by the bosses with all this talk about women. If, says one sharecropper to another, these whites were to join with us, we could tear this country to pieces. And a chorus of approval greets his words" (33).

James ends this phase of reporting on a complex note of frustration and opportunity. Though the workers are primed for action, nothing is happening, but this creates an opportunity for the Workers Party to make inroads (James 1996e, 31). During the lull between the end of the 1941 growing season and the following spring, James posted no reports from Missouri, but he continued to meet with the workers and help them develop their network. Organizational seeds planted in the fall and winter quickly bore radical fruit in April 1942. With James working as a scribe, the black sharecroppers issued a pamphlet, "Down with Starvation Wages in South-East Missouri," and launched a new sit-down strike. The standoff with landlords went on for three months, but in late June, rather than face the total loss of the cotton crop, landowners agreed to triple fieldworkers' wages from ten cents to thirty cents an hour. This may seem like a small victory, modest reformism at best, but what matters is that black and white sharecroppers persisted and won their demands despite hostility from landlords, state authorities, the F.B.I., and even Stalinist union leaders (who thought that strike actions at that time indirectly supported Germany's attack on Soviet Communism by weakening the U.S. war effort). Not only did collective struggle triumph over powerful forces arrayed against the sharecroppers, but the successful strike proved James' thesis that black self-organization could be the catalyst for effective mass action.

James annotates this period extensively in his unpublished autobiography. The pages dealing with his time in Missouri are filled with revealing anecdotes that add texture to the *Labor Action* reports and emphasize radical fieldwork as an occasion for James to put theories to the test, provide voice to the voiceless, and deepen his awareness of black popular culture as the instrument of self-organized masses moving through history with force. Of an organizing meeting one or two nights after his arrival in Lilbourn, he writes the following:

> So I had nothing to tell them, nothing of importance but I asked them to tell me about the situation that they were in. . . . I listened to their absolutely horrible stories of men living day by day and I asked them could anything be done. They said they were ready to do anything but they didn't know exactly [what] could be done. Then an idea struck me. I had noticed that about the six or seven men who spoke that they had spoken with a certain confidence and a certain attitude which showed that they were accustomed to speaking. So I turned to the first one and asked—"What do you do besides picking cotton in the cotton fields?" He told me that he was a parson, that he had a church, that people used to come to his church and he used to preach to them and [illegible]. I asked the other people who had spoken and then I found that the seven or eight of them were people who, in addition to working in the cotton fields, were people who had organized around themselves a church. So here was an organization. I asked them—"Do you think you could get your people to make a strike?" They said "yes," if the others are ready to join, we will organize a strike. I said, well then, let's organize a strike to take place at the time that the cotton work begins and you all are arranging about pay. They said, "We haven't got to arrange about pay,

we get so much an hour, and that's what we are going to get." One man said, "Well, I have about 40 or 50 people in my church but I could get about three or four hundred people to join in a strike. The men are desperate, they are ready to take part in anything."

So all the others who had spoken said, yes, that they were ready, that congregations were ready to take part in a strike and we agreed that night that we would organize a strike and the committee of organization would consist of the men who had spoken on that first night.

And they began to come and we began to organize the strike. (CL-RJI 806, see also Lopez, 86)

The 1942 pamphlet "Down with Starvation Wages in South-East Missouri" is rightly seen as a maximum example of James objectively testing out his ideas about how to build a spontaneous mass movement and provide effective leadership, while satisfying as well his concern as a radical historian to document the words and actions of "obscure leaders."[11] Whereas the pamphlet is a finished product, the autobiography shows James in process, actively pursuing his methods near the beginning of his time with the sharecroppers. As Jim Murray has noted, the pamphlet show James deploying vernacular rhetoric, particularly in the preacherly line that justifies strike actions through the biblical claim that "the laborer is worthy of his hire" (Murray n.d.). The autobiography, by giving more details about the organizing meetings and James' discovery that his cohort of strikers included several ministers, shows the source for his vernacular cadences.

While publicly distributed documents like the pamphlet and *Labor Action* reports show black self-organization in important political contexts—namely the highway sit-down of 1939 and the strike of 1942—James' autobiography reveals the freedom struggle being organized in everyday life. Given his underground status and the wide range of social forces arrayed against him, James traveled under the alias of "Brother Williams" and was constantly having to hide. Adults moved him around from house to house, and during the day black children fended off search parties. One day in particular, in the yard outside a house where James was concealed, several children met a posse of three men—one each from the F.B.I., the Communist Party, and the state police—and casually rebuffed them. James correctly sees this moment as the product of community training and organization: "Those children who had come from inside the house where I was staying and the ease with which the children put their feet on the running board and put their hands on the windows, and spoke . . . I was quite astonished. They were quite educated as to what was required in that situation" (James 1996e, 32).

Among the adults in James' orbit, Pete Wilderness is one person he remembers by name many years later. In telling a lengthy anecdote about how a young black man is abducted by a white driver who feels snubbed when the black man passes him on the highway—the climax of which is Wilderness's calm assertion that "Brother Williams, the day is coming when we got to put an end to all that sort of thing" (37)—James digresses to characterize Wilderness based on his habit of carefully reading every copy of *The Militant* that arrives from St. Louis. "That was the way he educated himself," James writes. "He wanted to know all that was happening. He read that paper every week. I used to look at him reading it and there were many things there that Pete had no background in but he read that paper and then he put it away" (34). Where the children show education as a communal process, Pete Wilderness embodies the individual for whom self-education is effective self-organization.

In treating James' fieldwork notes on African American popular culture, I have focused mostly on examples of successful black resistance in James' published and unpublished texts, both because this focus reflects the overall tenor of his post-1938 writing and because it helps sharpen the contrast with his earlier vision of African American experience as victimization. One of the things that gives his writing about black life its existential density, though, is that James also records the many dues he paid while being "initiated in the freemasonry, as it were, of the race," as James Weldon Johnson once put it (xii). Recounting his passage through New Orleans on the way back from Coyoacan, James tells several revealing stories about his induction into the harsher aspects of black manhood in the 1930s. In one incident, a black youth pulls James out of the street in New Orleans just in time to avoid being run down by a white cabbie who has become irate at the sight of James insistently hailing him for a ride (CLRJI 1020). Also in New Orleans, white women stare at James in a way that he has difficulty characterizing but that clearly makes him unsettled and nervous (Buhle 1988, 74). Interstate travel, a classic location for enacting U.S. race politics, has been a recurring theme in African American writing since the time of the slave narrative, and James' road stories echo the accounts of Ida B. Wells, James Weldon Johnson, Malcolm X, and others who have touched on this topic. Riding the bus north to New York,

James accommodates himself to Jim Crow directions, but after settling in with a volume of Hegel he is ordered to move further back (CLRJI 1020). On the train ride from St. Louis to southeastern Missouri, James' traveling companion predicts correctly that the behavior of whites will grow increasingly hostile the further south they reach. During his time on the scene in Lilbourn, James was witness to the kidnapping mentioned previously, as well as the aftermath of a lynching. In a lengthy account of the lynching incident, he demystifies the stereotypical explanation of taboo interracial sex, but the battle armor of dialectics and political economy do not minimize the impact of white terrorism on James, who writes, "I can tell you from my own experience, for weeks afterwards, whenever I met a white man at some distance from anybody, he looked at me and that lynching was there before us" (CLRJI 805). Throughout the 1940s, James wrote a now well-known series of love letters to Constance Webb in which his bitterness at segregation, though a comparatively minor thread, nevertheless surfaces with regularity.[12] Chronology should underscore the fact that James not only endured the rituals of segregation throughout his entire stay in the United States, he also recalled them vividly many decades later. His knowledge of the "humiliations and discriminations" referred to in *A History of Negro Revolt* was thus an intimate and lingering aspect of radical fieldwork, and yet it seems all the more noteworthy that the primary result produced in James' fieldwork notes is not bitterness but rather his emphatic focus on a successful black freedom struggle, and his classic interpretation of African American popular culture as a revolutionary force nationally and globally.

Postlude: Optimism

During the fifteen years of his first U.S. sojourn, James repeatedly used radical fieldwork to put himself in contact with living African American culture, thereby transforming the view of that culture expressed in *A History of African Revolt*. I want to conclude by reflecting on how this work of the late 1930s, 1940s, and 1950s connects with earlier and later periods in James' career, and how it sheds light on some theoretical legacy issues, particularly his philosophical and political optimism.

Brett St. Louis has made the case for writing "political ethnographies" of spontaneous popular movements in order to know and understand those movements in their specificity and concreteness, which is precisely the sort of thing we see in the *Labor Action* reports (St. Louis 1998, 7–8). In James' own discourse, an orientation toward political ethnography is routed consistently through the imperatives of radical history. James returned to the United States from 1968 to 1974, and in an unpublished speech titled "Black Struggle in the Caribbean," given in 1969, he tells a story about his driver in Washington, D.C., who promises in the wake of the fires of 1968 to show James "where they burnt and why they burnt and where they didn't. They knew what they were doing and I will take you to one or two people who have some part in this burning" (James 1969a). James compares this to urban unrest in Los Angeles, Newark, and Detroit and relates another fieldwork anecdote:

> I was talking to one of the boys in Detroit, and I remember one fellow he said to me, he said, you see they're moving us, and they want to get some of us from this part of the town, and put us there so they can surround us, but they can't do that. As long as we have this street, and that street, and that street, and that street, they can never surround us. We are in control. He was watching the city and what was taking place, and what the police were doing as though he were a general of a great army, and in command of the masses of the nation. (James 1969a, CLRJI 777)

Elsewhere in the speech, James interprets these episodes via the work of Georges Lefebvre, the French historian who insisted on the impact of "obscure leaders" during periods when Parisian masses pushed the French Revolution to its most radical phase. Readers of *The Black Jacobins* will likely recognize that James is revisiting a theme he first articulated in those terms more than thirty years earlier when writing his Marxist history of the Haitian revolution.[13] Clearly, though, even in his earlier work on Arthur Cipriani and the emerging Trinidad labor movement, as well as his theory and practice of yard fiction, James is interested in the voice of grass-roots leaders and the supporting masses. Jim Murray makes the persuasive argument in his essay, "The Boy at the Window," that James' modus operandi was already established by the time of his childhood involvement with the cricketers and their audience in Tunapuna (Murray 1996, 207, 210). Telescoping forward, the fact that Murray focuses on a passage from *Beyond a Boundary*, published in 1963, indicates that the radical fieldwork imperative is present not only in both North American stints but also during James' return to Trinidad from 1957 to 1966. Throughout this period, James continued to nurture ties at the grass-roots level through his cricket-related activities (including the popular success of *Beyond a Boundary*), editorship of the mass-distributed newspaper *The Nation*, free public lectures at the library, and concerted (albeit unsuccessful) efforts to organize the populist opposition Workers and Peasants Party. Without discounting completely the claims, mentioned above, that James became cut off from a popular base after his deportation from the United States, it seems hard to locate a post-1953 moment—particularly in the United States and Trinidad—when James was *not* making concerted efforts to establish contact with everyday people as an integral part of his revolutionary praxis.

Translating from Lefebvre's mimeographed lecture notes in French, James had quoted Lefebvre to the effect that historians face impenetrable lacunae when trying to assess the work of obscure leaders: "What we would most like to know is out of our reach; we would like to have the diary of the most obscure of these popular leaders; we would then be able to grasp, in the act so to speak, how one of these great revolutionary days began; we do not have it" (James 1989, 338 n. 39). Radical fieldwork, particularly when linked to fieldwork notes, is first and foremost a means of bridging a methodological gap by preserving the words and deeds of obscure leaders, such as the cutting batsman Matthew Bondman, the enslaved revolutionary songwriters of San Domingo, the autodidact Pete Wilderness in Lilbourn, Missouri, the poetically denunciatory landlady Mrs. Roach, the Port-of-Spain graffiti artists celebrating a historic inning by Sobers, the strategizing of street soldiers of Detroit, and more. By giving voice to the voiceless, James is ensuring that future historians and activists will face fewer reconstructive hurdles of the sort that frustrated Lefebvre as well as James himself.

James' political ethnography of the African American freedom struggle reveals another aspect of radical fieldwork, which is that such fieldwork serves to ground political and philosophical optimism. Lacking fieldwork experience in the United States, James at first equivocated and framed African American people as cowed by "humiliations and discriminations"; with the benefit of direct involvement, James adopted an optimistic revolutionary view and sustained it consistently down to his late essay on Alice Walker, Toni Morrison, and Ntozake Shange. Critics and biographers have accounted for Jamesian optimism by relating it to the influence of Hegelian philosophy (see Ross, 77, 84) and, in the case of African American issues, to a Caribbean immigrant experience that allowed him access to black life in the United States but left him comparatively free from alleged "nagging recollections of past defeats American Blacks held in their collective memory" (Buhle 1988, 74). Perhaps what this essay adds to the conversation is more evidence to support the claim that James' proximity to and active participation in popular movements throughout his long life is what funds his "enormous faith in the forms of organization and culture created by the masses themselves" (Kelley, 119). Radical fieldwork takes James beyond the stage of vindicating Africana history through reference to its great men. It projects him forward into the redemptionist discourse of dread history, grounding a seemingly unshakeable optimism about the eventual success of popular democratic struggles in the United States and elsewhere.[14] In one of his last interviews, from February 1989, James reiterates his faith in the historical force of everyday people: "That I believe—where it comes from I don't know. That is a psychological question. But I consistently stick to that because I find that all the great moments in history all originate not from the words and agitation and propaganda of gifted men—revolutionaries—but because that was coming from the population and they took it up" (Haut and Buhle 1989).

Finally, as well as fueling philosophical and political optimism, Jamesian radical fieldwork may even have therapeutic psychological value. In an interview in 1985 by the Mississippi activist Jan Hillegas, James insists that "we live in a tremendous world, and we have to have some idea of where it's going" (27). Outlining a program that sounds like a summary of James' own work with the Beacon Group, Fourth International elites, the Missouri sharecroppers, and the Johnson-Forrest Tendency, he tells Hillegas to find a suitable organization, get involved, begin to study the situation, issue a statement, and prepare to work for "at least ten years" (33). "And when you have got clear in your mind what you want to do and the organization you join has got a certain perspective," James continues, "then your mind will become at ease and you can devote yourself to the work with concentration and the determination to be effective there" (33). It is this practical optimism, as much as any particular doctrine, theory, or factoid, that links James to progressive humanist openings of the New Left, to civil rights and black power in the United States, to new social movements for gender, sexuality, and youth liberation, to national independence movements across the Caribbean, Africa, and elsewhere, and to new forms of labor internationalism. Such optimism is a large part of why James remains a necessary prophet as diverse freedom strugglers grapple with analytic and practical challenges posed by globalization in the post-Soviet era.

Notes

I wish to thank the University of Central Florida for a research grant that allowed me to spend a very productive month as fellow of the C.L.R. James Institute in New York. I would like to dedicate this essay to the memory of Jim Murray, typesetter, archivist, writer, teacher, and friend.

1. The phrase "popular culture" has a notoriously tangled frame of reference and invoking it requires some attempt to clarify the scope of usage here. In one strand of Marxist critique, deriving from Marx's study of commodities, superstructure, ideology, and false consciousness, popular culture signifies pop or mass culture, something that is debunked and either rejected or held with suspicion by thinkers such as Lukacs, Horkheimer, Adorno, Althusser, and others. Against this strand are critics such as Bakhtin, Gramsci, Brecht, Benjamin, Bloch, Barthes, Baudrillard, and Jameson, who in diverse ways embrace the ludic, utopian aspects of mass culture. See Grimshaw and Larsen.

2. Documents from the archives of the C.L.R. James Institute will be identified by the prefix CLRJI followed by the accession number. All such documents are cited courtesy of the institute.

3. Related in conversation by Jim Murray in January 2000. For other references to this passage, see Bogues 1997, 52; and Buhle 1988, 105.

4. I am borrowing the term "fieldwork" from its discursive home in cultural anthropology, where it refers to the scholar's immersion in daily life as a participant-observer outside one's home culture. Both participation and observation mark James' direct involvement with everyday people and mass movements throughout his life. An anthropological concept of fieldwork is also useful for framing James' encounters with popular culture as generative, dialectical engagements that shape researcher, informant, and the resulting texts.

5. James came to the United States under the aegis of Trotsky's Socialist Workers Party (SWP) and the U.S. party leader, James Cannon. When the SWP split in 1940, James followed Max Shachtman and became a founding member of the rival anti-Stalinist Workers Party (WP). The Johnson-Forrest Tendency (JFT), formed in 1941 as a semi-independent movement inside the WP, was named for J. R. Johnson, which was one of James aliases, and Freddy Forrest, which was an alias for Raya Dunayevskaya. Grace Lee (later Grace Lee Boggs) met James in 1941–42 in Chicago, published under the pseudonym Ria Stone, and was "the acknowledged philosopher of the Tendency" (Turner, 196). Johnsonites were known initially for their position on the Russian Question (they were among the first to criticize the Soviet Union as a form of state capitalism rather than viewing it as a degenerate worker's state to be defended against all attacks), later for their pro-autonomy stance on the Negro Question, and later still for publishing numerous pamphlets and translations such as the first English-language edition of Marx's 1844 *Economic and Philosophical Manuscripts*. In 1947, James led the JFT back into the Socialist Workers Party but eventually broke completely with Trotskyist groups in 1950. For more detail on the JFT, see Boggs 1993 38; Buhle 1988, 74–99; Worcester, 78–115. For more background on the anti-Stalinist left and the "Americanization of Bolshevism," see R. A. Hill 1993, 302–10 and 319–22.

6. See, for example, Buhle 1988, 16–26; Worcester, 7–8; Cudjoe , 41; Pyne-Timothy, 51–54.

7. By the mid-1930s, Robeson was a celebrity in England and in 1936 James recruited him to play the part of Toussaint in *Black Majesty*, a dramatized version of *The Black Jacobins*. James celebrated Robeson as a person who combined "immense power and great gentleness," as a forerunner of negritude, and as someone noteworthy for his "devotion to the world revolution" (James, 1996a, 256, 259–60, 262). James could also be critical about the extent of Robeson's cross-cultural awareness. "Occasionally," according to James, "Robeson spoke before the West African Student Union and the India League as well. But through it all, I think he never really understood Britain's imperialism" (Boyle and Bunie 2001, 299). For references to James in Robeson's biographies, see Boyle and Bunie 2001, 319–20, 339–40; and Duberman 1988, 171, 196–98.

8. I am citing from the typescript "The Negro Question," CLRJI 4493 (James 1939). This text is included as "Notes Following the Discussions" in James 1996b, 14–16. Ralph Dumain's annotation of this entry in the James Institute database places the manuscript in its proper chronological frame, that is, written during the Coyoacan summit. Dumain also comments on the unique ideological content of this document. Most notable are James' argument that Garvey, in appealing to darker-skinned people, was making "a veiled appeal to the lower classes," and his claim that the lower classes seemed more ready to accept the idea of a separate state, though this would have to be presented by black radical leaders rather than white ones.

9. See also Richardson, Chrysostom, and Grimshaw for a definitive statement from James on the nature and scope of the organization whose development was discussed at Coyoacan: "I am sure if you read the resolution, you will see that it makes clear that it was a political organization fighting for the position of rights in general and the black people in particular" (10). Here, James is reiterating his stance against separatist black nationalism by emphasizing "rights in general" and thus locating his fight within a discourse of civil rights.

10. Occasionally James makes reference to lived experience in order to drive home a point. For instance, in theorizing African American society as revolutionary, he tells Trotsky and the others, "I am informed that a new spirit is moving among the Negroes, in Harlem and elsewhere today" (James 1996b, 4), and later, in support of his argument for an independent Negro organization, he refers to his visit to Boston during the lecture tour: "I went to a Barbados organization and there found about twenty or thirty people who had some sort of free society, but after having spoken to them for five or ten minutes they became very much interested in the political questions that I raise; and the chairman told me that if I wanted to come back to Boston he could arrange a Negro meeting for one at which we would have about seven hundred people. I do not think that it is too much to say that that is characteristic of the general attitude of the Negroes in the various places at which I had meetings" (James 1984b, 41).

11. Regarding the pamphlet, see King (94–95) and Worcester, who notes that "James had written down the sharecroppers['] words rather than formulating their

demands" (72). The relationship of leaders to mass groups was always a core issue for James. That it was also in mind during his fieldwork in Missouri, in the preceding months, and indeed throughout the 1940s, is evident from the columns he published in *Labor Action,* including "Which Type of Leader Should Negroes Follow?" (September 2, 1940), "On Working Together with the Negro Masses" (October 13, 1941), and "Negroes and Bolshevism" (April 7, 1947). The phrase "obscure leaders" comes from the French historian Georges Lefebvre, to whom James made repeated reference over more than thirty years, and whose work I consider more closely in the conclusion below.

12. In 1948, for instance, writing from Reno, Nevada, where he had gone to secure a divorce in order that he and Webb could marry, James comments about an excursion around Lake Tahoe: "The lake was lovely, the drive splendid. It should have been a perfect outing." However, "there were no colored people in sight. We were excluded. All round there were houses, people, cabins, cars, people bathing. But Negroes were out. The exclusion was always present. It did not ruin the day but it poisoned it" (quoted in Worcester, 100–101). See also James 1996d.

13. The British Labour Party leader and historian Michael Foot has noted James' intellectual debt to Michelet (Foot , 99–103), but Lefebvre seems to have had a deeper and longer-lasting impact. References to Lefebvre appear twice in *The Black Jacobins,* once when James is writing about the insurrection against Toussaint's plan to restore the corvée (James 1989, 276), and later when he discusses the outbreak of fighting against Leclerc after the French general deports Toussaint (336). In each case, James uses Lefebvre to annotate the fact that resistance comes from rank and file soldiers who show "greater political understanding than their leaders" (339). James revisits Lefebvre, quoting him at length in "Black Sansculottes," an essay of 1964 concerning popular resistance to Haitian dictator François Duvalier (James 1984a, 161), and again in a speech of 1969 touching on black street leaders in the United States. These references, made over a span of thirty years, underscore the continuity of James' intent to inscribe the voices of "obscure leaders." Moreover, in the speech of 1969, African American people occupy the theoretical space previously reserved for Haiti's black sans-culottes, which indicates, from another conceptual angle, James's inclusion of African Americans in his maximum revolutionary category. Robert Hill also mentions James' debt to French historians, especially Michelet, Lefebvre, and Daniel Guérin (R. A. Hill, 340–45).

14. For a useful guide to the growing list of dread history's theorists and practitioners, see Bogues, 2000 and 2003. Bogues describes the field as follows: "A dread history is a different history that uses elite archives critically. More important, it develops a different set of optics and language for historical discourse while positing a radically different conception of history: old meanings of words become transformed when they are exposed to new discursive practices. A dread history recognizes that history in the modern period begins as written narratives grounded in European classifications and conquest, and that there is a difference between the making of history and descriptions of that making. A dread history moves along an historical axis

of redemption" (Bogue 2000, 117). While righteously honoring James as a radical forebear, Bogues confines James to vindication and "great man" history based on a reading of *The Black Jacobins* (116). Bogues is certainly right about that text, which (like Lefebvre's history) can only proceed far enough to pose the question of everyday popular agency, but my argument here includes the idea that James' method, specifically through radical fieldwork, contains the seeds of its own transformation into dread history.

5

Moving Metaphors

The Representation of AIDS in
Caribbean Literature and Visual Arts

IVETTE ROMERO-CESAREO

Because HIV/AIDS is the world's problem . . . and we are one world.
Advertisement for Squibbs Pharmaceuticals

Introduction: SIDA/AIDS, International Intercourse or the Global Gaze

Where the native territory had not yet received the contagion of the plague like
a recolonization through corporal fluids . . . the plague arrived like a new form of
colonization through contagion.

Pedro Lemebel, *Loco afán: Crónicas de Sidario*

A persistent complaint among Caribbean artists has been their insularity and
lack of intercommunication across the region. This isolation is understandable given the myriad hindrances to communication and productive interaction that emerge as barrier reefs in the very sea that joins us all—differences
in ideology, political structures, and the shared experiences of colonization
(from first "encounters" to subsequent plantation life, to present-day tourism). The historical development of each island has given birth to economic
disparities, topographic and demographic variations, and, most important,
linguistic diversity. The Caribbean islands consist of twenty-four to twenty-
eight countries (depending on the modes of classification) that fall within various political configurations (territories, dependencies, overseas departments,
and sovereign states) and which have several official languages (Dutch, Eng-

lish, French, Spanish, various forms of Creole, and Papiamento). Although porous borders make the Caribbean a cultural crossroads, and the area has been considered by many to be an exemplary locus of transnationalism, syncretism, and "creolization" or "hybridization," the islands remain relatively isolated from one another. While the flow of tourism from Europe and the United States is facilitated by numerous air travel and ocean cruise options, and the traffic of commodities (including peoples) between the Caribbean and metropolitan centers is determined by the needs of global markets, inter-island crossings are, to say the least, problematic. Because of airline corporation monopolies and varied political (dis)agreements, island-to-island movements are very costly for many, life-threatening for those who cannot afford "official" modes of transportation, and in all but a very few cases complex and time consuming. However, it can also be argued that none of these complications and disparities present insuperable obstacles to inter-island relations and that there are just as many or more elements connecting the islands than separating them—recognition of these underlying similarities may serve as a common "language." Furthermore, as modes of communication rapidly advance, as human mobility (or displacement) becomes, under better or worse conditions, much more prevalent, and as borders continue to shift, there have been new ways to connect across the territorial, economic, cultural, sociohistorical, and linguistic divides.

Artistic expression reflects these new ways of connecting, both within the Caribbean and beyond to international audiences and markets. The regional and international reception of Haitian art is a case in point, as major exhibitions and growing collections attest to the power of Caribbean-derived themes and subjects to elicit positive responses across national and transnational borders. Puerto Rican art is following a similar trajectory. A 2001 *New York Times* article by Luisita López Torregrosa, "Puerto Rican Art Moves Outward, and More Inward," focused on young artists who represent a major shift in local artistic traditions: "No one calls it a revolution, but in the last decade, especially in the last few years, young Puerto Rican artists have been pulling away from the island's insularity and traditional art forms and reaching out. They've mounted experimental installations and other provocative works in galleries and alternative spaces in parks and streets. The boundaries, they say, are being torn down" (33).

The same article cites Deborah Cullen, a curator at El Museo del Barrio, who compares "postmodern pioneers" such as Antonio Martorell and Pepón

Osorio to a younger generation of visual artists: "Today's younger group is very conversant with postmodern artists all over the world. They deal with Caribbean topics with more complex themes, breaking boundaries, exploring sexual identity and liberation from geopolitical borders" (López Torregrosa 33). Haitian-born Maud Duquella, manager of a large number of the leading Puerto Rican artists and co-owner of Puerto Rico's premier art gallery, Galería Botello, explains the change in economic terms, citing as examples visual artists who have shown their work internationally, such as Charles Juhasz, Arnaldo Roche, and María de Mater O'Neill, and noting that with a more prosperous economy, artists travel more readily and an increasing number of people are buying art. Although this is a very logical explanation in purely economic terms, it does not take into account the emotional and psychological shifts in the communities that have reconfigured artistic horizons. The artists, art promoters, curators, and gallery owners cited in this article all call attention to the transformations and breaking of boundaries that have occurred in the last twenty years. In addition to globalization—which has had both positive and negative effects, including increased communication and greater physical mobility, among other factors—traumatic historical events have also played a significant role in transforming the realm of representation.

In the Caribbean, the most harrowing and shattering development to affect broad sectors of the population at the end of the twentieth century and the beginning of the twenty-first has been the advent of the AIDS pandemic—a development seemingly far removed from trends in postmodern aesthetics. The very artists mentioned in the *New York Times* article are precisely those who, in the case of Puerto Rico, have lived through the most calamitous moments of the epidemic; many of them publicly articulated the ravages and losses caused by the disease. One of the artists featured in that article, María de Mater O'Neill, speaks of how strongly she was affected by the loss of loved ones to AIDS. Describing a period of mourning during which she stopped painting, O'Neill explains: "After [age] 30, I wasn't so innocent. People started to die. I lost friends in New York to AIDS" (López Torregrosa 33). In 1990 her close friend, the artist Carlos Collazo, died of AIDS in San Juan. During his final months he explored the mysterious nature of the illness, his declining health, and his approaching death in a haunting series of self-portraits.[1]

This loss affected the entire artistic community and sparked O'Neill's activism and volunteer work in breaking the silence surrounding the HIV/AIDS pandemic. In the same year, the newly founded Puerto Rican chapter of ACT UP led a march in Old San Juan. The demonstration ended in front of the governor's mansion, La Fortaleza, where protesters with red paint dripping from their hands led the chant "El gobierno tiene sangre en sus manos" (The government has blood on its hands). ACT UP members fell to the ground one by one, as symbolic dead bodies, their outlines chalked in as in homicide cases. Inspired by the demonstration, Teo Freytes, another artist cited by López Torregrosa, created an art book entitled *El gobierno tiene las manos llenas de sangre* (The government's hands are covered in blood, 1990) as well as a series of drawings, paintings, digital and linoleum prints, and a paper sculpture addressing the topic of AIDS. All of these works featured an angry male figure, with a face vaguely reminiscent of a death mask, bearing the ACT UP triangle (the "silence = death" slogan) on his chest and holding up a bloodied right hand. In some of the prints, the central figure is surrounded by numerous chalk outlines of the dead; in others, blood cells or spermatozoa frame the main image. These first attempts to express the anger and grief brought about by the still mysterious illness marked the beginning of a period of participation and outreach by the artistic community that we will see repeated across the region. The AIDS pandemic, more than a postmodern sensibility per se, has played the most substantial role in altering artistic horizons, breaking boundaries, expanding the exploration of sexual identity, and transforming geopolitical borders throughout the Caribbean. Like the Puerto Rican artists mentioned above, concerned artists in the region, regardless of their national (pre)conditions, have been trying to make sense of a disease that has, more than any other plague in history, transcended boundaries of all types.

Metaphors of Blame: Sexualized Monkeys, Zombies, Sodomizers, and Seductive She-Devils

> An illness that also connoted sexuality, poverty, race, drug use, and the wasting away of the body, AIDS was deemed shameful at multiple levels. But the transfiguration of the bearer's shame into art, political action, and community building saved the lives of many facing straight on the question of whose shame it was that HIV-positive people were dying.
>
> Frances Negrón-Muntaner, *Boricua Pop*

In the Caribbean, Haiti was the first country to face a steady bombardment of stigmatizing metaphors and regressive mythmaking related to HIV/AIDS. In

Aids and Accusation: Haiti and the Geography of Blame, Paul Farmer underscores how, early in the pandemic, U.S. professionals, including physicians, public health officials, and social scientists, insisted in linking the AIDS "mystery" with speculations about zombification and "voodoo" practices:

> In 1982, U.S. public health officials inferred that Haitians per se were in some way at risk for AIDS, and suggested that unraveling "the Haiti connection" would lead researchers to the culprit. In a sample of the melodramatic prose that came to typify commentary on Haitians with AIDS, one reporter termed the incidence of AIDS in Haitians "a clue from the grave, as though a zombie, leaving a trail of unwinding gauze bandages and rotting flesh, had come to the hospital's Grand Rounds to pronounce a curse." (2)

Using the economic framework Orlando Patterson identifies as the "West Atlantic system," Farmer redresses the focus of geographical blame by attributing the accelerated spread of AIDS in the Caribbean to the United States as a result of the unequal relationship ensured by its political and economic power. He points out that the countries more tightly enmeshed in this "West Atlantic system"—the Dominican Republic, the Bahamas, Trinidad and Tobago, Mexico, Haiti (and Puerto Rico, which he treats separately because it is not an independent country)—were also the ones with the highest percentages of AIDS cases in 1986: "And the [independent] country with the most cases, Haiti, was also the country most fully dependent on the United States. In the Caribbean basin, only Puerto Rico is more economically dependent on the United States. And only Puerto Rico has reported more cases of AIDS to the Pan American Health Organization" (Farmer, 149). Furthermore, Farmer points out the circumstantial nature of the spread of AIDS in view of U.S. domination and political intercourse within the Caribbean region. If the advent of the disease had occurred earlier in the twentieth century, when the economic forces at play were in a slightly different configuration, the focal point of the pandemic would not have been Haiti. He substantiates his point by comparing Haiti and Cuba, "the sole country not enmeshed in the West Atlantic system," and the strikingly dissimilar degrees of HIV prevalence rates in 1986. While Haiti showed prevalence rates of approximately 9 percent, in Cuba only 0.01 percent of one million people tested were found to have antibodies to HIV. As Farmer concludes, "Had the pandemic begun a few decades earlier, the epidemiology of HIV infection would have been different. Havana, once the 'tropical playground of the Americas,' might have been as much an epicenter of the pandemic as Carrefour" (150).

In its incipient stages, the HIV/AIDS monster was a racialized and gendered one. In the late 1970s and early 1980s, AIDS was popularly identified as a male malady, or more specifically, a homosexual plague. The media (particularly in the United States) focused on the three Hs—homosexuals, hemophiliacs, and Haitian men—as well as intravenous drug users. This historical moment is captured in Edwidge Danticat's novel *Breath, Eyes, Memory* (1994). The narrator expresses fear of going to school because of taunting by other children: "Many American kids even accused Haitians of having AIDS because they had heard on television that only the 'Four H's' got AIDS: Heroin addicts, Hemophiliacs, Homosexuals, and Haitians" (51).

In terms of race, common metaphors in the early stages of the AIDS outbreak oscillated from images of a dark bestiality (as in the once popular myth envisioning African "natives having sex with monkeys" (Wall), to speculations on vampirism, zombification, and "voodoo" worship. Even in this embryonic phase, links were being drawn between continents (with antiquated references to "dark Africa") and Caribbean islands. While poor, black men were blamed by the media, the official discourse of medical and political agencies focused on an assortment of culpable "others" such as homosexuals, drug addicts, and prostitutes. Detailing the nearsightedness and discriminatory language of pamphlets purporting to help the U.S. population avoid contagion by AIDS, Angela Wall explains that "it is not difficult to determine, then, who those 'Others' might be: they are those who engage in sharing needles and syringes; those who practice anal sex, 'with or without a condom'; and those who have sex with a 'pickup or prostitute or with someone they don't know well' . . . the drug addicts, homosexuals and sodomites . . . are the only ones at risk" (229). Wall states that "as a non-discriminatory virus which holds no race, class, or sexual prejudice, AIDS has successfully disrupted such traditional understandings and processes of moral value and belief legitimation: strong Christian values and high moral standards offer little protection against the HIV virus" (225). As she further explains, "a contradiction arises between the illicit, 'immoral' gay lifestyle lived out in excess by those supposedly responsible for the disease and the spread of disease into the 'decent' heterosexual community" (225–26).

By the mid-1980s, the percentage of male incidences of HIV/AIDS in the Caribbean was still fluctuating around 89 percent, but this allowed for a shift in the stigmatization of the "other," as women began to be portrayed as evil temptresses—receptacles of decay and destruction drawing innocent men to their doom. With the progression of HIV/AIDS throughout the years and the way it has afflicted the "normal" population, regardless of gender, age group, or sexual orientation, the stigmatization, while not eliminated, has become relatively de-centered.

In this trajectory, the role of Haiti's association with AIDS is of paramount importance. In the late 1980s, at the height of the Haitian refugee crisis in the United States, when Haitian migration to the United States was likened to a plague, the HIV scare served as justification for returning of boatloads of people to the island and isolating hundreds of Haitians in makeshift refugee camps on U.S. military bases in Puerto Rico, the Bahamas, and Cuba. Fear of contagion was used to justify virulent reactions to the waves of "boat people" who had already been treated as deviant and sickly "others" since the United States established the first detention facilities and processing centers in the early 1970s.[2] Ironically, during this period, Cuba was harshly criticized for its solution to the spread of the disease—the segregation of AIDS and HIV positive patients from public life in specialized sanatoriums (negatively referred to as *sidatorios*, from SIDA, the Spanish and French acronym for AIDS) where patients received what was deemed by many to be exceptional treatment. Coinciding with the first few years of Cuba's economic austerity in the 1990s, the "Período especial en tiempo de paz" (Special period in time of peace), wild rumors spread that perfectly healthy men were purposely injecting themselves with the virus in order to live comfortably in these medical colonies or, some surmised, as an act of protest. The policy of isolating those who were HIV positive came under such heavy criticism from numerous global human rights groups that the health centers reverted to outpatient services and voluntary inpatient care. Furthermore, in spite of economic restraints, Cuba intensified research efforts to develop immunization and was able to produce its own antiretroviral drugs, thus reducing the AIDS incidence in people between the ages of fifteen and forty-nine to 0.05 percent by 2002. Puerto Rico in the early 1990s ranked third in U.S. AIDS cases per capita (fifty-nine cases per one hundred thousand inhabitants) after the District of Columbia and New York, and sixth in the total number of AIDS cases after California, New York, Texas, New Jersey, and Florida (Migrants contre le SIDA 1997). By 1994 the mortality rate was forty-two per one hundred thousand persons (Gómez, Fernández, Otero, et al.). Today, although the rate of incidence has slowed down, the number of those afflicted has risen to thirty thousand.[3] According to Harvard University's Enhancing Care Initiative (ECI), "The island of Puerto Rico continues to be one of the epicenters of the AIDS pandemic in the Western Hemisphere."

The examples of Haiti, Cuba, and Puerto Rico demonstrate that perceptions of the illness are radically different depending on circumstances and contexts. In each case, the development of the epidemic has had much to do with political differences and the relationship between specific Caribbean countries and First World countries, such as the United States. As stated in the 2005 UN/AIDS Epidemic Update, "The Caribbean's status as the second most-affected region in the world masks substantial differences in the extent and intensity of its epidemics." National estimates of adult HIV prevalence surpass 1 percent in Barbados, the Dominican Republic, Jamaica, and Surinam, 2 percent in the Bahamas, Guyana, and Trinidad and Tobago, and 3 percent in Haiti, while in Cuba it remains close to 0.05 percent (UNAIDS statistics place it closer to 0.1 percent).

These disparities have much to do with patterns of sexual behavior, which account for variations in transmission of the disease; homophobia and social taboos that problematize the acknowledgment of same sex relations; the prevalence of condom use and safe sex practices; intravenous drug use, which contributes significantly to the spread of HIV only in Bermuda and Puerto Rico (2005 UN/AIDS Epidemic Update); incidence of commercial sex; economic dependence on tourism and variations in types of tourism; levels of education; degrees of poverty; and how individual countries address the epidemic by preventive measures, building health care facilities, and making treatments available. For example, "While universal treatment access is being achieved in Cuba, and coverage is relatively high in the Bahamas and Barbados, access to treatment is poor in three of the worst-affected countries in the Caribbean. About one third of people in need of antiretroviral treatment received it in Trinidad and Tobago in September 2005, as were a mere 12% in Haiti and 10% in the Dominican Republic" (PAHO 2005). In this context, the First World countries that directly control the tourist trade (including sex tourism), and those that produce antiretroviral drugs, control prices, and/or hinder their distribution, are intrinsically connected to the fates of these Caribbean countries.[4] Furthermore, the stigmatization of the most affected areas, such as African and Caribbean countries, inevitably obstructs large-scale efforts for prevention and treatment: "The paradigm of AIDS as a gay plague led to the categorization and stigmatization of risk groups, first identified as the four H's (homosexuals, heroin users, hemophiliacs, and Haitians)" and a consequent "delay in research funding, as public officials were hesitant to assign funds primarily benefiting stigmatized members of society" (Cunningham).

From the Caribbean perspective, there are still many sites from which to establish points of comparison reaching out to all parts of the globe, to the United States and Europe because of ongoing discussions about the availability and control of medications, to Latin America because of its geographic proximity, shared colonial experiences, and, in some cases linguistic ties, to Brazil because it produces antiretroviral drugs and has pledged to supply them to the Organization of Eastern Caribbean States (*Medical News Today* 2006), and, in particular, to Africa, which continues to get the most media coverage because of the extent to which poverty has magnified and accelerated the tragic onslaught of the illness. The raw facts about AIDS—such as the percentage of the population afflicted or the availability of health facilities and medication—have had a great impact on artistic creation addressing the pandemic.

Today, Haiti receives significantly less press coverage than other regions regarding HIV/AIDS. However, because it was the first country afflicted by a steady onslaught of stigmatizing mythmaking, it is not surprising that, despite the silence about the pandemic at many levels of public discourse, it was one of the first areas to represent HIV/AIDS in the visual arts, in particular, painting. An early example of a painting suggestive of the initial stages of the AIDS pandemic is Carlo Jean-Jacques' *Flanne* (in Creole "to rove" or "to wander," 1987). In this work, a central, ghost-like, male figure dressed in a white suit is surrounded by members of the community. Although there is no overt indication that the topic of the painting is illness, the main figure's emaciated frame, which seems to be fading away, and his skull-like countenance remind the viewer of the first victims of AIDS. Since Jean-Jacques himself died of AIDS in 1990, it is plausible to assume that he was representing the ravages of the illness and the consternation of the community.

In the context of the *botpippel* experience, Paravisini-Gebert and Kelehan (in this volume) discuss the work of Colin Anniser, a refugee at Camp Bulkeley, the section of the U.S. Naval Base at Guantánamo reserved for HIV positive "boat people." Anniser, who died from AIDS in 1996, emphasized the detention camp's oppressive atmosphere in *United States Navy Haitian*

Refugee Confinement Camp, Guantánamo Bay, Cuba (1993) (see fig. 6.9 in the next chapter). The artist presents a disquieting image of the refugee barracks, reminiscent of the urban cemeteries of Haiti. As in Jean-Jacques' *Flanne*, death seems to permeate the scene.

Two examples that provide more explicit commentary on AIDS in Haiti are Leopol Lymdor's *Anti-SIDA Demonstration* (circa 1990–94) and Frantz Zephirin's *A Prayer for the End of AIDS in the World* (1999). Lymdor's painting appears at first sight to be of a funeral, but closer examination reveals it to be an anti-AIDS demonstration. As bystanders, we see a group of townspeople carrying a coffin, and although we never know where the demonstration is headed, it is clear that this is a matter of breaking the silence: the wooden coffin bears the word SIDA written on it in large print and the determined demonstrators are led by drummers and other musicians. Zephirin's work features the deity Grande Brigitte praying for the souls of those who have died of AIDS and who have been carried into the hereafter by the AIDS Airlines 747.[5] Because of the circumstances surrounding the creation of these paintings, what they all have in common is the absence of hope. They may be marked by loss, suffering, or anger, but always by a sense of abjection.

Empty Beds: The Representation of AIDS and Abjection in Caribbean Artistic Production

> I walked silently to the place where I knew I would find him, but alas, as soon as I found it, I was surprised to see the empty bed.
>
> Felipe Rodríguez, "La cama vacía" (The empty bed)

I would like to focus here on two distinct types of artistic production reflecting on AIDS and its aftermath: literature and the visual arts. Jamaica Kincaid's *My Brother* (1999), in which the author tries to makes sense of her brother's gradual deterioration and death in Antigua, and Patricia Powell's *A Small Gathering of Bones* (1994), about the difficulties of being gay, and the shock and confusion caused by the first cases of AIDS in late 1970s Jamaica, are compared here to the photographic work of Puerto Rican artist Víctor Vázquez, who documents his friend's dying days in the book *El reino de la espera* (The realm of awaiting, 1991) and to other examples of artwork—paintings, installations, performance—produced by a variety of artists in the same historical context. These literary and visual texts are linked by a common metaphor, *the bed*, first occupied and then vacant, as the central image from which all other remembrances of the lost loved one arise. As opposed to the previously mentioned stigmatizing metaphors, which stemmed from a mixture of primal fears, confusion, and a desire to attribute blame, the metaphor of the occupied/empty bed reveals a more intimate and profound meditation on loss.

Kincaid's memoir begins with an image of her bedridden brother: "When I saw my brother again after a long while, he was lying in a bed in the Holberton Hospital, in the Gweneth O'Reilly ward, and he was said to be dying of AIDS. He was not born in this hospital. Of my mother's four children, he was the one born at home" (1999, 3). The sight of Devon battling AIDS brings back memories of his birth and how the very next day his life had been threatened by an army of red ants that would have devoured him had his mother not been with him in bed. Moving back and forth between the hospital bed and the bed at home (the bed metaphor being, at this point, an "inhabited" bed) the narrative ties in the memories evoked by Kincaid's brother's imminent death. The bed as a concrete reminder of forthcoming loss also appears in Powell's *A Small Gathering of Bones*. In this novel, Dale Singleton is confronted by the illness of his close friend, Ian Kaysen:

> The smell of antiseptic and illness embrace him, causing him to stiffen in its clasps. Him glance around the room, rectangular in shape, several large windows spilling bright light onto the thirty beds crowded in, fifteen on either side, a corridor in between. Except for scratchy sounds ejecting from the overhead intercom now and again, the humming of a respirator tank, and light snores coming from one or two of the beds, the room was silent and yellow. . . . Dale pull open the first curtain, the cloth tight in his grasp, uncertain of what to expect. But him didn't recognize Ian anywhere about. There was one person with general shape and length of Ian but the face was different, too frigid, jaw too plastic-like against the light fluffiness of the pillow. (Powell, 81–82)

Dale's inability to recognize his best friend's body is just the beginning of the ever-widening rift that this new illness creates between them. In an attempt to hold on to images of a healthy Ian, and perhaps to comprehend the nature of the illness, Dale reminisces about Ian's past and his joyful but reckless behavior, images that present a sharp contrast to the dissipation of a body framed by the sterility of the deathbed.

Víctor Vázquez's *The Realm of Awaiting* also opens with a comparison of past and present. He begins with an all-male family photo—presumably a childhood photo of his friend's father and uncle, flanking an austere grandfather—followed by pictures of his friend as a child and later, as an adult, hospitalized in the infirmary (see figs. 5.1 and 5.2).

After this, all photographs of the unnamed friend are framed by the hospital bed, which becomes progressively encumbered by medical equipment.

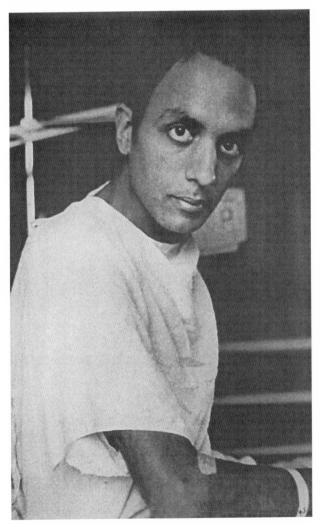

Figure 5.1. Víctor Vázquez, untitled photograph from *El reino de la espera* (The realm of awaiting). Reproduced with permission from the artist.

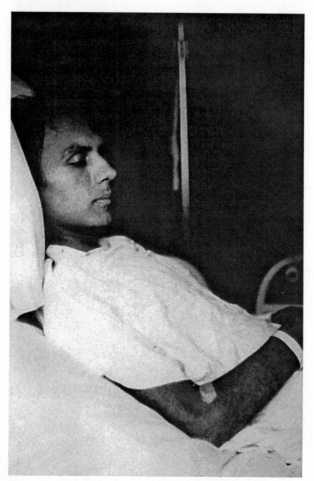

Figure 5.2. Víctor Vázquez, untitled photograph from *El reino de la espera* (The realm of awaiting). Reproduced with permission of the artist.

As Luis Rafael Sánchez describes in his prologue to this text, Vázquez "has constructed the realm of waiting out of bedrails, IV bottles and rubber tubing and plugs, out of bandages and sheets and pajamas, out of gauze pads and bits of cotton left on a night table, out of a glass, out of the unnatural atmosphere breathed in a hospital: cleanliness and asepsis, cold professionalism and loneliness" (Vázquez 1991, 11) (see figs. 5.3 and 5.4).

Far from being aseptic, the hospital room Kincaid describes is dirty, stained, and reeking of urine and undiluted bleach: "The metal [table] was rusty and the underside of the furniture was thick and covered with dirt. The walls of the room were dirty, the slats of the louvered windows were dirty, the blades

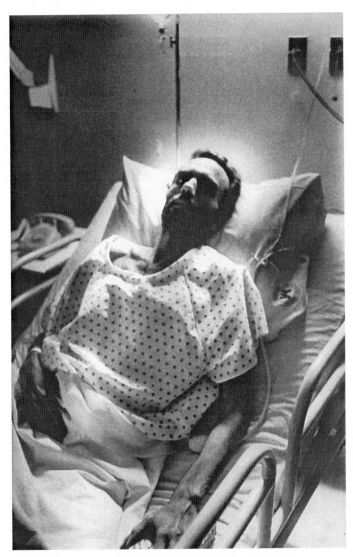

Figure 5.3. Víctor Vázquez, untitled photograph from *El reino de la espera* (The realm of awaiting). Reproduced with permission of the artist.

of the ceiling fan were dirty, and when it was turned on, sometimes pieces of dust would become dislodged. This was not a good thing for people who had trouble breathing" (1999, 22). Devoid of medical supplies, the only furnishings that surround the brother who is "lying there, dying faster than most people" are a broken television, a chair, two tables, and a bed. Representations of empty objects in various art forms have been used to evoke endings, ab-

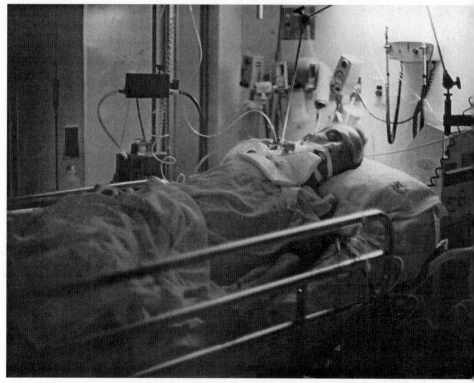

Figure 5.4. Víctor Vázquez, untitled photograph from *El reino de la espera* (The realm of awaiting). Reproduced with permission of the artist.

sence, and/or death. Vázquez's work is imbued by these popular metaphors, most notably the image of the empty bed.

While the bed, as a locus of memory, provides the stage for the patient's transformation, as well as the space from which all emotions and reactions surge, it is the body that offers concrete proof of prolonged agony, shrinking and sinking into the folds of the bedding. In *A Small Gathering of Bones*, the bed itself is the stage where the patient's passion is played out, mixing memories of carnal passion with the ongoing agony of the disease. Although the bed occasionally appears to be a protected space where Ian can meditate about his future, nurture fantasies about his mother's loving care, and hope for redemption through religion (especially when he is moved back to his bedroom at home), it is the stage where his increasing physical and emotional pain is made visible. But Ian refuses to die in this space. He returns to his estranged mother's house where he dies in a fatal accident (Powell 1994). In *My Brother* and *The Realm of Awaiting*, the diseased subject is resigned to dying in the

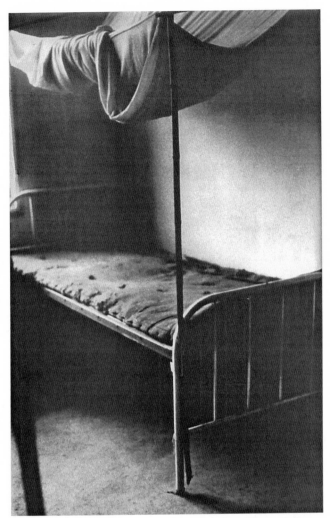

Figure 5.5. Víctor Vázquez, untitled photograph from *El reino de la espera* (The realm of awaiting). Reproduced with permission of the artist.

restricted space of the hospital bed, which anticipates, with its whiteness and paradoxical comfort, the padded coffin that will house his body. In Kincaid's and Vázquez's work, the absence of the body from the bed after the patient dies provides no relief; the body is as present and tangible as ever, as the narrator continues to grapple with the complexities of dying. The hospital bed comes to represent the interminable flow of other stricken occupants, past and present, and the impotence of being unable to consider the possibility of healing. The empty bed becomes the signifier of loss (see fig. 5.5).

In the context of Puerto Rican painting, the conscious elaboration of this metaphor is seen in the work of Antonio Martorell, notably in his series *Objetos del ausente* (Objects of the absent one, 1997) and his series of empty beds, *Camas vacías* (1998). In his statement for the collective show, titled *Memory and Mourning*, Martorell explains the evocative power of objects left behind: "Objects that belonged or were made by their owners, that dressed their humanity or addressed their desires. Everyday objects now named, baptized as art, undressed of their anonymous fashion and redressed with the sacredness of absence, the hierarchy of loss. . . . To begin with: Anselmo's shoes, Jorge's shirt, Alberto's mask. An urban planner, a concert pianist, a mask maker killed by AIDS" (Martorell 1997).

The artist accepts that he cannot escape popular icons and references. He credits popular music with being the strongest disseminator of these echoes and points out the resonances of the well-known Argentine tango "La cama vacía" (The empty bed; written by Carlos Spaventa and later rearranged in bolero form and popularized by singer Felipe Rodríguez in Puerto Rico in the 1950s and 1960s) in his series *Camas vacías*. The artist calls these pieces— mostly charcoal drawings on paper, canvas, or bed sheets—"bedscapes." He explains: "If I always return to objects, it is because in them we find the revelation and the trace of what is human. The beds I recreate are inhabited by absence." Other projects by Martorell that were developed as the AIDS pandemic gained momentum, such as *Sementerio* and *Cenatorio* (both created in 1991) and *Sí da* (1992), became all-encompassing events that included the participation of many sectors of the community. Similar to the coffins used in Pepón Osorio's installation *El Velorio/The Wake* (1991), in these works tombs were likened to beds, as spaces for eternal rest. Martorell's projects were large-scale, extraordinarily detailed installations cum performance art. For example, *Sementerio*—also called *Sementerio con "s"* (Sementerio with an "s") as a tongue-in-cheek clarification of the implicit play between the words "cementerio" (cemetery) and "semen"—was planned, as described by the artist, according to the following list:

1) A "lettered" fence with a corresponding gate that will close and open the Sementery; 2) A sky-painted canvas covering the floor; 3) A funeral monument made of candles; 4) Tombstones/kites at various levels of elevation with tails inscribed in silver and gold, like the ones adorning flower arrangements for the deceased; 5) An intermittent shower of

plastic flowers in various colors; 6) The visitors' shoes, which will be left lined up along the fence, awaiting the return; 7) The visitors will receive a small in memoriam card. (Martorell 1997)

Sementerio became an excellent example of "arte vivo" (live art) because every stage of the event became a performance: visitors became integral parts as potential mourners and people from the community as well as Martorell's friends, family members, and students from local universities and art institutes were invited to participate in the project by making kites and tails. Each kite (also representing a paper tombstone) became a separate piece of artwork dedicated to a deceased loved one. Although the many kites were just a small detail of the larger installation, they became a poignant testament to the number of losses to AIDS. In a symbolic gesture, linking two traumatic events with global repercussions, the kites were taken to the fortress walls of Old San Juan and, after a massive demonstration, were released into the wind as an anti-war statement (following Operation Desert Storm) and as a demand for an end to the silence surrounding AIDS/HIV. Moreover, the entire process, from beginning to end, was recorded for a documentary film (also titled *Sementerio*), a work of art in itself directed and produced by José Estrada for public television. Because of its emphasis on communal action, *Sementerio*, through all of its phases and transmutations, became a vehicle for collective catharsis and healing. The release of the kites expresses a desire to reach out beyond the sea walls of the city, to share the pain of bereavement and to proffer ties of solidarity.

The possibility of healing has changed the depiction of AIDS in contemporary art in some parts of the world. According to Gordon Nary in "Truth and Art in the New Age of AIDS," "While the old AIDS truths of alienation, a devalued life, and excruciating suffering and death still govern 94 percent of the global population with HIV disease and without access to AIDS drugs, the advent of available protease inhibitors and the success of the protean antiviral cocktails in the industrialized nations resulted in profound changes in the perception of the plague. Almost overnight . . . the in-your-face images of sex and rage were being replaced by more reflective expressions of challenged survival" (Nary). In Puerto Rico, however, views on this subject are polarized and have sparked much debate. Some critics deplore the insistence on representing AIDS patients as victims; they view this as a type of oppression (tantamount to condemning people to death in advance) and note that, because of the advances in medical research, death is no longer a foregone conclusion. Others, in particular such visual artists as Antonio Martorell, María de Mater O'Neill, Pepón Osorio, Marta Pérez García, Víctor Vázquez, Carlos Fajardo, and Teo Freytes, do not consider this an accurate observation. Although the majority of artists agree that more emphasis should be placed on demanding better medical attention for those afflicted by the virus, they are conscious of the fact that in Puerto Rico, as in the Caribbean at large and numerous other countries, the availability of antiviral cocktails is still far from a reality. As Kincaid points out in her memoir, for most people, the latest medication is not an option:

> The reason my brother was dying of AIDS at the time I saw him is that in Antigua if you are diagnosed with HIV virus you are considered to be dying; the drugs used for slowing the process are not available there. . . . It is felt in general, so I am told, that since there is no cure for AIDS it is useless to spend money on a medicine that will only slow the progress of the disease; the afflicted will die no matter what; there are limited resources to be spent on health care and these should be spent where they will do some good; not where it is known that the outcome is death. This was the reason why there was no AZT in the hospital; but even if a doctor had wanted to write a prescription for AZT for a patient, that prescription would not be filled at the chemist's; there was no AZT on the island, it was too expensive to be stocked, most people suffering from the disease could not afford to buy this medicine. (1999, 31–32)

In *The Biology of AIDS* (1994), it was estimated that the costs for AZT would run about $3,500 per year for one person. Without AZT, the average life expectancy of an AIDS patient who has an opportunistic infection—infections by common microorganisms that usually do not cause problems in healthy individuals, but which constitute the major health problems for AIDS patients—is about six months, whereas with the drug, life expectancy rises to one and a half years (Fan, Conner, and Villareal, 101). In *My Brother*, the use of AZT marks a literary shift—as the narrator manages to supply her brother with AZT from the United States, the reader is misled to believe, as Devon and his family were, that he will be a survivor. Devon improves radically—his lungs clear up, his infections heal, and he gains weight as well as renewed hope and appetite for life. He appears to recover his health and begins to plan a future, only to suddenly relapse, deteriorate, and die. The same false respite is featured in *A Small Gathering of Bones*, in which Ian first tries to show that he is still full of life, resuming his sexual escapades and insisting on going dancing, only to collapse after a debilitating coughing fit. He later tries to find rebirth by being baptized in a neo-Christian church (116–17).

As in Víctor Vázquez's work, a recurrent image in *My Brother* is the slow wasting away, the decaying of the body. "The realm of awaiting" in both texts is marked by disintegration. In Vázquez's work, the end of the waiting process is marked by an image of the diseased/deceased friend's feet. This potent signifier of trajectory, departure, and death is followed by a photographic collage crisscrossed with masking tape and with the years 1953–1983 scribbled at an angle. Heading this section we find a disturbing question, "¿Carne prohibida o carne podrida?" (Forbidden flesh or putrid flesh?). The question is asked twice with no apparent answer provided, but it is followed by several photos of a male torso, sometimes censored by a white or black stripe across the genital area, sometimes flanked by the floating head of the deceased (Vázquez, 47). Bodily deterioration is linked here to censorship, prohibition, and condemnation. In Kincaid's work, a similar fascination with the transformation of the flesh by the ravages of disease permeates the text, underlined by a subtext of blame or shame. At the beginning of Kincaid's memoir (and subsequently repeated several times in the text), the narrator points out that Devon's skin has become much blacker than usual, that "his lips [are] scarlet and covered with small sores that [have] a golden crust" (1999, 9), and that he can barely walk or sit up. Even eating is difficult. What begins as a small sore on his penis (discovered by his mother when she is bathing him) blooms into a horrifying sight that reminds the narrator of slides she has seen in an AIDS workshop. When she describes these slides in morbid detail, she relates sexuality to decay, decomposition, and aberration of sexual organs:

> The pictures were amazing. There were penises that looked like lady-fingers left in the oven too long and with a bite taken out of them that revealed a jam-filled center. There were labias [*sic*] covered with thick blue crusts, or black crusts, or crusts that were iridescent. There were breasts with large parts missing, eaten away, not from a large bite taken at once but nibbled, as if by an animal in a state of high enjoyment, each morsel savored for maximum pleasure. There were pictures of people emaciated by disease, who looked very different from people emaci-

ated from starvation; they did not have that parched look of flesh and blood evaporated, leaving a wreck of skin and bones; they looked like the remains of a black hole, something that had once burned brightly and then collapsed in on itself. These images of suffering and death were the result of sexual activity, and at the end of Dr. Ramsey's talk, I felt I would never have sex again . . . (37–38)

The connection she establishes between putrefaction and culpability is apparent in depictions of her brother's body. Evoking Vázquez's question—"¿Carne prohibida o carne podrida?"—Kincaid repeatedly describes the odor emanating from her brother's body: "The house had a funny smell, as if my mother no longer had time to be the immaculate housekeeper she had always been and some terrible dirty thing had gone unnoticed and was rotting away quietly" (1999, 90). In much the same way she had described the hospital room by repeating the word "dirty" over and over, she repeats the word "smell" in connection to what is dirty, the "terrible dirty thing . . . rotting away quietly" that is her brother's agonizing body. His horror, in observing his own body, is also emphasized. Immediately after the description of his smell, the narrator describes how her brother, upon realizing that she is watching him, suddenly throws off his sheets, tears his pajama bottoms away from his waist and, in deep panic and deep fear, says, "Jamaica, look at this, just look at this," while thrusting his penis toward her. She does not know how to react to the sight of her brother's intimate parts, which she had seen only as an infant, and which are now in a state of decay. She observes that "his penis looked like a bruised flower that had been cut short on the stem; it was covered with sores and on the sores was a white substance, almost creamy, almost floury, a fungus" (91). In the same way that her description of the slides culminates in denouncing sex, the scenes of her brother decomposing like a "bruised flower" or "evaporating slowly, drying out slowly" like a decaying house, are attached to notions of irresponsibility and flaw: "It was the sheer accident of life, it was his own fault, his not caring about himself and his not being able to carefully weigh and adjust to and accept the to-and-fro of life, the feasting and the famine of life or the times in between" (49).

Although Kincaid also makes a brief commentary on the government's capacity for letting so many people fall through the cracks, not caring whether they live or die, she underlines her brother's marginality. When she first learns that he is dying of AIDS, Kincaid is not taken aback because she knows he has been living a lifestyle that would not make his illness surprising. In her view, he lived a life that was conducive to contracting the virus: "He used drugs (I was only sure of marijuana and cocaine) and he had many sexual partners (I knew of only women). He was careless; I cannot imagine him taking the time to buy or use a condom" (1999, 7). Through the narrator's exploratory discursions Devon is presented as a figure of abjection—that is, what Agnes I. Lugo-Ortiz refers to as "the silent abject." As some critics (such as Lugo-Ortiz and Arnaldo Cruz-Malavé) have hypothesized about the characters in the works of Luis Rafael Sánchez and Manuel Ramos Otero. Devon, who lives on the margins of all possible territories—because of his race, class, homosexuality (as we discover late in the text), and disease—is a perfect illustration of the abject, as defined by Julia Kristeva: "It is thus not a lack of cleanliness or health that causes abjection but what disturbs identity, system, order. What does not respect borders, positions, rules. The in-between, the ambiguous, the composite" (4). Devon's state of deterioration due to a mode of living (and dying) that lacks meaning for "others," his progressive movement toward that deferred but certain death, and his "becoming" a corpse render him a sign of abjection: "It is death infecting life. Abject" (Kristeva, 4). Meaning and order are what the narrator seems to believe Devon's life lacks. Kincaid is horrified by the lack of respect he demonstrates for his own life as well as for the lives of those around him. Although Kincaid mourns the wasted life of her brother, she finds it abominable that after his radical improvement, he resumes his recklessness by taking drugs and living a lie—he denies his illness to himself and to those with whom he has unprotected sex. She mentions that he has done many "unspeakable things," such as stealing from his mother, perhaps killing a man in a gasoline station hold-up, and other deeds that remain untold. She compares her life, and how she has been able to make sense of it through writing, with the meaninglessness and disorder of his life, his inability to follow his dreams, to be whole, and to come to terms with his true identity. When the narrator reveals in the last section of the memoir that her brother had lived a double life, her anguish comes from knowing that he was never able to be himself—he had to hide his true identity from those who loved him the most. He was never able to reveal his homosexuality to his immediate family. She is appalled to discover that he had had to live his life in a complete denial of self, in a place where homosexuality was not considered as abominable as to speak about it (1999, 146). Her horror of abjection comes from the senselessness she perceives, and in this case, the madness of being forced to live a double life. The difficulty for Kincaid is to make "sense" of her brother's choices. His lack of meaning (in her eyes), rather than the signifying body per se, is what erects the boundaries between the narrating "I" and the "object" of her narrating impulse. As Kristeva details in "Approaching Abjection": "The abject is not an object facing me, which I name or imagine. . . . If the object, however, through its opposition, settles me within the fragile texture of a desire for meaning, which, as a matter of fact, makes me ceaselessly and infinitely homologous to it, what is *abject*, on the contrary, the jettisoned object, is radically excluded and draws me toward the place where meaning collapses" (2). Devon lies on the border between significance and meaninglessness. His body becomes, according to Kristeva's description of the abject, a "something" that the subject does not recognize as a thing, "[a] weight of meaninglessness, about which there is nothing insignificant, and which crushes me. On the edge of non-existence and hallucination, of a reality that, if I acknowledge it, annihilates me" (2). His dying body—soon to be "the corpse, the most sickening of wastes, is a border that has encroached upon everything" (3)—forces the narrator to face the border between life and death: "In that compelling, raw, insolent thing in the morgue's full sunlight, in that thing that no longer matches and therefore no longer signifies anything, I behold the breaking down of a world that has erased its borders: fainting away" (4).

In *The Realm of Awaiting* Vázquez's unnamed friend also reflects on life in terms of making sense of it. He speaks of his bodily pains, of his dreams—of dreaming about dying or not knowing whether he was dead or alive—and of how he lived his life: "I dreamed that I had lived pleasure and that the body was everything—that was my meaning in life. And I rejoiced. . . . I dream that I have lived life with meaning. What do you think? I don't know, but I think meaning is everything" (Vázquez 1991, 26). The text on this page reveals that the speaker is in an "in-between" state. The text shifts between different realms—the borders between dreams and wakefulness, night and day, life and death. He tries to make sense of his identity and life by reflecting upon his body and its trajectory through time and space.

Faced with the impossibility of making sense of death or of proposing a definitive solution for a community faced with an epidemic, the only healing possible for the survivors who narrate the trauma is presented through art. Kincaid never brings religious reflection into the text, apart from a short anecdote involving Obeah and her mother's attempt to save her from certain death. In contrast, Vázquez adds the dimension of religious imagery. First, he inserts quotes from the Upanishads regarding life, and then he superimposes faded images of his deceased friend on representations of the Madonna and child, saints, and angels, sometimes partly obscured by a silhouette of a male body. Compassion, wonder, and a large dose of irony provide closure to the text. As we close the book, the photograph of the friend's soles reminds us of the rawness of this particular type of death, denuded of any romantic notions. Kincaid, on the other hand, ends her memoir with a degree of expectation and, as she had done in *Lucy*, with the act of writing. She stresses how writing has saved her life:

> I became a *writer* out of desperation, so when I first heard my brother was dying I was familiar with the act of saving myself: I would *write about* him. I would *write about* his dying. When I was young, younger than I am now, I started to *write about* my own life and I came to see that this act saved my life. When I heard about my brother's illness and his dying, I knew, instinctively, that to understand it, or to make an attempt at understanding his dying, and not to die with him, I would *write about* it. (196, emphasis added)

Conclusion: Art as Cathartic Space

> Neither nostalgia nor celebration, the objects of the absent try to grasp some of the essence of loss, recapturing and transforming grief into art, pain into joy. A quiet joy, but nonetheless a joy, the joy of creation.
>
> Antonio Martorell, "Artist's Statement," *Memory and Mourning: Shared Cultural Experience*

> The various means of purifying the abject—the various catharses—make up the history of religions, and end up with that catharsis par excellence called art.
>
> Julia Kristeva, *Powers of Horror: An Essay on Abjection*

When Jamaica Kincaid claimed to have written about her brother to understand and "not die with him," she enraged a large part of her readership. Somehow it seemed that the author/narrator was expected, perhaps because of her gender, to couch her study of death in more compassionate terms. Some critics were particularly disconcerted by the attribution of fault to the one afflicted by such an unforgiving disease, or the demonization of the victim, who, in this case, was the author's own kin. I argue that the memoir's strength lies precisely in its portrayal of the confusion, pain, and complex constructions of survivors faced by the loss of friends or family members to an illness that is still barely understood. What is interesting about this text is that the narrator sways back and forth between various standpoints. At times, she is a jealous Antiguan "daughter" yearning for the past—when she conjures up loving memories of the "garden paradise" where she grew up, occasionally revealing a desire to return to the supposedly "simple pleasures" of Caribbean life in "a small place." At other textual moments, she is a First World professional pampered in the lap of relative comfort, returning from the prosperous, First World country as a heroic prodigal daughter—a woman with the means to supply the miracle antiviral cocktail AZT. The self-conscious author does not reserve her harsh and sometimes sarcastic judgment only for her mother and brother, but rather turns the critical gaze toward herself, her life trajectory, her weaknesses, and her motivations. While at times she reacts with anger toward the deceased by asking herself why he continued his "shameless" dissoluteness after apparently having been given another chance to live, in other instances she lays the blame on the unequal distribution of wealth and control of the treasured antiviral medication as well as on the continued social acceptance of male promiscuity.

Instead of delineating the contours of Devon's emotional agony as he approaches death, Kincaid emphasizes the materiality of that progression: his mouth, his skin, his eyes, and his emaciated frame all attest to the physical agony. Moreover, his penis is highlighted, not only as the locus marking his "failure" as a male (a man who has not fathered children, we are reminded), but also as the focal point of his abjection and consequent suffering. Perhaps the author's flaw lies in her inability to translate her brother's anguish and physical pain, but as Elaine Scarry states in *The Body in Pain,* "Whatever pain achieves, it achieves in part through its unsharability and it ensures this unsharability through its resistance to language" (4).

The unsharability of pain is effectively depicted by the closing image of Vázquez's book. Throughout the interior of *The Realm of Awaiting,* as we are confronted by the constant gaze of the afflicted, we are made to witness, and, to a certain extent, identify with his psychic pain. The back cover, in contrast, presents the soles of his lifeless feet. This marks the limits of our ability, partial as it may be, to share physical pain and the agony of the dying. "When one hears about another person's physical pain, the events happening within the interior of that person's body may seem to have the remote character of some deep subterranean fact, belonging to an *invisible geography* that, however portentous, has no reality because it has not yet manifested itself on the visible surface of the earth" (Scarry, 3, emphasis added). As we close the book, the only sharability we can attain is the shared pain of the survivors. We, as spectators, may be able to share the multiple emotions experienced in the realm of "awaiting"—but we cannot enter the uncharted territory of death.

The artists (visual artists and writers) discussed in this study attempt to bridge the chasm of abjection and death through creation; they try "to grasp some of the essence of loss, recapturing and transforming grief into art, pain into joy" (Martorell). In order to survive trauma then, art becomes the channel for personal and communal catharsis. Catharsis, from the Greek *kathairein*, meaning to purify, cleanse, or purge, represents a conduit for "the purgation or purification of the emotions (as pity and fear) primarily through art . . . used by Aristotle in his description of the effect of tragedy" or a purification process "that brings a spiritual renewal or a satisfying release from tension" (Gove, 353). But, as Martorell's "tombstone kites" exemplify, the catharsis is achieved not only through the purification of emotions and release of tension: it is also achieved through the attempt to give substance and visibility to the invisible geographies of pain, and by leaving the confines of our individual "islands" to reach beyond our isolation. By turning their gaze outward, Caribbean artists try to make sense of the tragedy of the HIV/AIDS pandemic and to extend their solidarity. While simultaneously inhabiting and departing from their insularity, they endeavor to share the unsharable.

Notes

1. In 1994, a retrospective exhibition was organized in honor of the artist—*Carlos Collazo 1956–1990: Exposición Homenaje*—at the Antiguo Arsenal de la Marina Española in Old San Juan. In the same year, the filmmaker Sonia Fritz produced and directed the documentary film *Un retrato de Carlos Collazo* (A portrait of Carlos Collazo). Both the exhibition catalogue and the film include testimonial excerpts by various artists and other members of the art world who knew him well.

2. These centers were likened to concentration camps by many. As J. Michael Dash explains: "Ostracism is the penalty that must be paid for cultural deviance. In December 1972 'Detention Facilities' or 'Processing Centres' were established to deal with the first wave of Haitian refugees washed up on the shores of Florida. This was the sobering experience that awaited thousands of Haitians feeling economic hardship and political persecution. Jean-Claude Charles is correct when he describes these camps as the 'univers concentrationnaire' which lurks behind 'de si jolies petites plages' in Florida, the Bahamas and Puerto Rico" (118).

3. By September 30, 2005, there were 30,541 cases of AIDS reported in Puerto Rico. There is an incidence of 76 men to 24 women, a ratio of 3.2 to 1. The highest propor-

tion of cases (42.7 percent of the population) is found among people between thirty and thirty-nine years of age, followed by people between forty and forty-nine years of age (representing 26.2 percent of the population). For a more detailed study, see Edna Marrero, Cruz, and Miranda de León.

4. Although Cuba's epidemic remains by far the smallest in the Caribbean, the UN/ AIDS Epidemic Update states that its preventive measures may not be keeping pace with conditions that favor the spread of HIV, including widening income inequalities and a growing sex industry.

5. The works mentioned here and other examples of Haitian artwork are discussed in detail in my book *Blood, Boats, and Empty Beds: Representations of AIDS in the Caribbean* (in progress).

6

The "Children of the Sea"

Uncovering Images of the *Botpippel* Experience in Caribbean Art and Literature

LIZABETH PARAVISINI-GEBERT AND MARTHA DAISY KELEHAN

though of course they said nothing at all just
went lobbying by with their heads up & down in the
corvée of water & their arms still vainly trying to
reach Miami & Judge Thomas & the US Supreme Court & their mouths wise
Open drinking dream & seawater . . .

Edward Kamau Brathwaite, "Dream Haiti"

Botpippel—the Kreyol rendering of the term used to designate the undocumented Haitian immigrants who began attempting the treacherous voyage to the United States around 1972—are one of the most poignant symbols of the heartrending trajectory of Haitian history in the late twentieth century. Unable to afford exit visas or airplane tickets, the "boat people"—most of them rural Haitians—ventured on the 700–mile crossing, financing their dangerous undertaking with the proceeds of the sale of their land and belongings, and fleeing repressive political conditions, ecological devastation, and economic stagnation at home for freedom and opportunity abroad. Of the estimated 100,000 Haitian refugees who arrived illegally in Florida during the 1970s and 1980s—more than 55,000 between 1972 and 1981 alone—many attempted the treacherous sea crossing to Miami in unsafe boats, risking their lives in the hope of a better life and often falling into the clutches of unscrupulous smugglers (Arthur, 180). For those who made the crossing safely only to fall into the hands of the Immigration and Naturalization Service (INS), flight often led to incarceration in refugee camps and, all too frequently, repatriation and death. Unknown thousands died in the attempt, disappearing into the oblivion of a watery grave.

For those who survived the crossing and escaped detection, the ghosts of those thousands lost to the sea, many of them their traveling companions, are a poignant reminder of the price paid for their own freedom and opportunities. Those remaining behind in Haiti, for whose sake the travelers ventured forth, remember them as the lost ones, irretrievable and gone. Their memories remain, like the haunting presence of a revenant, unburied and unmemorialized. Our question then is, what would be a suitable memorial for those who lack a place for a headstone? If they are not likely to be properly commemorated by the Haitian state, who will seek to immortalize their deaths? How can the horrors and losses of those many crossings be conveyed and remembered? How have the arts and literature sought to crystallize one of the most traumatizing chapters of Haiti's recent past?

In this survey of the art inspired by the plight of the Haitian *botpippel* we will argue that Haitian painters have developed a highly stylized and eloquent iconography to create history paintings that seek to synthesize onto canvas one of the salient experiences of Haitian history in the last quarter of the twentieth century and the first decade of the twenty-first. This iconography is built upon repeating elements—a sinking boat in a stormy sea to which people in rags cling desperately, an awaiting U.S. Coast Guard ship, the distant and unattainable U.S. shoreline, the Haitian flag, images of the Vodou *lwa* or spirits, menacing sharks, the Guantánamo refugee camps—which, although limited in themselves, have allowed for a broad and nuanced range of representations of the haunting *botpippel* experience. The creation of these nightmarish seascapes, often by painters with little formal education or artistic training, represents the most significant creative response to an unfolding drama that, although eloquently addressed by a handful of pan-Caribbean writers, has been slow to engage Haitian authors. The nuances of these artistic representations encapsulate a wealth of political, social, and cultural responses to the conditions that have driven so many thousands of Haitians to a risky and often fatal sea crossing.[1] In these images, historical memory operates through representation (Küchler and Melion, 7), as the paintings constitute the most salient vehicle for reconstructing an untold, often unwitnessed history. They posit "a dynamic of mnemonic processing" through which traumatic memory can be addressed personally and collectively (7).

For the refugees who survived the crossing, the Haitian people as a whole, and the world at large, these are images through which all "can come to know and process the collective experience" of the *botpippel* (Bennett, 31).

Botpippel art, however, is not, for the most part, public art. Public art—often supported and authorized by government institutions, well-funded organizations, or wealthy corporations—requires either official sponsorship or access to funding sources and systems of patronage that are far removed from the realities of the large majority of Haitian immigrants. Other than the occasional example of *botpippel*-related graffiti or unauthorized murals found in Port-au-Prince and the streets of Little Havana in Miami, we have come across only three examples of public *botpippel* art—one, a monument erected in 1995 on the Tabarre Road in Port-au-Prince; the other two, murals in the lobby of the office occupied by the Haitian Refugee Center in Miami in 1997.

The memorial, a stone and metal sculpture in the shape of a *kannté*, one of the small rickety boats on which refugees have sailed from Haiti, is on the Tabarre Road—the only major new road built after President Jean-Bertrand Aristide's return to power in 1994—just past the headquarters of his Foundation for Democracy in Port-au-Prince. The memorial, sponsored by the Aristide government, has been described as "a sculptor's rendition of a brick and concrete boat which was hurriedly constructed" to be unveiled during President Bill Clinton's visit to Haiti in March 1995 (Ruth). Its place of honor as the only state-sponsored memorial to the *botpippel* has been overshadowed by the violence that has taken hold of its surroundings, especially after Aristide's departure in 2004; it is now sited in one of the most troubled neighborhoods in Port-au-Prince and has not escaped being marred by the graffiti, slogans, accusations, and insults of Haiti's political turmoil. It stands amid the rubbish of a collapsed urban infrastructure. It is also infamously linked to the persistent rumor that it was built to conceal a "magic well" where Clinton was to be initiated into Vodou by Aristide himself. Aristide, according to the *Haiti Observateur*, had dedicated the sacred well by shedding the blood "of a newborn infant in gratitude to the gods whom he believes allowed his return to power," while Clinton's initiation was meant to "keep him impervious to Republican attacks and to guarantee his re-election" (McLeod). The superimposition of these two narratives—centered on the machinations required to gain and maintain political power—over what had been meant as a memorial to the victims of the failure of such power in Haiti, signals the monument's inability to encompass and represent the national trauma of the *botpippel* experience.

The other two examples of *botpippel* public art are murals at the Haitian Refugee Center in Miami. One, titled *Haitian Tragedy*, depicts a shipwreck painted with broad brushstrokes that evoke the movement and danger of the boat crossing. It is a painting of a boat going down into the sea, the Haitian flag on its mast, with two female figures reaching into the water in an attempt to save their fellow shipmates by pulling them back into the boat. It encapsulates the narrative of the *botpippel* experience while reminding those coming to seek help that the center understands the dangers involved in undertaking the journey that brought them to the city and is willing to provide the services—be it personal, legal, professional, or educational—that the refugee needs to integrate successfully into American society. Like the female figures in the mural, the center is there to pull them metaphorically out of the water.

The second mural shows another group of Haitians spilling out of their shattered boat onto a Florida beach. The mural is centered against the backdrop of the Haitian flag, with the words "Haitian Refugee Center" appearing in both English and Kreyol. The red and blue of the Haitian flag is continued throughout the shipwreck scene in the people's clothing, anchoring the scene and offering a thematic continuity between the plight of the shipwrecked refugees and the center's mandate. The faceless human figures are scattered across the beach in various poses of extreme physical distress, but they are nonetheless alive. The mural also alludes indirectly to the center's role in helping Haitian refugees remain in the United States once they had set foot on land, since for Haitians there was no "wet foot/dry foot" policy. (Under this policy, put into effect in 1994, Cuban refugees intercepted while still at sea were returned to Cuba; those who had reached U.S. soil were allowed to stay.) The two murals are among the earliest, and certainly the most public, of a painting tradition that has produced primarily medium size paintings for display in museums and private collections. In "Art and Resistance: Haiti's Political Murals, October 1994," Karen McCarthy Brown identifies only one mural in Port-au-Prince that alludes to the *botpippel* experience, which she describes thus: "[A] group of Haitians, some light-skinned and some dark, are at sea during a serious storm. Their boat is made of the most sacred of Vodou drums, the *asotò*, the one believed to be the voice of the ancestors. Lasirèn, a Vodou sea spirit, here appearing in the form of a large pink fish, pushes the boat from behind while the radiant head and shoulders of Jesus hover benevolently above" (Brown 1996, 55).

One *botpippel* painting, nonetheless, fulfilled a public art role during a march organized in February 1993 to call for equality of treatment for Haitian and Cuban refugees. Organized by Miami's black leadership in "unprecedented support" for the plight of Haitian refugees, the march recalled the spirited demonstrations of the civil rights movement. The speakers, which included the Reverend Jesse Jackson, called for American help to restore deposed president Aristide and condemned the confinement of Haitian refugees at the Krome Detention Center in Florida and the U.S. naval base at Guantánamo. They also demanded "that Haitian refugees receive the same welcome to the United States as Cuban rafters and defectors, who under a special law are quickly freed and granted nearly automatic legal U.S. residency" (Viglucci, 2B). They linked the unequal treatment of Haitian refugees to the Jim Crow laws that limited the participation of African Americans in economic and political society before the civil rights movement.

The focus of the speakers' protest was what they saw as a double standard in U.S. policy toward illegal immigrants arriving from Cuba and Haiti. Official policy dictated that most illegal immigrants be detained on arrival, unless immigration officials judged that they met the criteria for release while awaiting a status hearing, which usually entailed local sponsorship and evidence of political persecution at home. Cuban immigrants, however, were rarely held in custody, as they qualified for special provisions under the law. Haitians were seldom released to the custody of friends and relatives and underwent detention while their cases were reviewed. Most were denied entrance into the United States; a significant number were repatriated to uncertain fates in Haiti.

Among the symbols displayed by marchers were a banner with a likeness of Martin Luther King and the words "Let my people go!" and "a man holding up a framed painting of a sailboat on a rough sea. Loaded with Haitian refugees, the boat is accosted by a Coast Guard helicopter and a Coast Guard ship" (Viglucci, 2B). Its date and artist unknown, the painting's deployment as a wordless political banner during such a demonstration attests to its power to represent through its elements the narrative of the Haitian *botpippel* and the urgency of their plight. Private art becomes public here through its insertion into an act of mass political expression.

The spirit of the march, during which ministers, veterans of the civil rights movement, and Haitian leaders expressed variations of the same message— "Just as segregation laws once kept blacks on one side of town, government policies now keep Haitians out of the country because of their skin color" (Viglucci, 2B)—echoed feelings expressed in Felix Morrisseau-Leroy's 1991 poem, "Boat People." The poem invites Haitians to embrace the "boat people" term, despite its pejorative connotations in American society, since the *botpippel* experience is only one more stage in the Haitian migratory history.

> We don't bring drugs in our bags
> But courage and strength to work
> Boat people—yes, that's alright, boat people
> We don't come to make trouble
> We come with all respect
> It's them who calls us boat people
> We have no need to yell or scream
> But all boat people are equal, the same
> All boat people are boat people
> One day we'll stand up, put down our feet
> As we did at St. Domingue
> They'll know who are boat people
>
> (184–85)

Botpippel art belongs to a long established tradition of history painting that dates back to the Renaissance. Its defining characteristics as a genre—"its public and ethical form; its principles of historicity and narrativity; and its didactic intent" (Green and Seddon, 82)—have been characteristic of a subgenre of Haitian painting that includes Gary Dorsainvil's *Haitian Military Open Fire on Demonstrators* (1986), Etienne Chavannes' *President Aristide Returns to the National Palace October 15, 1994* (1994), and Paul Jean-Pierre's *Bill Clinton 30 Avril 95* (1995), among many. History painting, a genre particularly associated with French painting of the eighteenth century, placed its emphasis

> on the choice of a significant moment or action in the story chosen, one in which the immediate antecedents and consequences of the action depicted would be suggested in a clear, accessible and meaningful way. History painting displayed not only *narrativity* but a second characteristic as part of its ambition, that of *didactic intent*. History painting, in other words, had an ethical and moral dimension in which viewers would in some sense perceive virtue, a virtue both relevant to their own time and one of a universal timeless kind. (Green and Seddon 7)

The characteristic elements of history painting, as found in *botpippel* paintings, offer a point of departure for our analysis. If, as Green and Seddon argue, "it is only through the forms of its representation—'the thumb print on a glass wall'—that the past exists for us at all" (1), Haitian painters have taken the notion of history painting, with its connection to the bourgeois political sphere and its "suitability as a voice through which the very idea of the public could be spoken of and spoken for" (9), and appropriated it as a vehicle for recording, denouncing, and memorializing the plight of the forgotten *botpippel*.

Botpippel paintings are first and foremost encapsulated narratives of shipwreck. Shipwrecks were a common enough theme in Haitian painting before the *botpippel* phenomenon—one has only to think of Rigaud Benoît's masterpiece, *Shipwreck* (1965), which depicts a group of people lost at sea, making offerings to the Vodou spirit or *lwa* La Sirène in a plea for rescue. The painting is of interest in our context because it contains many of the narrative elements that will be combined and recombined in paintings of *botpippel*: the unstable, unsafe boat in which the people have ventured out, the collapsed sails, the flailing arms and naked torsos, the frayed flag, the menacing sharks, the offering to the *lwa*, and the rescue boat in the distance.

The basic narrative aspects of *botpippel* paintings can be read most vividly in Fritz Mistira's *Boat People Tragedy* (1987), a painting on masonite commissioned by the collector Jonathan Demme (see fig. 6.1). Mistira, a young college student at the time, elaborated his narrative through layers of action that become more dramatic and personal as the eye moves from background to foreground. The background depicts rolling brown hills—deforested and devoid of vegetation, an allusion to the desert-like conditions that have resulted from intense deforestation and soil erosion in Haiti. The central element of the painting is the large sinking boat that bears the Haitian flag—a sturdy looking but nonetheless capsizing boat in vivid red standing for the sinking nation of the last years of the Duvalier regime. The human figures (some of them children) assume one of two stances: they either face the viewer, arms extended in desperate pleas for help, or attempt to hold on to the boat, their backs to the viewer. One figure in the lower right corner has already drowned. The sharks surrounding the boat also encircle the viewer, who is invited to enter through a shark-free lower right corner into the world of the painting, either to assist, as we are compelled to do, or to share the shipwrecks' fate.[2] The position of the viewer is a puzzling one, as we look at this scene from what

Figure 6.1. Fritz Mistira, *Boat People Tragedy*. Jonathan Demme Collection of Haitian Art. Reproduced by permission.

could most logically be another boat (perhaps a U.S. Coast Guard ship). All hope of rescue comes from the viewer's perspective, since the desolate landscape of the background offers no hope and the sharks block all possible retreat.

The elements in the painting are similar to those woven together by Edwidge Danticat in "The Children of the Sea," the opening story in *Krik? Krak?* (1996), about two lovers, one of whom is on an over-packed and sinking boat headed for Miami. Forced to flee Haiti after speaking against the Duvalier government on his radio show, the young protagonist leaves with a handful of *gourdes* and a notebook in which he records his troubled crossing. His entries alternate with the narrative addressed to him by the girlfriend he left behind. "Children of the Sea" serves as a parallel text to *Boat People Tragedy*, fleshing out and giving voice to the narrative elements the painting encapsulates so economically. Political repression, exploitation, and the deepest poverty, like the barren hills of the painting, serve as push factors leading people out to sea. "You could fill a museum with the sights you have here," the man in

Danticat's story says of his companions, alluding to the potential effectiveness of art to express the tragedy of the *botpippel*'s crossing (15).

Danticat draws several poignant parallels between the *botpippel*'s crossing and the Middle Passage, a reference that is never far from the surface meaning of these paintings, elements as they are of the Haitian historical narrative. The *botpippel* narrative is also strongly anchored in culture and religion. In Haitian Vodou, the Africans who leapt to their deaths from the slave ships rather than accept slavery are said to reside under the water; upon death one follows the ancestors down to the depths of the ocean where the *lwa* or spirits reside (Brown 1991, 223). The young man in Danticat's story understands his experience as a refugee through the prism of Haitian history and religion: "I feel like we are sailing for Africa. Maybe we will go to Guinin, to live with the spirits, to be with everyone who has come and has died before us" (Danticat 1996, 14). This "walk back to Africa" across the water becomes a powerful metaphor when considering the risks of undertaking to cross the Atlantic on a frail boat or a makeshift raft. The phrase used to describe where the *lwas* and ancestors reside, *lòt boa*, "on the other side," is also used in common speech to refer to relatives living in America. They are only *lòt boa*, able to return at any time from across and below the water to their families (Arthurs, 205). "Walking back to Africa" parallels the potentially self-sacrificing act of fleeing freedomless Haiti for a chance at liberty in the United States, with the belief in the American dream as a sustaining element.

Danticat addresses the blind faith that Haitians place in the existence of the American dream and their ability to gain access to it in her novel *Breath, Eyes, Memory* (1994). Louise, a middle-aged Haitian street vendor, is willing to risk her life at sea in order to reach the gold-paved streets of the United States:

"It is very dangerous by boat."

"I have heard everything. It has been a long time since our people walked to Africa, they say. The sea, it has no doors. They say the sharks from here to there, they can eat only Haitian flesh. That is all they know how to eat."

"Why should you want to make the trip if you've heard all that?"

"Spilled water is better than a broken jar. All I need is five hundred *gourdes*. (1994, 99)

The day Louise finally scrapes together the last of the five hundred *gourdes* needed for the voyage she leaves the village and is never heard from again.

Other painters have added a variety of narrative elements to those that appear in Mistira's painting, complicating the emplotment of the *botpippels*' story as told through painting. Whereas Mistira's *botpippel* are drowning within view of the land, the land is that of Haiti and therefore not a refuge or a place from which to expect aid. They turn instead to the viewer, hinting at a possible intention to engage him or her in a participatory act of rescue. The sharks, therefore, have not come full circle, as an opening must be left for us to engage with the world of the *botpippel*.

Chavannes Jeanty's hauntingly beautiful *Boat People* painting closes Mistira's circle, thereby turning the viewer into a powerless spectator (see fig. 6.2). One of the three boats in the painting has already capsized, spilling its human cargo into the turbulent, shark-infested waters, where they are graphically depicted in a losing battle against these predators. Here the sharks surround two of the three boats—two of them moving away from their ready prey to encircle a second boat—as if actively and meaningfully seeking to capsize it. The proportions between the sharks and the boats are cleverly controlled by placing the sharks in the foreground, where they loom almost as large as the boats themselves. The composition allows them equal narrative and formal importance. Their circular motion contributes to the impression of a vortex in the center of the painting in which the hapless refugees are caught. The sharks' strength, movement, and apparent sense of purpose contrast with the comparative passivity of the boat's occupants, who sit in motionless stupor as waves crash against them from the right; their fear is more palpable than their horror. The strength of the painting comes primarily from the illusion of motion it creates—the motion of sharks, water, and clouds becoming the principal way of conveying the peril faced by the refugees.

The cross-like mast and flowing sails of the boats recall the voyages of discovery and the Middle Passage. Most significant, however, is the merging of the turbulent waters and the stormy sky, which eliminates the horizon, with all that conveys of hopelessness and despair. The viewer is not invited to enter into the scene; the sharks stand between us and any possible rescue. They also stand between the boats and any progress toward their goal. The point of view is somewhat ambiguous here, although the position of the jibs and fullness of the sails would indicate that the boats are moving toward the viewer. The figures in the boat and in the water, moreover, are not seeking to engage the viewer, anticipating no rescue from that direction. Here we are indeed witnessing the un-witnessable; the painting records what no eyes have seen.

Figure 6.2. Chavannes Jeanty, *Boat People*. Collection of Lizabeth Paravisini-Gebert.

(Kedon Estigène, one of Haiti's best "jungle" painters, uses a similar composition in his 1996 painting, "Refugees," with the striking difference that his refugees are fanciful, multi-colored doves.)

Frantz Zephirin's *M'ap Cherche la Vie* (1998, acrylic on canvas), adds a new spatial dimension to the *botpippel* narrative. Zephirin, born in 1968 in

Cap-Haitien, started his apprenticeship as a painter under his uncle Antoine Obin, a master painter of the highly stylized Cap-Haitien school, which Zephirin has subsequently abandoned. He has met with considerable success as a painter and was featured in the *Sacred Arts of Haitian Vodou* traveling

Figure 6.3. Frantz Zephirin, *M'ap Cherche la Vie*. Collection of Janet Feldman, Waterloo Center for the Arts (Waterloo, Iowa). Courtesy of Janet Feldman.

exhibit (1997–98). In *M'ap Cherche la Vie*, the *botpippel* are almost indistinguishable in the middle ground, struggling in the water near their frail sinking boat, small and seemingly insignificant. The foreground is occupied by the menacing figure of an alligator framed by two tall and ominous rock outcroppings against which the boat in the background has crashed (see fig. 6.3).

The painting, by invoking Ulysses' dangerous crossing between Scylla and Charybdis, brings the focus away from the details of the *botpippels'* situation and onto the difficulties of the crossing and the harsh conditions of reception. The alligator, Cerberus-like, signals the lack of welcome for the *botpippel* in the United States through its connection to Florida's swamps and the monsters of *The Odyssey*. Here, as with the sharks in Chavannes Jeanty's painting, the placement of the menacing alligator in the foreground reinforces the threat to the comparatively powerless *botpippel*. The richly textured cliffs mirror the jewel-like rendering of the alligator's skin, unifying them as allied in their purpose of keeping the refugees from crossing through. The huge rocks, resembling menacing jaws, reinforce the idea of the devouring power of the sea and of the unwelcoming, rocky shores they will not be lucky enough to reach. There is no beach for landing and no shelter in these vertical cliffs.

Zephirin's contribution to the narrative of the *botpippel* experience links it to European mythology, thereby seeking to make the Haitian people's plight understandable to a non-Haitian audience. He works with another master narrative, that of the flood and Noah's Ark, in an untitled painting from Bill Bollendorf's collection (Galerie Macondo; see fig. 6.4). Here a menagerie of predominantly African animals, anthropomorphically depicted as dressed in their traveling best, are standing in the water, lowering a boat into the sea as they prepare to board with their scant belongings. A horse-headed figure (lower right) carries a box that reads "Boat People, Caution, Danger"; an elephant holds a bottle labeled "The Hope Water." Zephirin's weaving of the narrative of Noah's Ark (with its theme of hope emerging out of adversity) with the hopefulness of these travelers (as caught in their colorful attire and confident gazes, and in their almost jubilant hoisting of their newly built boat) speaks to a seldom-invoked aspect of the *botpippel* narrative, that of the dreams and anticipation of those setting forth toward new lives and greater prosperity, an optimism they will seek to sustain with the "hope water" they will be carrying with them in their travels. The painting is not without its irony, as one of the figures auto-denominates the refugees "dangerous" and

Figure 6.4. Frantz Zephirin, untitled painting. Collection of Bill Bollendorf at Gallerie Macondo. Courtesy of Bill Bollendorf.

counsels "caution." Nothing, however, could be safer that these domesticated anthropomorphic creatures with roots in the African plains.

Zephirin's juxtaposition of narratives as the means of increasing the viewer's understanding and identification with the situation of the *botpippel* is echoed in the concurrence of images in Ernst Louis-Jean's re-rendering of Théodore Géricault's *The Raft of the "Medusa"—Se sa ou se pa sa* (That or nothing; not pictured), which takes its title from the Kreyol translation of Hamlet's initial question in his famous soliloquy, "To be or not to be."[3] Louis-Jean, an architect from Port-au-Prince now living in the United States, is drawn to significant historical moments as subjects for his increasingly popular history paintings. In *Misery*, for example, one of the early historical works that brought him to the attention of galleries and critics, he depicted his nightmarish vision of the election-day massacre in Haiti in November 1987.

In *Se pa ou se pa sa* Louis-Jean draws on the familiar images of Géricault's painting—one of the most famous of European history paintings, now at the Louvre—to draw attention to the graphic, thematic, and historical similarities between his work and that of the early nineteenth-century French Romantic painter. The shipwreck of the *Medusa* was one of the most glaring European scandals of the early part of the nineteenth century. The ship, a French government vessel, had sunk off the coast of Senegal in 1816 while bringing a new governor to take possession of the port of St. Louis, which had recently been ceded to France by the British. Of the 150 survivors who tried to hold on to life on a raft, only 13 were still alive when the raft was found, among them the ship's inept and cowardly aristocratic captain, later brought to trial for his criminal mishandling of the ship and its passengers and crew. They were believed to have survived by practicing cannibalism. Géricault depicts the moment when the survivors catch their first glimpse of the rescue ship.

In Louis-Jean's painting, there is no rescue ship in sight, but two contending mirages occupy the upper corners of the canvas showing the options open to the refugees. On the right side we see the architectural symbols of New York City (including the Statue of Liberty and the Empire State Building); on the left side we have a typical Haitian graveyard.[4] By including the symbols of New York City as representative of the refugees' goal, Louis-Jean underscores the ironic inapplicability of the words of Emma Lazarus's "The New Colossus" inscribed on the Statue of Liberty ("Give me your tired, your poor, your huddled masses yearning to breathe free") to Haitian refugees who are not as welcome as earlier arrivals to the United States. The cemetery points to death as their only other option, either death at sea or death in Haiti if they are repatriated to the island by the U.S. Coast Guard.

Louis-Jean's interpellation of Géricault's masterpiece eschews the realism of the latter (who was said to have interviewed and sketched survivors in preparation and had a replica of the raft built) and accentuates instead the perhaps forlorn hopes of reaching (and being allowed to remain in) the promised land that shines brightly ahead as a mirage floating in the sky like an unattainable illusion. By linking his painting to Géricault's famous work, however, Louis-Jean's painting resonates with the connection to another "headline-making" case, to the governmental ineptitude that lead to the *Medusa* tragedy, and most poignantly, to the human costs, despair, and suffering of the sea crossing with which Géricault's painting is identified. *The Raft of the Medusa*, through which Géricault sought to express "the predicament of the shipwrecked everywhere in the world" and to proclaim his "scrupulous respect for the truth," here becomes a vehicle for a new painting conveying the truth of yet another episode of historical shame (Géricault).

The perils of the *botpippel's* sea crossing—brought to poignant life by Louis-Jean through his evocation of the *Medusa* tragedy in *Se pa ou se pa sa*—find a literary echo in Russell Banks's *Continental Drift* (1985). The novel narrates the travails of a young Haitian woman trying to reach the United States, Vanise Dorsinville, in quasi-Odyssean terms. All the money her family has saved to allow her to leave Haiti only takes her as far as North Caicos Island. In transit from there to the Bahamas she and her teenage nephew are brutally and repeatedly gang raped, after which she is sold to a house of prostitution. Only after the murder of her pimp is she able to save the necessary amount to secure passage on a charter boat that deals in small time tourism out of the Florida Keys with a sideline in illegal drug and immigrant trafficking. She arrives in Miami traumatized after her nephew and baby are thrown overboard and drowned during a U.S. Coast Guard raid, a mere hundred feet off the coast of Florida, by the Americans who had promised them passage. Of the sixteen Haitians on board, she alone makes it to shore and to a relative living in Little Haiti.

The power of Banks' narrative stems from the matter-of-fact, nonchalant style through which he conveys the unspeakable horrors of the *botpippel* experience. The utter plausibility of the story, which is rooted in so many real narratives of the dangers implicit in reaching the U.S. coast illegally, are exacerbated by the impossibility of redress, as his protagonist's illegal status shuts her off from any appeal to justice. Vanise is thus reduced to muteness, a speechlessness that reflects her inability to speak the unspeakable. Like the survivors of the *Medusa*, many of whom had descended into madness by the time they were rescued, Vanise must find a way to psychological wholeness. She looks for healing through her initiation as a *manbo* or priestess in Vodou, healing her broken spirit through a return to the religion of her ancestors.

The lack of welcome on the part of the people of the United States and their institutions is further developed by Wilfrid Guerrier in a group of four paintings titled *Boat People #1* through *#4*. The series, which focuses on various stages of interaction between Haitian refugees and the U.S. Coast Guard, articulates the history of active interdiction of *botpippel* at sea following the intensification of the flow of refugees after the overthrow of the Aristide government in 1991, following which a flotilla of Coast Guard ships was deployed to block their passage. Guerrier worked on this series during the height of international awareness and most vocal opposition to American policies concerning the reception of refugees that the INS insisted on categorizing as economic refugees while many saw them clearly as political refugees. During the year that followed the coup—"as a United Nations economic embargo eroded living standards in Haiti still further, as political repression intensified and as hopes of return to democracy evaporated" (Arthur 181)—the U.S. Coast Guard intercepted about forty-two thousand refugees, more than the total for the previous ten years combined.

Figure 6.5. Wilfrid Guerrier, *Boat People #1*. Jonathan Demme Collection of Haitian Art. Reproduced by permission.

Guerrier understands the power of the narrative element in his paintings: "When I paint," he has said, "I tell a lot of stories . . . something that can help the country" (Lavaud). In this series he weaves and reweaves these elements in compositions that underscore the uneven dynamics of power between the boat people and the U.S. Coast Guard. His *Boat People #1, Haitian Refugees Encounter US Navy* (1995, see fig. 6.5), for example, revolves the perspective of Zephirin's painting. Here, the shipwrecks are struggling in pools of bloody, shark-infested water in the foreground of the painting, and the Scylla and Charybdis they must pass through are two U.S. Navy ships standing between them and the brilliant sun and verdant background that represent the promised land of the United States.

The painting is awash in motion—the refugees struggling in the water in the foreground, the waves crashing against the sinking boat, the tempestuous horizon, and the exploding rays of the setting sun. The eye is struck by the movement of all the elements in the painting except for the Coast Guard ships themselves, whose fixity recalls the immovable U.S. policies they represent. Guerrier works here with corresponding, parallel elements—not only the two American ships but also the two masts, one on the Coast Guard ship to the left of the painting (standing erect), the other on the sinking boat (ready to topple into the sea). The latter holds the last remaining shreds of the Haitian flag, while the U.S. boats display three flowing and intact American flags. The refugees are likewise divided into two groups; those in the foreground, struggling in blood-tinged water, appear to be beyond help while the refugees in the middle ground, those closest to the Coast Guard ships, are swimming energetically toward rescue. Their frantic activity contrasts sharply with the passivity of the Coast Guard vessels and their crews, who seem to be waiting for the refugees to come to them instead of providing the prompt and determined help that could save many from drowning.

The slowness and lack of energy of the Coast Guard rescue effort is a constant theme in this series of paintings, whose principal subtheme is the ambiguous nature of the U.S. response to the *botpippel* crisis. Underscoring this implicit critique in Guerrier's work are the repeating elements in his compositions, where the refugees are consistently placed in frantic motion in the foreground while the rescue vessels remain in the background, equipped and ready for deployment, but slow in undertaking any action. The discrepancy between the urgent plight of those whose boat has crashed against the waves and are now desperately flailing amid the remains of their vessel and the comparative passivity of the boats and hovering helicopter in the background—as Guerrier depicts in *Boat People #2* (not pictured)—encapsulates the artist's emplotment of the elements of the *botpippel* narrative. Curiously, in *Boat People #4 (Helicopter Rescue,* not pictured), where the rescue helicopters have moved from the background to the foreground of the painting (one of them hovers over the figures struggling in the crashing waves) the human figures have turned their backs to the helicopter and look toward the viewer, as if true help were only to come from that direction. The painting, whose composition is very similar to that of *Boat People #2*, is particularly notable for the effects Guerrier creates with the light emanating from the helicopter's searchlights, as it dominates the center and upper left quadrant of the image.

E. Bien-Aimé's untitled boat people painting (fig. 6.6) also features a Coast Guard rescue helicopter on the upper quadrant, but here it remains behind the crumbling sailboat, whose frantic passengers face the sharks awaiting them in the tempestuous waters. The sharks, in turn, flank La Sirène, the

Figure 6.6. E. Bien-Aimé, untitled painting. Collection of Janet Feldman, Waterloo Center for the Arts (Waterloo, Iowa). Courtesy of Janet Feldman.

marine avatar of Erzulie, *lwa* or spirit of love, consort of Agwé, master of the seas. The presence of the *lwa* appears to offer comfort and protection, but most particularly it seems to counsel calm and patience. This is one of the few *botpippel* paintings to show passengers in the hull of a ship—visible here through a missing chunk on the side of the boat. The Coast Guard vessels—a helicopter and a ship—appear here as secondary elements in the painting. The ship is barely sketched, while the helicopter sports a clownish grin like a character in a children's animated show.

One of the most compelling images of the confrontation of Haitian refugees with the Coast Guard comes from Edouard Duval-Carrié's series *Milocan, ou La migration des esprits* (1996). Duval-Carrié, one of the best-known Haitian-American artists, evokes in his work "the magic and mystery of the Vaudou universe and comments on Haiti's history and socio-political realities with sharp, surreal wit" (Poupeye 89). In this series, now at the Bass Museum, the painter/sculptor addresses the departure of the Haitian *lwa* or spirits to follow the *botpippel* to their fate at sea. One of the paintings in the series (not pictured) shows the *lwa* in a dinghy arriving at the shores of the United States. In *Le Monde Actuel ou Erzulie Interceptée* (see fig. 6.7), Erzuli (Ezili), the Vodou spirit of sensuality and love, descends in tears from a Coast Guard ship, the stark steel and immutable expressions of the guards contrasting with her coquettish Creole dress with its diaphanous sleeves and her bejeweled fingers. Tucked in the sash of her dress is the small figure of a refugee symbolizing the failure to guide and protect, which explains her tears. The dagger piercing her halo recalls Cupid's love arrows (symbol of her powers to confer and withdraw love) but also the wounds inflicted on the Haitian people by the *botpippel* tragedy. The painting's composition, which places Erzulie in the very center of the canvas, uses the angularity of the boat's gangplank and the steely demeanor of the flanking guards to underscore the thematic contrast between the *lwa*'s distress and the soldiers' (and by definition the American nation's) indifference to her anguish.

Botpippel paintings include a number of canvases that address the encampment of Haitians in the U.S. naval base at Guantánamo Bay, Cuba and at the NIS Krome Center in Miami. Within days of the 1991 coup that toppled the Aristide government, President George H. Bush ordered the Coast Guard to take all Haitian refugees to the U. S. military base at Guantánamo where INS officials would determine whether or not they met the requirements for admission into the United States. The makeshift refugee camp soon proved

Figure 6.7. Edouard Duval-Carrié, *Le Monde Actuel ou Erzulie Interceptée*. Collection Bass Museum of Art, Miami Beach. Gift of Sanford A. Rubenstein. Courtesy Bass Museum of Art.

catastrophically unsuitable to hold the thousands of refugees (up to twenty thousand of them) who needed processing at any one time. Ultimately, most of the more than forty-five thousand Haitians processed through Guantánamo were deemed to be economic, rather that political, refugees and repatriated to Haiti.

During the early stages of the *botpippel* migration in the 1980s, Haitian refugees had been held in Fort Allen, on the southern coast of Puerto Rico. They were the subject of a haunting short story by Puerto Rican writer Ana Lydia Vega, "La alambrada" (The barbed-wire fence), from her award-winning collection *Encancaranublado y otros cuentos de naufragio* (*Cloud-Cover Caribbean and Other Tales of Shipwreck, 1989*).[5] Told from the perspective of a child who watches as layers of barbed wire were coiled into an impregnable fence around the camp's perimeter, the story describes the silent despair of the refugees in poignant terms:

> Rumors were spreading, strange tales: they had taken their clothes away, they had been forbidden to talk to each other, they had changed their names. We didn't know anything. We couldn't know anything. Perhaps we were making things up. We never heard anything except for their monotonous chant in the night. And even that merged with the distant chant of the sea.
>
> One thing was certain: they continued to arrive. The barbed-wire fence would swallow them one by one and we could do nothing but watch. (Vega 1982, 50, our translation)

Guantánamo—and to a lesser extent Fort Allen—are "imperial location[s], close to home, in the ambiguous border between the domestic and the foreign" (A. Kaplan, 12). As such it is *of* the United States, but worlds away from the intended place of arrival. Their place in the *botpippel* narrative transcends the mere fact of their having become the frustrating spaces of confinement for Haitian refugees, a way-station where U.S. immigration authorities can go through the motions of their performance of justice before returning them to uncertain fates in Haiti. As colonized spaces they link the *botpippel* story to the continuum of U.S. imperial history in the Caribbean. The power of Vega's narrative stems precisely from the young narrator's acknowledgment that as a colonial—as a Puerto Rican and a woman—she possesses no knowledge and is powerless to understand or address the pain she observes. In "Haiti, Guantánamo, and the 'One Indispensable Nation,'" Jana Evans Braziel argues that the U.S. naval base in Guantánamo "remains rooted, historically, militarily, and juridically . . . within the domain of U.S. policy, connected to legal and extralegal forms of violence (and militarized prison systems) as both deployed within the domestic borders of the U.S. (against citizens and immigrants) and imposed on foreign occupied terrains" (127):

> In the case of Haitian "boat people" seeking refuge in the United States, the period from 1970 to the present has witnessed an increasingly restrictive and even repressed policy of detainment and deportation, with few individuals actually granted asylum, despite evidence of pervasive forms of political retaliation and torture suffered by those applying. The U.S.-INS system—or *regime of control*, as [Michel] Laguerre accurately coins it—relies directly on five mechanisms of control: *departure or embarkation control*; *disembarkation* or *border control*; *maritime control*; *internal control*; and, as the ultimate mechanism of surveillance, *carceral control*. These "control procedures" of the U.S.-INS, Laguerre explains, operate as mechanisms of "exclusion and admission." (137)

Michelet, in *United States Soldiers Beat Protesting Detained Haitian Refugees at Confinement Camp, Guantánamo Bay, Cuba* (1993), brings together quite economically the salient elements of the Guantánamo narrative from the perspective of one who had himself fled the 1991 military coup against Aristide by sea and had been one of the camp's detainees (see fig. 6.8). Michelet layers his painting with a series of small narratives that together weave the story of the Haitian encampment in Guantánamo as a persistent nightmare of physical abuse, showing us the details of what takes place in those round enclosures encircled by barbed wire that make up the geographical boundaries of the military camp. Like in the circles of hell, here Michelet links the notion of enclosure with that of corporeal punishment—punishment that is visibly racialized and which recalls the restraints and poses made familiar by white dominion under slavery. Inscribed "GTMO God is Good," the painting underscores the very absence of God.

Michelet's multiple narratives of abuse are centered round a row of U.S. soldiers in riot gear deploying their collective and individual force against a number of hapless and unarmed refugees. Behind them, forming the painting's background, are the huts encircled by barbed wire from behind which young refugees embody their protests through poses that suggest yelling. The painting suggests sound as well as movement, since the acts of violence com-

Figure 6.8. Michelet, *United States Soldiers Beat Protesting Detained Haitian Refugees at Confinement Camp, Guantanamo Bay, Cuba.* Jonathan Demme Collection of Haitian Art. Reproduced by permission.

piled here preclude silence. The actions against which the painting articulates its denunciation are made explicit through a series of pictorial vignettes arranged as a semicircle in the foreground of the painting, framing the central row of soldiers. Moving counterclockwise from the left corner of the painting, these vignettes include poses later made infamous by the Abu Ghraib prison photographs: a man with arms bound behind his back is being forced to kneel while a soldier holds him by the hair; a man lies on his side, arms and legs bound, while a soldier with a club poses in an attitude of mastery behind him; a man lies dead or unconscious at the feet of the row of armed soldiers, his blood flowing to the ground; a woman bends down to succor the wounded figure of what could be a child; a man cowers as a soldier aims his club at his head or back; another is in the very motion of collapse, having sustained a blow to the back of the neck. As an indictment of the violence perpetrated against Haitian refugees, Michelet's painting gathers narratives that stand here in place of the testimony to the mistreatment refugees like the painter himself endured in Guantánamo. The images stand for that which words have conveyed but has fallen on deaf ears.

Colin Anniser, like Michelet a refugee at Guantánamo, produced a series of paintings of Camp Bulkeley, the section of the Guantánamo base reserved for HIV-positive refugees. Among those of the Guantánamo detainees who were declared by the INS to be political refugees in the early 1990s, there were approximately 310 refugees who had tested positive for the AIDS virus and whose detention at Guantánamo was continued under a 1987 law barring immigrants with HIV from entering the United States. The group, which included women and children, was held prisoner at Camp Bulkeley, "the world's first and only detention camp for refugees with HIV" (Dayan, 158).

Joan Dayan, in "A Few Stories about Haiti, or Stigma Revisited," described the HIV-positive refugees as "fenced in by barbed wire and guarded by Marines armed with automatic machine guns" while "living in tin-roofed huts, using rarely cleaned portable toilets . . . surrounded by vermin and rats" and "subject to disciplinary action and pre-dawn raids of their sleeping quarters" (158). She quotes from Judge Sterling Johnson's opinion in *Haitian Centers Council v. Sale* (1993) describing Camp Bulkeley's conditions:

> They live in camps surrounded by razor barbed wire. They tie plastic garbage bags to the sides of the building to keep the rain out. They sleep on cots and hang sheets to create some semblance of privacy. They are guarded by the military and are not permitted to leave the camp, except under military escort. The Haitian detainees have been subjected to predawn military sweeps as they sleep by as many as 400 soldiers dressed in full riot gear. They are confined like prisoners and are subject to detention in the brig without a hearing for camp rule infractions. . . . (158)

The 1993 judicial decision declaring that the refugees were "entitled to constitutional due process" (Goldstein) and forcing the Clinton administration to close the camps spoke of the "Haitians' plight" as "a tragedy of immense proportion." It was a welcome decision for the numerous activists who had taken up the Haitians' cause in the United States, among them actors Tim Robbins and Susan Sarandon (who spoke against the camp at the 1993 Academy Awards), the Yale Law School students who had helped file the legal challenges against the government's policy and who had joined the

Figure 6.9. Colin Anniser, *United States Navy Haitian Refugee Confinement Camp, Guantá-namo Bay, Cuba.* Jonathan Demme Collection of Haitian Art. Reproduced by permission.

detainees in a hunger strike to proclaim their solidarity, and legendary dancer and choreographer Katherine Dunham, who had, at the age of eighty-two, staged a forty-seven-day hunger strike of her own to protest against the repatriation of the *botpippel* (Anderson).

Colin Anniser, himself an HIV-positive Guantánamo refugee, offers in *United States Navy Haitian Refugee Confinement Camp, Guantánamo Bay, Cuba* (1993), a disturbing "map" of the portion of the Guantánamo camp reserved for people with the AIDS virus (see fig. 6.9). Camp Bulkeley is seen here in all its well-ordered, barbed-wire brutality. As in Mistira's *Boat People Tragedy*, here the viewer approaches the scene from the sea, facing the refugees, some of whom, arms extended, clamor toward the viewer for help and release. Built around a series of enclosures that separate the soldiers from the refugees, the arrangement of the huts resembles that of the prototypical plantation barracks inserted into what can only be described as a prison compound.

At the center of Anniser's painting of Camp Bulkeley is an arrangement of huts whose architecture recalls that of the urban cemeteries of Port-au-Prince. For the prisoners encamped in this section of the base, the placement of these huts (halfway buried in the earth) reminds us that death hovers over them in many forms—from the threat of being returned to Haiti to the plight of being encamped without access to proper treatment after an HIV diagnosis that in many cases came as an unwelcome surprise during their confinement. (Anniser, diagnosed with HIV while in Guantánamo, died from AIDS in 1996, after he had been granted temporary asylum in the United States.) The importance to Anniser of this central image is underscored in another of his paintings (*Camp Bulkele* 1993), which concentrates exclusively on what here becomes the centerpiece, the very heart, of his composition.

Jean Ricardo Domond's *Under Glass*, from the collection of naval historian Marcus Rediker, is one of the few paintings that address the detention of Haitians at the Krome Center in Miami. The INS's Krome Detention Center is a sprawling complex on the edge of the Everglades, about thirty miles from Miami, which includes a shooting range for guards and Miami area police officers and two courtrooms for judges to hear immigration cases without refugees having to leave the facility. Over the years during which it has served as the main facility for detention of Haitian refugees seeking asylum, Krome has become synonymous with abuses of detainees. In *American Gulag: Inside U.S. Immigration Prisons*, Mark Dow details incidents of beatings, illegal searches, sexual abuse, violations of civil and human rights, and torture, which he sees as stemming from the increasing criminalization of refugees: "From the early 1980s, the beginning of what might be called the contemporary era of INS detentions, crucial inadequacies have been in place.... 'Processing centers' were prisons, and everyone knew it, even if they had to deny it in public. Pacification and repression were, therefore, in order and inevitable" (Dow 55). Giorgio Agamben, in his book *State of Exception* (2005), echoes Dow's concerns with the impact that extensions of power during times of crisis—which could range from measures to contain an influx of undesirable aliens to the post-9/11 Patriot Act—can have on the curtailment or suppression of citizenship and individual rights. Since these extensions of power, which he calls "states of exception," extend the rule and authority of certain persons, institutions, and governments well beyond where the law had existed in the past, Agamben fears that they "mark a threshold at which logic and praxis blur with each other and a pure violence without logos claims to realize an enunciation without any real reference" (40). Dow would argue that the INS, particularly at Krome, has turned the incarceration of refugees—deemed necessary by the Reagan administration in the early 1980s to contain undesirable Haitian and Mariel-boatlift Cubans and extended by the Bush administration under the Patriot Act—into a quasi-permanent state of being.

Haitian novelist Edwidge Danticat describes Krome as a place of "silent despair" that "had always seemed like a strange myth to me, a cross between Alcatraz and hell." "I'd imagined it as something like the Brooklyn Navy Yard detention center, where my parents had taken me on Sunday afternoons in the early 1980s, when I was a teenager in New York, to visit with Haitian asylum seekers we did not know but feared we might, people who, as my father used to say, 'could have very well been us'" (Danticat 2005). In 2004, the horrors of Krome spilled into Danticat's life in an ironic and tragic way when her uncle Joseph Dantica died while in the custody of Krome officials. Danticat, whose passionate commitment to Haiti and to Haitians in the diaspora has been in evidence through her writing and activism, has long been a critic of U.S. immigration policies toward Haitians. Her uncle had been forced to flee his church and school after it had been ransacked by armed gangs of youths, some of whom he had helped throughout the years. At the age of eighty-one, he had arrived at the Miami airport seeking political asylum and had been detained by the INS despite having a multiple-entry U.S. visa. He was held without being allowed to see Danticat or any other member of his family because of "security reasons." Deprived of his medicine and transferred to the prison wing of a local hospital, he died in custody five days later, in her words, a "casualty of both the conflict in Haiti and an inhumane and discriminatory US immigration system" (Jaggi).

Domond's *Under Glass* (see fig. 6.10) captures the hopelessness of imprisonment at Krome through the conflation of the experiences of the slave ship and the refugee boat. Seven refugees are shown trapped in a glass bottle looming large at the very center of the painting, dominating the space. The background shows cement-block walls in the process of being constructed—a reference perhaps to the growth the facility has undergone in order to handle a growing number of asylum seekers—and behind the walls the urban geography of Miami is depicted. Gourds hanging from steel rods in the construction speak

Figure 6.10. Jean Ricardo Domond, *Under Glass*. Collection of Marcus Rediker. Courtesy of Marcus Rediker.

to the Haitian provenance of the trapped refugees and hint at a connection to Vodou and the *lwa* or spirits. (Gourds are used for a variety of purposes in Vodou altars, among them for holding food offerings for the spirits.)

In *Under Glass*, Domond plays with the proportions of the figures and objects in the painting, thereby destabilizing the scene and underscoring the importance of the trapped human figures as they sit incongruently inside the small bottle resting on a tray, dwarfing the prison walls that form the background. The oversized padlock and key—the latter resting just outside the bottle, tantalizingly close but yet unreachable to the men and women trapped in the bottle—serve to underscore the impossibility of an exit already signaled by the entrapment of the human figures. The key, like freedom and an entry into the United States, is inaccessible. Confinement appears to be fixed and immutable, while the broken chain, which proportionately belongs with the keys, points to the breaking of the chains of slavery only to see them exchanged for this entrapment under glass.

Domond plays with a multiplicity of elements to bring to the viewer the horrors of confinement. Chief among them is the use of a bottle that could serve both as a ship-in-a-bottle container or as a receptacle for the preservation of a laboratory specimen. Hallucinatingly trapped in a viscous reddish fluid that could be blood, amniotic fluid, formaldehyde, or a flavored liquor to offer a guest (hence the liquor glass resting on the table), the bottled figures look stupefied, as if zombified in their entrapment. Their entrapment in the bottle reminds us of the process of zombification itself, in which a *bokor* or sorcerer seizes the victim's *ti bon ange*—the component of the soul where personality, character, and volition reside—and traps it in a bottle, leaving behind the body as an empty vessel subject to the commands of others. *Under Glass*, moreover, speaks to the viewers' voyeuristic inclinations, reminding us that, like figures under glass, we can look at the situation of the refugees without really making a connection. And that the key to the refugees' freedom, sitting so prominently on the table, is within our reach—if we can only stir ourselves into action.

Today, more than a decade after the court-ordered closing of the Guantánamo refugee camps, the *botpippel* experience continues to resonate in Haitian art even though the tide of refugees had slowed down until Aristide's second ouster in 2004. We find the characteristic elements of the genre in a recent series of haunting, brooding works by Jean Idelus Edmé, a painter associated with the Centre D'Art in Port-au-Prince. Edmé has painted boat people since as far back as 1988, inspired by a relative who made the crossing to Miami by boat and is now a U.S. citizen. His recent work, particularly his *Botpippel* (2003), invokes both the breathtaking power of the sea and the memory of the Middle Passage, which he links to Christian symbolism (a favorite element being the mast of the ship used to symbolize a Christian cross). He is among a group of artists who have revived the *botpippel* genre in recent years, and that includes a number of young sculptors working in wood, such as Melio Jeanty, whose work can be seen at the Musée d'Art in Port-au-Prince and who produces relatively simple carvings depicting eight or ten people in a boat, typically accompanied by either a mermaid or a sea monster. Gabriel Volcy, a former policeman and native of Leogane who works with Galerie Monnin, produced in 2003 an impressive rendering in wood of a boatload

Figure 6.11. Rejin Leys *Wherever There's Someone Fighting.* Reproduced by permission of the artist.

of refugees in imminent danger of capsizing. Marked by the skill with which he has captured the almost palpable expression of horror on the faces of the boat's occupants, the work is a most impressive example of the possibilities of using sculpture to address the history of the Haitian refugees.

Haitian refugees, particularly those who had been held in Guantánamo Bay awaiting processing, are also the focus of the work of Rejin Leys, a Haitian artist living in New York. Leys is one of several young artists featured in a 1988 *New York Times* article on Haitian art in New York. Her *Wherever There's Someone Fighting,* an ink and paper work reproduced in the *2002 Social Justice Calendar* published by the Bread and Roses Cultural Project in New York City, brings the elements characteristic of the *botpippel* iconography to greater focus through their abstraction (see fig. 6.11). The work is part of a series of works on boat people that explores the links between labor and migration. Here, the refugees' dreams of financial prosperity in the United

States become the ragged corners of a dollar bill framing the drawing; the waves of the sea become blue veins on a polished white marble surface and in turn transform before our eyes into the barbed wire that restricted the refugees' movement within Guantánamo base. Reyes' boat, a stylized shape with seven protruding black feet, refers both to walking out of the sea onto the shore as well as to the myths of walking over the waters to return to Africa. Leys also meant the boat with feet to literally represent the "boat people." "If the terms boat people and illegal alien are used to dehumanize," she has said, "then what would this non-human creature look like?"[6] Textured to recall a wooden vessel, the boat has angel-like wings in lieu of sails, pointing to the lightness of flight. The words that frame the boat, "Wherever there's someone struggling to be free, look in their eyes, you'll see me," drawn from Bruce Springsteen's "The Ghost of Tom Joad"—adapted in turn from John Steinbeck's *The Grapes of Wrath*—provide a link between the refugees' struggles and other migrations of the displaced and hopeful poor. Springsteen's song (1995) provides a suitable link to the *botpippel's* struggle through its exploration of "an America that has turned its back on the working class and the foreign-born" (Deming).

The unfortunate legacy of the Haitian refugee camps was revived following the attacks of September 11, 2001 against the United States with the arrival of the first prisoners of the war against terrorism at Guantánamo base. Less than a decade after the closing of the Haitian containment camps the nightmare they represented had returned as Guantánamo has once again become the space for confinement, torture, and death. Could it indeed be the case that people have forgotten that history has not opened a new chapter but is merely repeating itself? As Joan Dayan writes:

> Within a maze of chain-link fences, razor wire and guard towers, metal cages baked in the tropical heat, the inmates inhabited what was described in the early months of its existence in *The Guardian* as a "densely packed zoo." Soon afterwards the cages were replaced with a penal colony designed to hold indefinitely up to 2,000 prisoners. How do these images of incarceration tell a history of punishment and retribution in the United States? What is the standard for treatment of prisoners taken in the current "war against terrorism"? For the prisoners sent from Afghanistan and other sites to Guantánamo, mistreatment begins during transport. The prisoners are shackled by the hands and limbs,

made to wear ear cuffs, blindfolded by blacked-out goggles, and then hooded. . . . At Guantánamo they were forced to kneel with their legs crossed for long periods of time. Exposed to the sun, they were held until September 2002 in cages measuring 1.8 by 2.4 meters. (Dayan, 158)

"Guantánamo is not a spa, but neither is it an inhumane torture camp"— so claimed Colleen P. Graffy, U.S. deputy assistant secretary for public diplomacy, seeking to contain the international backlash against the United States as stories of atrocities in Guantánamo poured out. "It is a prison," she has argued, "and as prisons go, it is well-run and humane" (Sweig). The world, it would seem, disagrees, as would those who like Michelet and Anniser left their paintings as testimony to the despair of a confinement that only ended when they and other Haitian refugees were vindicated by the courts. As the debate over immigration and the closing of the U.S. borders rages, threatening to become the dominant issues in current U.S. politics, the *botpippel* paintings remain to illustrate past efforts at the curtailment and deterrence of earlier waves of undesired refugees, many of whose voices were silenced by death.

Russell Banks, in *Continental Drift*, writes of the mysterious inability (or unwillingness) to speak of the Haitians fleeing to America. His Haitian characters had seen too much, gone through too much to speak of simple, everyday matters. Bob Dubois, his protagonist, describes the Haitians he brings on his boat to Miami as "a quiescent, silent, shy people who seem fatalistic almost, who seem ready and even willing to accept whatever is given them (Banks 305). It is an assessment shared by Karen McCarthy Brown, who while working with Haitian refugees in Brooklyn noted the same silence among those who, like Banks' Vanise Dorsinvile, had turned to Vodou for wordless comfort after their harrowing experiences at sea or in refugee camps (Brown 1996). Haitian writers have been equally silent about the painful experiences of the *botpippel* and the many losses of life their story contains. Marie-José N'Zengo-Tayo explains the difficulty of writing about the *botpippel* experience, arguing that "the reason for this 'absence' can be found in the impossibility of transforming this reality into a meaningful metaphor" (93).

It has been the painters, then, who have found the visual language and artistic metaphors to record the narrative of this tragic episode in Haitian history. As artists, they have also become memorialists, historians, witnesses who have brought to life on canvas a narrative that seems to many forgotten, a story brought to life again only occasionally when the debate over containing immigration blazes anew or when the base at Guantánamo once again makes headlines. In *Empathic Vision: Affect, Trauma, and Contemporary Art*, Jill Bennet asks how art can convey the force of trauma, how it can "register pain's call for acknowledgement . . . an antiphony of language and silence" (50). The *botpippel* painters, whose exploration of the narrative of the Haitian refugees—the lucky ones who made it to shore and the unlucky ones lost at sea or repatriated to a yet more inhospitable home—saw them become secondary witnesses to their national tragedy, have sought through their art to trigger within us an affective response, another mode of witnessing. They ask us to become, as spectators to the trauma of the *botpippel*, the living memorials—and the living memories—of another chapter in Haiti's tragic history.

Notes

We would like to thank Bill Bollendorf of Galerie Macondo, Janet Feldman (and the Janet Feldman Collection at the Waterloo Center for the Arts in Iowa), Marcus Rediker, and Pebo Voss (curator of the Jonathan Demme collection of Haitian paintings) for their help with the writing of this essay.

1. The plight of the *botpippel* also became a theme for young Haitian musicians. Magnum Band, a Haitian-American Kompa band based in Miami, recorded several songs that asked for better treatment and sympathy for the plight of Haitian refugees arriving in the United States. In "Liberty" (1982), they asked listeners to imagine what happened to the refugees who spent all they had to make the sea crossing, people who "sold everything they had at home/to look for a better life/when they arrive they're put in prison/some never arrive/sharks ate them en route/they sank in terrible weather" (Arthur 196).

2. Encircling sharks will be a leitmotiv in *botpippel* paintings. They figure most prominently in and black and white ink drawing by J. J. Georges (from Galerie Macondo) that graphically depicts sharks at the bottom of the sea feeding on drowned Haitian refugees. The constant presence of sharks in *botpippel* paintings and narratives contrasts sharply with the oft-repeated tale of Elián González, that most famous of Cuban proto-refugees, saved from the sharks that encircled him by dolphins that kept him afloat until he was rescued.

3. See Jan-Franns Gasyon's Kreyol adaptation of Shakespeare's *Hamlet*, *Amlèt: Trajedi youn nèg ki pa ka deside*, where the soliloquy begins thus: "Se sa ou se pa sa. Men kesyon an. Èske youn nonm ki sere dan-l, ki kontinye ap soufri an silans tout move kou ke lavi a pote-l pi brav ke youn lòt ki pito touye tèt li pou-l fin ak sa? Mouri ak dòmi se menm bagay; epi, kalite dòmi sa a ede-n fini ak tout soufrans ki lan kè-n ansanm avèk tout doulè ke kò-n santi . . . se sa nou ta renmen ki rive, e byen vit tou. Mouri ak dòmi!" (22).

4. These elements are also present in an untitled watercolor painting by Jean Ernst Domond (Bill Bollendorf/Galerie Macondo) that juxtaposes a series of miragelike images whose central theme is that of death at sea. A cemetery occupies the upper left-hand corner and the eye moves counterclockwise to encompass a skeletal figure and a masked figure half-submerged in the sea, where small broken boats are dwarfed by a war ship (an allusion to the U.S. Coast Guard) over which armed military figures hover menacingly, blocking access to a city of skyscrapers.

5. Vega addresses "boat people" and their experience through humor in the title story from this collection, "Encancaranublado" ("Cloud Cover Caribbean"), where she places three potential refugees, a Dominican, a Haitian, and a Cuban trying to reach the United States, on a shaky raft in the middle of the sea. Her interest lies in highlighting how, despite their inter-island tensions and differences, they face similar challenges in their relationship to the United States. Their in-fighting capsizes the raft, at which point they are "saved" by an American fisherman who is unable to distinguish among them and sends his Puerto Rican crewman to deal with them. He, in turn, counsels against their naïve visions of the United States as paradise: "If you want to feed your bellies here you're going to have to work, and I mean work. A gringo don't give nothing away. Not to his own mother" (Vega 1989, 111).

6. E-mail exchange with author, January 19, 2007.

7

Testimonial Intent and Narrative Dissonance

The Marginal Heroes of Miguel Barnet

MICHAEL ARONNA

Art, however, is social not only because of its mode of production, in which the dialectic of the forces and relations of production is concentrated, nor simply because of the social derivation of its thematic material. Much more important, art becomes social by its opposition to society, and it occupies this position only as autonomous art. By crystallizing itself as something unique to itself, rather than complying with existing social norms and qualifying as "socially useful," it criticizes society by merely existing, for which puritans of all stripes condemn it.

Theodor Adorno, *Aesthetic Theory*

Within Latin American and Caribbean studies and critical theory, testimonial narrative has been the site of multiple ideological, cultural, ethnographic, historiographic, and aesthetic projects. The many claims made by and against these projects have their roots in specific political, epistemological, and disciplinary frameworks that tend to freeze testimonial narrative within a particular status as practice, art, or science. Hermeneutic partisans of *testimonio* have fixed on three unique aspects of this genre: the reconfiguration of power and labor relations engendered by testimonial collaboration, the recovery of marginalized ethnographic histories, and the transformation of the speaking subject into a written voice. Each of these points to significant political and cultural issues and outcomes in and of themselves. However, when considered within disciplinary rigidity and political prudishness of all stripes, predetermined disciplinary and political lenses of analysis often reduce the social and aesthetic scope of testimonial narrative as practice and text.

The richness of this type of collaborative documentary narrative in Latin

America and the Hispanic Caribbean, both as an instrument for social change and as a constructed object in itself, lies in the negotiation between intentionality on the one hand, and the relative autonomy of the discursive artifact on the other. This is a constitutive tension that runs horizontally and vertically throughout *testimonio*. The modal conventions for the transmission and control of knowledge are inescapably linked, as Gramsci has indicated, to specific articulations of cultural hegemony. Egalitarian social contracts and relations of production between intellectuals and informants in the invention of testimonial narrative, when combined with explicit relations of solidarity between producers and readers, can alter the historically oppressive function of intellectual discourse in the Americas. Nevertheless, such contracts are inexorably linked to intention and faith in ideology and truth, qualities that are ultimately unverifiable at the level of discourse. Even when we accept intention at face value, the political and aesthetic goals of documentary narrative do not necessarily correspond to the effects produced in the reader. The complexity and ambiguity of the discursive object is not completely exhausted by intention, which, as Phyllis Frus has stated, weakens the authorial interpellation of the reader: "We read a true story and an invented one in much the same way, giving ourselves over to the illusion of reality that is created and neglecting the medium of narration, unless it becomes other than transparent" (160).

Far from reducing an understanding of the social to an essentially textual exegesis, the recognition of the non-transparency of narration breaks with the reification or naturalizing effects of bourgeois realist discourse in order to redefine self-referentiality as a social as well as meta-textual act. Some critics of testimonial narrative have mistakenly classified this self-indexing of the relationship between the subjectivity of the observer and social reality as "literary," understood as a "fictional" or less than scientific feature, thus failing to recognize narrative's own inner dynamic and the role this positional tension plays in all narrative modes. The observation that documentary nonfiction carries the markers of its invention in narrative does not essentially discount its truth-effect any more than it does for the social and natural sciences that are likewise constituted through representation and discourse. As Michel Foucault has signaled in his archeology of scientific discourse, the overdetermined interplay between social relations, the discursive field, and subject position is also a constitutive feature of scientific knowledge: "The human sciences are not, then, an analysis of what man is by nature; but rather an analysis that extends from what man is in his positivity (living, speaking, labouring, being) to what enables this same being to know (or seek to know) what life is, in what the essence of labour and its laws consist, and in what way he is able to speak" (353). Thus the instances in which *testimonio* foregrounds its constructed nature as narrative follow from Marx's notion that reification, or the naturalization of class antagonisms, is avoided when humanity is not estranged from the relations and conditions of labor (Frus 170). Thus the historical conditions that inform the at times contradictory negotiation between the egalitarian aims of testimonial collaboration and the irreducible and potentially prickly countereffects of narration underscore that the self-reflexive moments of documentary narrative simultaneously ground the text in the real through social activity.

This investigation of Hispanic Caribbean testimonial narrative comes out of my own desire to explore what Alberto Moreiras has characterized as the "unguarded possibility of the real" of testimonial literature and the ways in which different interpretative communities have constituted this sense of the real in relation to the text's alleged formal intention. Yet as Moreiras suggests, this sense of the real is a liminal space of the sublime wherein the reader performs an overly determined socio-aesthetic reading (195). The changing and historically contingent nature and location of this reading leads me to pose the following questions: What precisely is the irreducible agency of the act of textual self-narration in this collective or individual act of reading and how does this contingent narrative autonomy engage different readings of the text across time, race, class, and gender? How have the accumulated instances of doubt and scandal surrounding testimonial and autobiographical narrative in the political sphere and in the publishing industry questioned and/or strengthened specific communities' interpretations of the text? Have traditional notions of "the real" and "the literary" been redefined by the palimpsest of competing subjective readings of testimonial and documentary literature? In the context of testimonial and documentary literature, are these categories obsolete?

It is in this light that I wish to focus on my own perception of disjuncture between intention and the relative autonomy of narrative effects in Miguel Barnet's *The Autobiography of a Runaway Slave* (1966) and *Rachel's Song* (1969). My interest in Barnet's practice of testimonial narrative over that of other Caribbean and Latin American examples is linked to Barnet's awareness of the invented nature of his collaborative projects. For Barnet, "invention" does not connote fiction; rather, it refers to the belief that the self-identification and definition of the people is an ongoing historical process. In an analogous manner, Barnet's vision of the people and its communicative modalities is also plastic in that he denies the assumptions of "authentic" simplicity, transparency, and spontaneity of the narrative informant and his or her language. Accordingly, the historiographic, cultural, and political force of Barnet's work is not premised on notions of the "purity" of the constitution of the speaking subject or on unrealizable methodological protocols for purging narrative discourse of its imaginary components. As a consequence, the collaborative autobiographical narrators of Barnet's work are themselves the products of their historical epochs and the social and communicative exchange of the ethnographic process. Like the process itself, or the history they narrate, the informants of *The Autobiography of a Runaway Slave* and *Rachel's Song* are complex social figures who contradict themselves and frustrate those who seek redemption through a pure subaltern subject.

Practitioners of testimonial narrative posit these texts as collaborative postcolonial projects that create new agents, circuits, and relations of power in the production and dissemination of knowledge. While this is in part undeniably the case, what I nevertheless find particularly complex about these texts is the degree to which they simultaneously posit a critique of subalternization from the perspective of subaltern experience, knowledge, and communication. The perceived silences, misunderstandings, and (mis)representations of the subaltern indicate that the subaltern possess what Walter Mignolo has termed as a "consciousness that exists for itself" (111). In his well-known description of his objectives and methodology for testimonial narrative, *The Documentary Novel,* Barnet lays out the design of the relationship between social history, collective sensibility, and specific protagonists: "it should unravel reality, focus on key historical events that have affected the sensibilities of a people the most, and it should be presented through the eyes of the protagonist" (1979, 4). This brief statement of purpose establishes an internal tension between significant historical moments and the specific perception of a witness whose credibility is linked to his or her involvement in these epochal events. Likewise, this credibility is also contingent on Barnet's deliberate choice of which events to include or omit. As we shall see, this editorial selection establishes or undermines the informant's reliability.

Barnet links the ability of the informant to get to the bottom of reality to his or her particular suitability. Beyond the question of direct participation in the historical events narrated, the fitting nature of Barnet's testimonial witness is also linked to the narrative style, ideology, and temperament of the informant. Undoubtedly, the significance of these factors is heavily mediated through the intervention of Barnet's editing of the material. In fact, Barnet is quite frank in his discussion of the methods he employs to achieve a desired effect in the formal act of narration as well as in the containment of the ideological point of view of the speaking subject. Nevertheless, the complete realization of Barnet's aesthetic and political intent runs up against the formal and ideological resistance embedded in the relative autonomy of the discourse of the narrated self. This autonomy is the product of the tension between the intent of Barnet's form and the praxis of his witness. While Barnet is largely successful in his stated objectives, the characters conjured up out of the real-life stories of Montejo and Rachel maintain a degree of irreducible indeterminacy. As J. M. Bernstein indicates, the mercurial aspect of the narrated self resists formal or intentional closure: "Self narration is the excessive truth of narrative form; autobiographical excess reveals the self as twisting free from form and universality even as it appropriates it to itself" (65).

The broad outline of the life of Esteban Montejo, the sole witness and collaborator with Barnet on *The Autobiography of a Runaway Slave*, unfolds in intimate relation with the sweeping historical transformation of Cuba from a slave-holding colony to an independent republic. Montejo's active agency from runaway to independence fighter lends him an epic heroic stature that grounds him in the post-revolutionary moment of his narrative utterance. Montejo's past actions of independence and resistance make him, as Barnet affirms in his introduction to the original Spanish version of the text, "a good example of revolutionary conduct and quality" (1968, 10, my translation). Montejo's engagement with the social in a society undergoing radical transformation also underscores the social variant on the discursive concept of excessive meaning. As Roman de la Campa suggests, Ernesto Laclau's concept of the infinity of the social addresses persistent political and economic antagonisms that challenge an exclusively discursive understanding of new forms of social agency and knowledge production (137). In this context, the relative narrative autonomy of Montejo as speaking subject must be considered alongside the dynamics of the excess of meaning of his social acts and positions.

Barnet's vision of a new social totality departing from Montejo's enunciative and social protagonism is difficult to dispute, particularly if we limit ourselves to the chronology of Montejo's life as presented by Barnet. Yet if we consider this selective life span in the light of the German historian Michael Zeuske's archival findings concerning Montejo's activity subsequent to the periods covered by Barnet, we see that the long and complex life of this informant resists univocal closure. Zeuske's discovery of Montejo's contractual ties to a political boss subsequently associated with the Machado dictatorship indicates that he may have benefited from this association and become a small land-owning peasant after independence (Walter, 21). The possibility that Montejo may not have always been a simple, long-suffering peon may disappoint those who place the burden of universal redemption on a fetishized idealization of the subaltern. On the contrary, Montejo's modest social mobility and involvement in the Independent Party of Colored People during the racial disturbances of 1912 traces the complicated and shifting social and ethnic politics of post-independence Cuba. A tumultuous historical period produces contradictory heroes and witnesses, not impeccable legends. As John Beverley asserts, the subaltern subject is not "totalizable as the 'people as one' of nationalist or populist discourse" (52). Rather, the site of the subaltern's agency is not theoretical or textual but historical and contingent.

Moreover, a close reading of the temperament, memory, and rhetorical structure of Montejo's autobiographical practice in *The Autobiography of a Runaway Slave* as edited by Barnet reveals a narrative excess that cannot be entirely subsumed under a one-dimensional epic intent. Recent archival findings about Montejo's later life are not entirely at odds with the collaborative recollection of his life in terms of content, performance, and tone. In this sense, the chronological and thematic unity imposed on a spontaneously recalled life, a technique analogous to Hayden White's notion of emplotment, does not exhaust the complexity of Montejo as a social agent and narrative figure. His life, as told by Montejo and Barnet, is politically inspiring and aesthetically engaging, but nevertheless produces other countereffects of indeterminate volition.

The narrative character that Montejo constructs in the telling of his life is a complex invented figure that occupies a liminal position between the real and the imaginary. While it is important to underline that the character of Montejo is an invention of his own memory and speech, this should not be confused with fiction or literature in the narrow sense of the term. Rather, the ontological autonomy of the textual Montejo is a function of narrative, or as Roland Barthes has stated: "Narrator and characters, however, at least from our perspective, are essentially 'paper beings'; the (material) author of a narrative is in no way to be confused with the narrator of the narrative" (111). Barthes's absolute separation of the performing narrator from his or her textual manifestation appears extreme in the context of the faith-based belief of the testimonial homology of witness and narrative informant characteristic of the proponents of *testimonio*. Nevertheless I posit that his notion of narrative autonomy is useful in this consideration of Barnet's collaborative creations. Whether we consider the "real" or the "paper" Montejo, the reader is faced with a complex negotiation between a wily informant and a sympathetic and focused ethnographer. As Roberto González Echevarría points out, the narrative conceit of the figure of Montejo "is no naïve Sancho and certainly not the Rousseau-inspired native who is going to save Barnet from the complexities of writing" (120).

The most outstanding feature that contrasts with the epic tone and "calidad revolucionaria" of Montejo's life is his extreme misanthropy and acute pessimism. The vehemently anti-social core of Montejo's personality undermines the unifying heroic emplotment that Barnet constructs around Montejo's deeds. What is striking about this pessimism and isolation is the vehemence with which Montejo posits these qualities as motivating factors for his life of action, as if to contradict nobler attributions. Montejo's cynical distance from his surrounding community is constant throughout the three sections of *The Autobiography of a Runaway Slave*. Although there are significant moments of a spirit of collective struggle in Montejo's account, his narrative is nonetheless delivered by an "I" whose essential cynicism places him at odds with his community.

Montejo's picaresque skepticism and alienation has its origins in the physical, moral, and social degradation of slavery. As Montejo affirms in the following passage, the debilitating conditions of forced labor and the sickly environment of the slave barracks led him to flee both slave labor and society for the healthy solitude and freedom of nature: "Life was hard and bodies wore out. Anyone who did not take to the hills as a runaway when he was young had to become a slave. It was preferable to be on your own on the loose than locked up in all that dirt and rottenness" (Barnet 1968, 40–41). Although Montejo's association of freedom with solitude is rooted in his rejection of the institution of slavery, his strong isolationist temperament is also linked to an explicit desire to avoid the company and culture of his fellow slaves in bondage and runaway communities. In this sense, Montejo never seems to transcend entirely an anti-social survival strategy grounded in his experience of slavery. Montejo describes his estrangement from the runaway community or *palenque* in cynically practical terms: "The other runaways always stayed in groups of twos and threes, but this was dangerous because when it rained their footprints showed up in the mud, and lots of idiots were caught that way" (49). The expedience of Montejo's logic is self-evident in the success of his flight. Yet the underlying principle of his distrust and disdain for his peers in slavery belies a skepticism that undermines his function as an epic figure: "I did not let the other runaways catch sight of me: 'Runaway meets runaway, sells runaway'" (49). As the quotation marks in the text indicate, the adage of "Runaway meets runaway, sells runaway" signals that this notion is inscribed within Montejo's consciousness as a kind of proverbial wisdom that he emphatically articulates in a post-revolutionary site of enunciation. In this way the social estrangement originating in the period of slavery leaks into the contemporary moment of narration.

In the section titled "Abolition" there is a clear correspondence between Montejo's belief that the exploitation of blacks continued in modified form after abolition and his ingrained philosophy of anti-social skepticism. An important element introduced into Montejo's account at this juncture is a disbelief in official policy and discourse. Despite assurances that slavery was over, Montejo saw continuity within the new system of peon labor: "Negroes were free now, or so they said. But I could not help noticing that bad things still went on. There were bosses who still believed that the blacks were created for locks and bolts and whips, and treated them as before. It struck me that many Negroes did not know that things had changed, because they went on saying, 'Give me your blessing, my master'" (Barnet 1968, 64). As Gerard Aching has indicated, Montejo's suspicion of social and economic transformation during abolition extends to official accounts of this period (39). Thus Montejo challenges Barnet's emplotment of a successive emancipation and inclusion of blacks in Cuba leading up to and including the post-revolutionary period (40). In this manner the formal intent of Barnet's chronology is thwarted by Montejo's narrative process. The misanthropic attitude toward his fellow emancipated blacks and official discourse voiced by Montejo cannot be isolated within the injustices of the past and spills into the present of his narration.

In Montejo's description of life during abolition he appears to cling to his solitary ways and only grudgingly frequents the sites of black social life in search of female companionship. He characterizes his life during this period as one guided by a strong work ethic and the pursuit of women. The scenes of taverns, gambling, and dances he narrates are places of gossip, intrigue, and disputes he preferred to avoid. Significantly, in these descriptions he continues to speak of black Creoles in the third person in contrast to his first person narration: "If the Negroes had had things their way, they would always have stayed dancing till dawn. I know how it is with them. Even now, if you go to a dance, the last person to leave will be a Negro. Personally, I won't say I don't like dancing and rumbas, but I have come to take a long view of these things" (Barnet 1968, 63).

In the third and final section of *The Autobiography . . . ,,* "The War of Independence," we witness a significant change in Montejo's estrangement from historical events and a larger Cuban society. At this point Montejo includes himself in the collective undertaking of the War of Independence: "What all of us wanted, as Cubans, was the freedom of Cuba. We wanted the Spanish to go and leave us alone, 'Freedom or Death,' people said, or, 'Free Cuba'" (Barnet 1968, 111). But as Aching has pointed out, even in this moment of inclusion in a national struggle Montejo distinguishes black involvement in the war from the Cuban elite's interests: "We Negroes protested too—our grievances went back years" (Barnet 1968, 37). In this way the united front of the struggle is fractured and black interests are not posited as identical with those of the national independence movement. As Montejo's experience as a runaway exemplifies, black resistance to colonial rule predates the war of independence. Nevertheless, Montejo's participation in this national conflict is evidenced by a linguistic shift to the first personal plural, *we,* particularly with verbs indicating an active, collective participation in the struggle against Spain: "Then we reached El Mamey, where there was hard fighting. Our side was united, and though the Spanish put up some resistance we taught them another lesson. Then we headed for other plantations. We were approaching Matanzas by now, still without fixed leadership. We passed through the España and Hatuey plantations and seized a load of arms" (183).

Although Montejo's active involvement in the War of Independence approximates him to the kind of recuperated epic hero of Barnet's design, Montejo's narration of this period undercuts its heroic effect. He undermines the epic character of the independence struggle by blurring the distinction between banditry and rebellion. He spends as much if not more time detailing the non-military pillaging of the countryside as he does describing the heroic defeat of the Spaniards at Mal Tiempo. Montejo describes the leaders of the independence army as little more than common bandits ready to surrender to the Spaniards when hard-pressed. This banditry with a noble cause disillusioned Montejo, whose own proclivity for stealing livestock was jaded by the unbridled greed of the leader, Tajó: "I stayed three months with Tajó, but one day I decided I had had enough and I left. He went too far, he stole and sold livestock, in short he was a disaster, a cattle-thief masquerading as a liberator. There were many others like him" (Barnet 1968, 186). With the exception of Martí, for Montejo, Tajó was the rule rather than the exception among the independence leaders, a point made clear when he tells of his desertion of the latter for Cayito's battalion, only to discover that "from one thief to another thief, from one assassin to another."

Significantly then, the moment of Montejo's deepest involvement in a national movement for emancipation is perhaps also the occasion for the ultimate confirmation of his pessimistic and anti-social philosophy. It is very indicative that Montejo experiences the greatest instance of disillusionment with the War of Independence at the personal level. He speaks of the extreme difficulty he had forming friendships inside and outside the independence army. It is a severe emotional and social blow to him when his best and only friend, Juan Fabregas, turns himself into the Spanish forces: "At last I heard that he had surrendered to the Spanish. When I heard that I went cold all over. Then I fell into a rage, angry and contemptuous all at once. I went on fighting in the war for honour's sake" (Barnet 1968, 208). With the betrayal of his best friend and comrade-in-arms, Montejo's slavery-inspired proverb, "Runaway meets runaway, sells runaway," is confirmed. Faced with the loss of his social bond to the struggle he falls back on the code of the lone individual, personal honor. Thus the lesson that Montejo takes away from his participation in a collective national movement is distrust at the official and personal level: "The best thing in war is not to trust people, and the same is true in peace, though it's more essential in wartime. You should never trust anyone. This isn't sad because it's true" (196).

William Luis has argued that Barnet's intent in the final section of *The Autobiography of a Runaway Slave* was to establish an epic link of continuity between the Ten Years' War and the Cuban Revolution (483). Beyond the chronological irregularities Luis points to in this heroic teleology, what stands out in this constructed bridge is the undercurrent of distrust for the leadership, rhetoric, and motives of the independence movement. Although there is a sense of historical agency and direction within Barnet's design, Montejo's narrative practice eludes intentional closure. One may well ask what is the effect of the linkage between the Ten Years' War and the Revolution when Montejo muddies his details of military victory with tales of banditry, sloganeering, and the poor treatment of blacks after the war. This section can be read, along with its intention, as a progressive yet flawed stage toward the egalitarian triumph of the revolution. Nevertheless, the cyclical narrative syntax and cynicism of Montejo's performance suggests that little had changed after independence. He lives alone in a plantation barrack, defiantly friendless and states: ". . . The same work as before. It seemed as though everything had gone back in time" (Barnet 1968, 222). In this way Montejo's contradictory account of the Ten Years' War simultaneously traces the historically complex motives within the independence movement as it escapes confinement within a one-dimensional epic of national liberation.

Another salient countereffect produced by Montejo's narrative excess is an underlying notion that life was somehow better in the past. This is a vague nostalgia that runs counter to the explicit narrative of the progressive improvement of the situation of blacks in Cuba after the abolition of slavery and the advent of national independence and culminating in the revolutionary period. While the nostalgic tone of the narrative can be attributed to his general crankiness and the mediation of old age, it also suggests a curiously counterintuitive ideological effect. The reader's first impression that Montejo feels that his life was better in the past is linked to his blissful account of his years of solitude and communion with nature during his years as a maroon. According to Montejo, during his years as a runaway he had access to meat, vegetables, coffee, tobacco, honey, and herbal medicines. In contrast to the ecological and social alienation of plantation monoculture, Montejo lived in harmony in a community of trees: "I got used to living with trees in the forest," he wrote (Barnet 1968, 57). "I felt they were taking care of me" (56). He lived a Golden Age of natural abundance, which he took advantage of with Robinson Crusoe-like industry. He states that he lived better than the free peasant *guajiros*: "The truth is I never lacked for nothing in the forest" (53). This idyllic correspondence between freedom, youthful vigor, and nature comes to an end with abolition. Significantly, the end of this rare and happy period of Montejo's life is announced by an anonymous and boisterous chorus: "I realized from the way people were cheering and shouting that slavery ended, and so I came out of the forest. They were shouting, 'We're free now.' But I didn't join in, I thought it might be a lie" (59). The beginning of official freedom and the return to society and the drudgery of work are perceived as a fall from grace rather than as an improvement by Montejo. Thus in a paradoxical fashion for Barnet's emplotment, Montejo the narrator situates the happiest moment of his life in the most exploitative and retrograde period of Cuban history.

A less clear yet equally nagging countereffect of Montejo's narration concerns his sense that the quality of daily life has become impoverished over time. Such observations are interspersed throughout the text but do not constitute a unified discourse. According to Montejo, children were raised properly, women were more fun, food tasted better, and elders were respected in the past. Beyond these banal observations that can once again be attributed to a particularly crotchety senior citizen, in a broader plane Montejo's commentaries recall a lost sense of spectacle, religiosity, magic, and community in Cuban society. What contributes to the complexity and richness of these observations is that at other moments in the text Montejo proclaims his indifference to these same practices and institutions.

At one level Montejo's discourse of cultural loss coincides with Barnet's original intention of conducting ethnographic interviews with Montejo about African religion and culture. Of all the subnations (*chinos, gallegos, congos, lucumí, canarios, criollos, gitanos,* and so forth) into which Montejo divides Cuban society, he reserves his greatest admiration for those of African birth. He perceives in the Africans an integrity, self-knowledge, mutual understanding, and unifying philosophy he finds lacking in other segments of Cuban society, particularly in the black Creoles. Montejo describes African storytelling traditions, healing practices, and religious ceremonies in a positive light. In contrast to the scenes of black Creole gatherings, which he attends only to find female company, Montejo states that the African ceremonies were more fun, spectacular, and sublime: "The African religions are more entertaining because you dance, sing, amuse yourself, fight. There is no maní dance, the stick game and *quimbumbia*" (Barnet 1968, 142). Yet for Montejo, the African world of his youth no longer exists at the time of his narration. Moreover, as the following passage suggests, no other belief system has filled the void left by its disappearance: "There aren't any Africans in Cuba now, and the new people couldn't care less about religion, all they think about is eating, sleeping and having lots of money to throw around. That's why we're in this state, wars here, wars there" (140). As the final sentence of this passage indicates, Montejo's remembrance of lost African traditions goes beyond the nostalgia of the aged and reflects negatively on the moment of enunciation.

Another instance wherein Montejo speaks of a lost sense of community is his description of the mutual aid and solidarity of the rural communities in the area of Las Villas. The utopian vision of collective labor, shared resources, fraternity, and joviality of these communities is the only moment of the text that rivals the Golden Age of his youth as a maroon in the wild. It is quite poignant then, that this praise is uttered in a post-revolutionary narrative position in which collective agriculture, campaigns of mutual aid, and the rhetoric of solidarity lie at the root of revolutionary policy and discourse. It is in this light that we consider Montejo's assessment of contemporary Cuban society: "People don't behave like that nowadays. Everywhere you look now there is envy and jealousy. That's why I like solitary life. I don't meddle with other people, so they won't meddle with me" (Barnet 1968, 158). Thus Montejo situates his vision of a utopian society in a pre-revolutionary past and characterizes the socialist period of his speech as rancorous and noncooperative. His behavior and attitude are constants that undermine the progressive chronology of Barnet's outline.

As Barnet acknowledges in his introduction, Montejo's will to self-invention was evident during the ethnographic interviews that Barnet later edited to form the text. Although he was at first a difficult informant, as Montejo became aware of the value his unique knowledge and experience held for Barnet, he actively engaged the interviewer to direct the conversation according to his interests. Despite Barnet's editorial efforts to structure Montejo's account in terms of a purposeful chronology and writerly aesthetic, Montejo's consciousness of the role he played in constructing a personal and national history achieves formal immanence within the text itself. Although Montejo's narrative agency at times coincides with Barnet's political, ethnographic, and aesthetic objectives, Montejo's distinct agenda is also linked to a personal desire to construct a narrative character that will entertain, instruct, and mold the listener and reader. The character that Barnet and Montejo create out of Montejo's utterances is a narrative figure that can only be consciously controlled to the degree that discourse itself can be instrumentally bottled. The relative autonomy of Montejo's narrative praxis is at times difficult to isolate because of its inscription within the additional layer of Barnet's written discourse. Yet one should not view this encapsulation as ultimately determinant either. As Luiz Costa Lima suggests, Barnet's written transcription of Montejo's performance faces internal semiotic limits as well: "It is the case, of course, that in writing, no one has total control over this process—except if we consider the recopying of what has already been written. Only hard practice or an intuitive eye to the competency expected of the projected reader will tell when the development threatens to overturn expository harmony, thus necessitating a new *emplotment*" (Costa Lima, 122). In this way *The Autobiography of a Runaway Slave* is the product of a complex palimpsest of intent and autonomy that challenges assumptions of a teleological emplotment.

Although we have already pointed to dissonances between intent and effect in the natural or transparent discourse of the text, the impact of these countercurrents is underscored by instances of narrative rupture or non-transparency within the text that bring the irreducible autonomy of Montejo's narration to the surface. Specifically, these are moments when Montejo explicitly refers to himself as a character within his own self-invention and as a practitioner of a tradition of Afro-Cuban storytelling. In this sense these moments are in synch with Barnet's ethnographic project while they also constitute meta-discursive moments that posit the composition of the text as a theme in itself.

In his description of the African oral tradition in Cuba Montejo affirms that storytelling was the particular function of community elders whose stories were a mix of history, folk knowledge, and magic that one ignored at one's own risk: "They talked about the land, African animals and apparitions. They didn't go in for gossip and quarrels, and anyone who lied to them was severely punished. You had to be quiet and respectful to get along with the elders. A boy once made fun of one elder, and he said, 'Listen, when the sun sets you'll be on your way too'" (Barnet 1968, 160). Montejo also states that the storytelling tradition was also rooted in the logic of entertainment, aesthetics, and performative competence: "What the old men enjoyed most was telling jokes and stories. They told stories all the time, morning, noon and night, they were at it constantly" (161). The parallels between these elders and Montejo is implicit and points to Montejo as a practitioner of an oral tradition with its own formal and thematic history. This connection is made clearer when Montejo explicitly inserts himself in the story as a character who is being instructed in the art of oral narrative: "One day she called me and said, 'You're a good, quiet man, I'm going to tell you something,' and she began telling me all sorts of African tales" (162). In this way Barnet's attempt to create a new kind of cultural artifact for a "new man" runs into a more ancient and entrenched narrative tradition with its own internal laws. Yet it is as much an overdetermined collaboration as it is a collision. In this sense it would be inaccurate to reduce this negotiation to an interplay of textual modalities inasmuch as the text maintains a unique relation to the real in terms of the autobiographical referent and in terms of its self-referencing as the product of a specific historical process of collaboration.

In *Rachel's Song* the negotiation between Barnet's intention and the relative autonomy of his informant's narrative practice is complicated by a number of thematic and formal factors. First, in terms of the informant's social and narrative agency, the gender, class, race, and occupation of the text's namesake, Rachel, significantly differentiate her from the direct, active, and sympathetic role Montejo plays in the construction of his life in *The Autobiography*. . . . In contrast to the epic value of the social transformation from slave to maroon to independence fighter that constitutes the significant chronology of Montejo's life, the recollection of the apolitical and socially ambiguous career of the chorus girl Rachel does not offer an analogous progression. Whereas Montejo's life seemingly unfolds on the broad stage of Cuban history, Rachel's life is literally encased in the dimly lit space of the cabaret stage and the boudoir of early twentieth-century Havana (Sklodowska 1977, 117). Within both of these spaces Rachel negotiates a precarious path of independence and dependency on male desire and support. Working as a cabaret actress who attracts wealthy admirers, she performs for men in both her professional and intimate life in a manner that blurs the distinction between the two spheres.

The social milieu of Rachel's world consists of envious co-performers, shady impresarios, ostracized homosexuals, corrupt patrons, and pimps. For Barnet it is a fascinating underworld of decaying glamour and social corruption that corresponds to a historical period of enervating underdevelopment: "The rides around town in Macorina's bishop-purple convertible, red headed, obese, conversations in Prado cafes, the almost decrepit stage hands, survivors of the shipwreck of the Alhambra; filters of Cuba's social and political life, the moving presence of the tattered curtains, all contributed a great deal to inspire this book" (Barnet 1979, 15). As the low-born daughter of poor European immigrants who led a marginal life as an actress, kept woman, and madam of a brothel, Rachel is cast as an outsider in terms of her gender and class. Her status as a working woman within the entertainment industry, as well as her retrograde racist opinions, influences the nature of the collaboration between Barnet and his female subject. In contrast to the broad solidarity and shared agency Barnet experienced with Montejo in the earlier project, Barnet felt the need to distance himself from the at once attractive and "*lumpen*" account of Rachel's life. At one level Barnet assumes that the marginal content and counter-revolutionary attitude of Rachel's narration will in effect speak for themselves. Nevertheless, at the formal level, Barnet juxtaposes Rachel's narrative with other voices from her contemporaries and the popular press to contextualize and correct her version of her own life as well as her interpretation of national history. Barnet has stated that this bricolage of points of view was a deliberate attempt to challenge the reader to actively assume a position concerning Rachel's life and thoughts: "In *Rachel* I have used a counterpoint technique or a Rashomon system. It's as if we were looking through a concave lens, so that the public can identify itself in the book and take a stand either for or against Rachel" (7).

As Elzbieta Sklodowska has demonstrated, the technique of narrative counterpoint and the unequal relations of power between an educated anthropologist and an enfeebled dance-hall performer conspire to undermine female consciousness and narrative self-definition in the text (1977, 118). Yet despite the overwhelming evidence of Sklodowska's assertion, I propose that contrary to the ethnographic and formal intent of the text, the content and performance of Rachel's voice resists absolute enclosure within a one-dimensional design. Whereas the corrective technique of conflicting narrative accounts is particularly effective in challenging the racist worldview and sketchy understanding of broader social and political history within Rachel's speech, it is, however, less effective in undoing her construction of her life as a glamorous tale of the social mobility and defiant marginality of a working-class woman in the face of moral censure, hostile rivals, and limited resources.

The shadow of a circumscribed yet significant narrative autonomy in Rachel's recollections can be attributed to the overlapping and interaction of her story with other established popular narrative forms of female agency, representation, and consumption. I am referring to the language, imagery, and tone that approximate that of popular film and music, the picaresque, melodrama, and the tabloid press. These popular forms champion a life guided by guile, hope, passion, beauty, artifice, and vanity, all of which are grounded in an economic necessity specific to women's social roles and options. Within traditional male socialist criticism this popular female narrative tradition has been negatively categorized as narcissist alienation and what Barnet terms as a "language of underdevelopment" (1979, 9). Yet at the same time it is possible to recognize the relationship between these popular forms and poverty without reducing them to some notion of false consciousness or delusion.

In terms of narrative history the more modern discourses of female survival and glamorous upward mobility associated with popular film in *Rachel's Song* are rooted in the older literary tradition of picaresque hunger and a particular female response along the lines of Defoe's *Moll Flanders*. Rachel points to the specific female response to poverty in the justification of her conventionally illicit actions: "It was the need for food. In those years there was hunger in Cuba. And many political whirlwinds" (Barnet 1991, 52). Thus we can see how Rachel's aestheticized melodramatic self-definition is tied to underdevelopment, but not necessarily in the restricted sense described by Barnet. At the outset of the text Rachel establishes a model of willful self-invention informed by the cinematic conventions of glamour: "The loveliest thing is to look back with happiness. To see yourself like in a movie, as a playful child, just sitting straight up in an armchair, playing the piano . . . I love that" (13). Thus Rachel chooses a gilded filter for her own life story derived in part from the glossy images and uplifting plots of popular film. Accordingly, Rachel recalls the episodes of her life through the cinematic narrative language of flashback, a storytelling modality that reflexively recreates her struggle to achieve stardom against all odds.

In effect, the emplotment of her life as constructed by Rachel, namely, that of a working-class girl who achieves financial stability, fame, and glamour through a career in show business, simultaneously corresponds to the development of the culture industry in the early twentieth century and to the meta-cinematic storyline of popular film, which sentimentally fictionalized the triumphs and tragedies of working-class women in their struggle to become stars of the stage in such American films as *Rolled Stockings* (1927), *Our Dancing Daughters* (1928), *Hollywood Revue of 1929* (1929), *Dance Fools Dance* (1931), *42nd Street* (1933), *Dancing Lady* (1933), *Footlight Parade* (1933), *The Gold Diggers of 1933* (1933), *Dames* (1934), and countless others. Ironically, the stars of many of these films were recreating on screen their own rise from humble and/or immigrant origins to professional and international prominence through stage performance in much the same way Rachel chronicles her own cabaret career.

The storyline of these Hollywood musicals about chorus-girl life originated in the silent era and thus enjoyed transnational popularity. In Latin

America, the influential Mexican film industry gave a culturally recognizable "Latin" face to this plotline, which dealt with the interrelated social realities of urban migration, an emerging entertainment industry, and changing female roles in the public and private spheres. During the early 1930s, the Mexican cabaret performer Celia Montalván made Spanish-language films in Hollywood, starred in a French film under the direction of Jean Renoir, and, in her only Mexican Film, *Club Verde*, portrayed a perfidious vedette during the Revolution (Monsiváis, 35). A handful of these early Mexican stars, such as Dolores del Río and Lupe Vélez, crossed over into the early Hollywood period of chorus-girl and flapper films and instilled what American directors construed as an exotic Latin sensuality into the genre. Thus in such del Río vehicles as *High Steppers* (1926), *Flying Down to Río* (1933), and *Wonder Bar* (1934), and such Vélez features as *Lady of the Pavements* (1929), *Mr. Broadway* (1933), and *Hot Pepper* (1933), Latin American actresses played a foundational role in the tradition of reflexive films about the lives of the stars. Moreover, as Vélez's career underscores, this reflexivity was not merely a narrative ploy; it often had its roots in personal survival and the marginal area between dance-hall performance and the sex industry. When Lupe portrayed hellacious yet glamorous vedettes, she could well have been calling on her own reputed past as a burlesque performer, stripper, and prostitute (Conner, 3). In this sense the continuity between the life of the film star Vélez and Rachel's narrative of self-invention is real.

Ambiguities in the author-function of *Rachel's Song* underline the connection between Rachel's textual (and theatrical) performance and the history of the self-reflexive representation of the chorus girl on stage and in film. As Sklodowska has signaled, disputes over theories of authorship have occupied a central position in the debates between cultural studies, postcolonial studies, and responses to traveling theory on the Other (2002, 206). In this context I propose that questioning the concept/reality of the author is directly linked to the textual and social context of *Rachel's Song* on the one hand, and the collaborative, innovative, and heterogeneous production of knowledge at the root of testimonial narrative on the other. The very constitution of the "real life" character of Rachel from various chorus girls interviewed by Barnet speaks to the link between the illusory storyline of stardom and the social realities of women in the early twentieth-century entertainment industry. In the preliminary note to the original Spanish-language version of the text, Barnet describes Rachel in the following manner: "She is somewhat of a synthesis of all the show girls who appeared at the defunct Alhambra Theater, a true gauge of the country's social and political activities" (iii). Whether this pretextual disclaimer weakens or strengthens Rachel's relationship to the social is open to debate. While this admission does pose a challenge to a traditional notion of an author or personhood, the "real life" and textual character of Rachel does not passively slip into the realm of fiction. In the social instance her origins in ethnographic interviews remain and the trans-individual nature of her experience in the theater is representative and constitutive of a broader constituency of her female contemporaries in Cuban cabaret. Rachel's claim to the social is thus greater as a synthesis of witnesses than as an individual testimony. As in the chorus-girl films she consciously invokes, Rachel is a character and an actress literally performing her real culture industry role as a showgirl. Moreover, Barnet's note is external to the text as such and is not necessarily reflected in the function of Rachel as speaking subject or in the response of the surrounding voices that refer to her as a unified subject. To discredit her social and textual agency is to limit oneself to what Barnet says he intended to do in the work. Just what Barnet intends is unclear and often at odds with other meanings generated by the text.

In 1989, Cuban novelist and film director Enrique Piñeda Barnet recognized the historical and narrative connection between Rachel's life and its textual reconfiguration as film in his adaptation of *Rachel's Song* into a feature film. The result, *La Bella del Alhambra*, is a musical that draws on the tradition of meta-cinematic films about the struggles of the stars of stage and screen within the specific context of the Cuban music hall of the 1920s and 1930s. In this way the happy blur through which Rachel recalls her past is linked to concrete historical openings and professional independence that existed in the emerging entertainment industry of the early twentieth century. No matter how few and illusory such cases may have in fact been, this storyline nevertheless became a source of vicarious solidarity and luxurious hope for the female consumers of film, the tabloid press, and sundry film magazines. Rachel herself addresses the real and lived value of just such an illusion when she states: "Never have I wanted to take away anyone's fantasy. Because a fantasy realized is worth anything" (Barnet 1991, 15). The rosy filmic lens through which she views her life does not correspond to the emplotment envisioned by an elite male anthropologist such as Barnet, who states: "I prefer informants who see the sad, the rough side of life, the suffering side, to those who cover things with a mask of fatuous happiness" (Barnet 1979, 18).

Yet Rachel's emplotment is no less arbitrary than his. On the contrary, we must underscore that it is her life she is narrating and therefore she selects an interpretive model that is structurally intrinsic to the autobiographical construction of memory and socially related to the material conditions of her life. In this sense her dreamy filmic model has a historical affinity with her identity as a working-class woman and a stage actress.

The autonomy from the bonds of family and marriage that female performers such as Rachel found resulted in their moral censure by traditional authorities within the church, "decent society," and the state. We see such censure played out in *Rachel's Song*. Rachel recalls and rejects the religious criticism of "those censors of public evil, dressed in black, those catholic ladies" (Barnet 1991, 15). She decries the ruinous gossip of her neighbors: "'That gal, what's she up to, she's going to ruin the man, soaks him dry, the poor wife' and things like that, because there's no enemy worse than a neighbor. There isn't!" (75). And she abhors the political censure of the Machado dictatorship: "The Machado regime made that theater into hell, like the whole country" (117). The illicit display of the body, suggestive lyrics, and political satire emanating from a young woman provoked members of the social and political elite. Thus the social, moral, and political censure Rachel experienced because of her stage career and its tenuous relationship to prostitution is present in many of the defining moments of her private and professional life. Important, these incidents are recalled in the images and language of popular theater, melodrama, and film. One such incident is the story of her tragic love affair with Eusebio, a young member of the Cuban elite whose mother vehemently opposed the relationship between a showgirl of ill repute and the scion of a powerful family. The story of star-crossed lovers separated by social class and family intervention ends in abortion, Eusebio's suicide, and tabloid scandal. Rachel herself comments on the melodramatic and social familiarity of this narrative: "Between the two of us it was a Greek tragedy" (22).

In terms of Rachel's narrative stance and consciousness, it is important to underline that she does not internalize or accept the social and moral reproach leveled at her throughout her life. We can see that she was aware that conventional social and moral authorities disapproved of her career and cast her as a moral if not legal outlaw. Her defiance of this censure points to a conscious motivation at the root of her will to speak. As Anthony Zahareas has stated, this desire for vindication often lies at the root of first-person narratives of marginality in both fiction and nonfiction: "The narration in first-person of one's own misdeeds usually provides, at least implicitly, the very reason for bothering to write, 'to tell it like it is.' Thus the one factor that these and other female narrators share is the presentation of a situation in which each narrator, in her own particular way, is extremely conscious" (133).

It is in this light that we should consider Rachel's affirmative recollection of the social underworld in which she moved. One such example is her memory of the grand public funeral for the pimp Yarini. Rachel brushes aside any indignation at Yarini's profession and praises him as an example of lost manhood: "He was something impossible. The type of male who didn't give himself easily. You had to beg him, tell him stories, give him winks. What an age! Today you don't see that. Today love is a vulgarity. Sign a paper, have a pack of kids, like little rabbits, a mother-in-law . . . Horrors!" (Barnet 1991, 36). Rachel's humorous comparison of the mysterious glamour of illicit love in the past with the perfunctory drudgery of marriage in the present makes visible that she is aware of the negative interpretation her life receives in the moment of her narration. Thus Rachel is conscious that the marginal life she has led on and off stage conflicts with conventional definitions of womanhood in both bourgeois and socialist societies. Rachel does not express remorse whatsoever for not fulfilling the different yet intersecting prescribed roles of wife, mother, and worker in the past and present. On the contrary, Rachel openly embraces her picaresque life of performance, marginality, and survival in all of its aspects. When her gay mentor and confidant Adolfo attempts to euphemize her life as a cabaret actress and prostitute as that of a pure artist, Rachel confides to the listener/reader: "I was not only a, how to say it, budding actress, but a social barometer, what my country remembers me for" (42). Like the unapologetic and notorious stars of stage and screen such as Mae West in Hollywood and María Félix throughout the Spanish-speaking world, Rachel realizes that her fame and power are indelibly linked to a certain degree of scandal and moral censure.

Thus despite moments of apparent weakness in the chronology and accuracy of Rachel's narration, her affirmative self-concept of her marginality is a contradictory mixture of occlusion and honesty. Rachel's consciousness of her position outside of past and present societal norms for women informs her narrative strategy of vindication at the same time that it requires a degree of truth. As Anthony Zahareas indicates, this desire to outline and defend a marginal life renders the first-person narrator both extremely credible and very unreliable: "In this sense, a social offender's narrative of past experiences is, historically speaking, the most authentic available but, given the historical context of presenting oneself before others, it is also, ironically, *the least* reliable" (150).

Clearly, the unreliability of Rachel's account is underscored by Barnet's formal conceit of juxtaposing her narration with other voices and witnesses from the period. Barnet's intent of countering Rachel's voice is most effective when he opposes her racist appraisal of the rebellion of blacks in 1912 who fought for the implementation of reforms made after independence and to guarantee their access to representation through the Independent Party of Colored People, which the government had made illegal. Rachel attributes the uprising to rum, banditry, and, ironically, black racism. It is quite significant, then, that Barnet corrects Rachel's interpretation of the racial tension of 1912 through the voice of Esteban Montejo, a testimonial informant of epic and sympathetic national stature:

> They called us savages, little patent leather boys and a thousand other insults, but since when in this country has a program more democratic than that of the Independents of Color been brought before the people than when we fought tooth and nail to the benefit for us Negroes, who had come out of the war barefooted and in rags, hungry, just like Quintín Banderas, who was killed a year later while he was gathering water from the well in his house? Let's not hear any more cheap talk. The moment of justice has arrived. (Barnet 1968, 58)

In this way Barnet pits the socially and morally legitimate account of a heroic male informant against that of a marginal and ideologically flawed female witness. In this instance, Barnet employs the technique of counterpoint to provoke a negative reaction in the reader toward Rachel's racist social history and testimony.

Thus in large measure, Sklodowska's argument that Barnet's use of counterpoint "dispossesses" Rachel of her voice is corroborated (1977, 114). Nevertheless, although the technique of countering Rachel's point of view is particularly effective in parts of the text where she addresses broader questions of social and national scope, the voices of contemporary performers, scriptwriters, managers, pimps, and tabloid reporters who comment on her career and character do not carry the same critical weight as the corrective critique offered by Esteban Montejo. Unlike Montejo, these voices come from the same marginal demimonde as Rachel, and as such they do not differ qualitatively from her in terms of sympathy or reliability. Rather, these opposing accounts can be viewed as co-characters in the filmic narration of petty infighting, professional envy, and melodrama of both Rachel's narration and the historical tradition of films about egomaniacal directors and back-stabbing stars who climb the ladder of success on the bodies of their less successful and bitter co-stars and supporting staff.

In yet another level of meaningful reflexivity between memory, narration, and film, Enrique Piñeda Barnet's film adaptation of *Rachel's Song, La Bella del Alhambra*, underscores this traditional cinematic storyline when he includes a bodice-ripping and hair-pulling fight between Rachel and La Mexicana, the aging diva whom Rachel progressively upstages. This scene is itself a historical fetish of the masculine gaze of film, conventionally known as the "catfight," which depicts the narrative unreliability of Rachel's peers in show business. This conflict between performers and narrators is a feature of the emplotment of stardom, a time-worn storyline that opposes an unrepentant actress and woman against her detractors much in the way Paco Ignacio Taibo I has characterized the reflexively scandalous and triumphant career of María Félix: "Writers, directors, dressmakers, conspire against her and she beats them all " (13, my translation). In this way we observe that Barnet's formal intent of counterpoint is realized at the larger level of a historiographical narrative concerned with national sociopolitical questions while it perhaps unwittingly mobilizes other popular cultural forms and narratives in its consideration of female identity and agency.

Moreover, the narrative strategy of counterpoint employed by Barnet underscores that the social and editorial composition of *Rachel's Song* is as much a subject of the text as the informant's life story. The constant shifting of voice and interpretation brings to the surface the constructed nature of memory and narrative in the text as well as in the fields of the human and social sciences. In this way the formal non-transparency of narration in *Rachel's Song* not only serves to contextualize and critique the capricious and unenlightened aspects of Rachel's account, but also points to the difficulty in telling the "truth" from a single totalizing point of view. Although Barnet compiles these conflicting voices in his guise as unifying editor, the fragmented worldview presented by these accounts is not reconciled through the conscious design of his written text. This non-transparency of the text is at once an overt meta-commentary on the production of the text itself and a broader observation on reflexivity in social narrative. The reflexivity of the text is at once found within the counterpoint narration and the social relations of collaboration and difference among the witnesses on the one hand and between these witnesses and Barnet on the other. In this way the reflexivity of the method of narration in *Rachel's Song* transcends textual closure and grounds the text in the socially constitutive process of its production.

Despite the significant erasure of her voice in the face of critically opposing counter-narratives and witnesses, Rachel is, in the ultimate instance, the "star of the show" in her memory and in the written text. Although her control and competence concerning the autobiographical site of enunciation is contested, the overwhelming force of her self-affirmation cannot be completely dissolved: "In such and such a play there was a queen, she was me. There was an aristocratic lady, she was me. There was a sexy lady, she was me and so, me, me, me (Barnet 1991, 82). Once again we see how Rachel consciously links her stardom to female roles of power, glamour, and promiscuity while she directly ridicules traditional social and stage roles as housewife and folkloric woman. In this way the degree to which Rachel's relative narrative autonomy, as a real testimonial subject and/or character of her own narration, is subsumed by Barnet's design is in question. Nor should we be simplistic in our consideration of Barnet's ethnographic and aesthetic intention in *Rachel's Song*. As his commentary on the work suggests, his thematic design for the text is somewhat less clear than the epic progression toward an egalitarian society he envisioned in *The Autobiography of a Runaway Slave*. Barnet has said that he was not so much interested in Rachel's egocentric, racist, and limited point of view, but rather that his focus lay in demonstrating how her less enlightened opinions were contradicted by other more comprehensive and perceptive insights. The result, for Barnet, is a woman and/or character developmentally stunted by the social conditions of the Cuban belle époque, an impasse he termed as "the frustrations of a life in a specific social context" (Barnet 1979, 21). Yet as we have seen, Rachel herself does not characterize her life as frustrated, but as triumphant. Curiously, Barnet's examination of the psychology of a Cuban flapper does not challenge this self-concept. Whereas Barnet's editing and counterpoint is very effective at revealing the limits of Rachel as a social historian and arbiter of social and racial conflict, his editorial intervention does not overcome the autobiographical and popular narrative of a socially climbing cabaret actress.

In his prologue to the text, Barnet anticipates this tension between his control over the direction of the text and the degree of autonomy exercised by his informant in the telling of her story: "*Rachel's Song* speaks of the person, of her life, as she told it to me and as I told it to her" (Barnet 1979, iii). For Barnet, the text was a collaborative retelling of a recalled life that gave him the final word. But a close reading of the text gives one the impression that Rachel is not listening to Barnet's interpretation. Borrowing from Daniel W. Lehman's reading of the power struggle at the center of Freud's clinical writings in his interpretive construction of the life of his patient Dora, I propose that Rachel, like Dora, escapes the confinement of the scientist's methodology and retains partial control in the generation of meaning in the invention of her life story (Lehman, 62). In this way Rachel resists becoming a character in the version of her life that Barnet creates for her. She ends her tale in the same dreamy and defiant tone with which she reviewed her career and private life: "You have to dream. If this life is everything, if it all ends at that, holy shit. I, at least, don't accept that" (Barnet 1991, 121). Significantly, she speaks unapologetically of her income as a brothel owner and expresses her desire to be beautifully attired for her funeral. Rachel is to the end the rough-and-tumble survivor and glamorous star of her own filmic imagination. She remains conscious, despite eccentric talk of extraterrestrial travel, of the relationship between the public nature of her fame and ill repute and the gaze of the audience. In the final moments of the text she requests that a mirror be placed on her chest in death: "That's my dream. I'd like my public to remember me just as I was" (125). It is yet another image of her life projected as a self-invented spectacle. It is a spectacle rooted in the material and social circumstances of her life as a low-born immigrant woman and stage performer.

The ultimate meaning of this memory as spectacle is not confined to a one-dimensional emplotment. Rather, the negotiated tension between Barnet's intention and Rachel's reflexive self-invention as a character within an established popular storyline underlines Barnet's interest and respect for his informants, whether they come from the epic stage of Cuba's transition from slave-holding colony to independent republic or from the cabaret stage of the Cuban dance hall of the early twentieth century. As we have seen, the specific formal strategies of univocal and counterpoint narration correspond to different social spheres, agents, and collaborative relationships. Yet despite the differences in narrative voice and collaborative tone in *The Autobiography of a Runaway Slave* and *Rachel's Song*, the underlying reflexivity and narrative excess of the informant's practice in both texts break with conventional expectations of transparency in nonfiction, documentary, and testimonial narrative. In his rejection of naturalized, transparent, or reified ethnographic narrative, Barnet indicates the social, contrived, and ultimately uncontrollable process of his and all narrative projects to represent social, political, and cultural history with absolute totality. The puritans have yet to sort out their stripes.

8

Off-Beat Migrancies

Musical Displacements in the Hispanic Caribbean

YOLANDA MARTÍNEZ SAN MIGUEL

Introduction

> Migration is a one-way trip. There is no "home" to go back to.
> Stuart Hall, "Minimal Selves"

Stuart Hall's work on the reconfiguration of identities in a global and migra-tory age frames my analysis of contemporary Hispanic Caribbean music. If, as has been frequently argued, the "beginnings" of Caribbean identity can be described as the creation of a culture composed by a multiplicity of trans-planted subjectivities—that is, Europeans and African slaves—I would like to rethink the notions of globalization and migration as they are applied to the most recent massive displacements taking place in Cuba, the Dominican Republic, and Puerto Rico.[1] Since displacement has been a constant element in the configuration of a cultural identity in the Caribbean (see Glissant, 139; and Benítez Rojo, xxxii), what does it mean to be a transnational, translocal, and global subject during the second half of the twentieth century and the opening decade of the twenty-first? What are the limits and problems posed by current studies on those fluid identities, and what meaning do the "local" and the "regional" have in a context of constant movement and exchange of cultural referents and experiences? Is it possible to talk about a common experience of displacement and globalization in the Caribbean? If it is true that, as Hall suggests, migration completely alters notions of "home" and be-longing, what happens when cultural productions from migrant populations are appropriated by the members of a community that has not been displaced from its place of origin? Do culture and identity travel freely in this global age? We should consider some of Caren Kaplan's theoretical concerns in her essay "Transporting the Subject: Technologies of Mobility and Location in an Era of Globalization":

> The trajectory of knowledge and idea as they "begin and end some-where" speaks to a vital aspect of subject formation in modernity. In the current moment in metropolitan life, when so much of the world appears to be linked by global media, transnational finance and culture, and other manifestations of contemporary mobility and speed, how do we understand "points of origin" and the "where" of "somewhere"? How do we theorize the locatedness of travel in an era of globalization? (C. Kaplan, 33)

These and other questions have been central to my study of Hispanic Caribbean migrations during the second half of the twentieth century. I am specifically interested in analyzing the ways in which insular cultures experi-ence the massive emigration and immigration of other Caribbean popula-tions. Thus, I have researched the cultural impact of Cuban and Dominican immigration to Puerto Rico, as well as the local identity reconfigurations in Cuba and the Dominican Republic that incorporate massive emigration as a key element in their definitions of contemporary Cubanness and Domini-canness.[2]

In this essay, however, I would like to focus on "local" readings of musi-cal productions within the Hispanic Caribbean. I am particularly inter-ested in exploring the limits of cultural exchange, and I have chosen music as one of the artistic expressions that travels most easily between different countries and social contexts. If music is a key element in the definition of Caribbean identity (Carpentier, 2–8), and if it is one of the cultural mani-festations that so evidently illustrates the pulses of a transnational market, what are some of the local interpretations—within and between commu-nities—that it makes possible? What happens when meaning is produced in more than one location, and when the "original meaning" of a cultural production is as important as the "multiple meanings" that same artifact or piece acquires in the different contexts of its circulation, reproduction, and re-enactment?

I examine here two different examples of a similar experience. First, I ana-lyze the local readings of merengue hits in Puerto Rico and then I use Carlos

Varela's and Pablo Milanés's songs to illustrate different interpretations of the experience of "exile" by Cuban audiences living on the island and in the United States. I contend that these two cases illustrate how this music circulates in a transnational circuit even as it is also resignified by each one of its local performances. Therefore this essay concludes with some reconsideration of the limits of globalization and migration as central categories in current definitions of Caribbeanness in order to incorporate this reflection into a broader debate on identity discourses.

Rereadings of the Merengue in Puerto Rico

> The past is not waiting for us back there to recoup our identities against. It is always retold, rediscovered, reinvented. It has to be narrativized. We go to our own pasts through history, through memory, through desire, not as a literal fact.
>
> Stuart Hall, "Old and New Identities, Old and New Ethnicities"

Let us consider popular music as one of the defining elements of the Dominican cultural enclaves in Puerto Rico. I consider merengue to be one of the most popular symbols of Dominican national and transnational identity, particularly at the international level (see Duany 1994, Austerlitz, and Batista Matos). The origins of the merengue already illustrate the translocal character of Caribbean cultures through its combination of Hispanic and Afro-Caribbean influences. This musical genre combines elements of the Hispanic *danza*, the Haitian *mereng*, and various African rhythms (Austerlitz, 2–4). Almost all of the texts are composed of *coplas, décimas,* or *seguidillas*, with a refrain performed by a chorus, while the music is produced with a combination of various Creole instruments, such as the *tres* or *cuatro* guitars, the accordion, the *charrasca* (metalscraper) or *güira*, the *tambora* (double-headed drum), and the bass, among others (Gradente, 12: 180; Duany 1994, 67). Rhythmic improvisation, polymetry, and the use of the debate or counterpoint are part of the African influences in this musical genre. Examples dating back to the nineteenth century were divided in three parts: a *paseo,* the main part of the merengue (*coplas*), and the *jaleo*. In the twentieth century the genre retained mostly the *coplas* and the *estribillo* (refrain) or *jaleo*, where the voice of the singer and the chorus alternate (Ramón y Rivera 5: 536). The tempo of the music tends to be fast and changes very little throughout the piece, so there is not a very dynamic contrast between the *coplas* and the *jaleo* (Ramón y Rivera, 5: 536).

Merengue has served as one of the points of contact between Dominicans and Puerto Ricans, to the degree that it has enjoyed widespread popularity in both communities in the last three decades. For Dominican migrants, merengue allows a contact with their country of origin, since it is a cultural practice that links and transports them to the country they left behind. At the same time, music offers displaced Dominicans a way of incorporating themselves into their new social space, thanks to the widespread popularity this musical genre has enjoyed in Puerto Rico, New York City, and around the world. For Puerto Ricans, the merengue is part of a repertoire of dance music whose rhythm is contagious, and which enjoys the support of an ample local and international audience. This is why there has been a gesture of "appropriation" of this musical genre by Puerto Rican performers (including numerous women) who have incorporated into this cheerful rhythm a great variety of ballads and popular songs, increasing the thematic and linguistic register of the merengue in Puerto Rico and the United States (see Duany 1998). This process peaked in 1995, when there were more groups performing merengue than salsa in Puerto Rico (Batista Matos, 188).

Paul Austerlitz dates the origins of this musical genre to 1844, basing his conclusions on Pedro Henríquez Ureña's theory that the first known merengue was a text that satirized a soldier who had deserted from the army during the War of Independence (Austerlitz, 1; also Batista Matos, 201). For this reason, this musical genre has been linked from the outset to the proclamation of the republic and the emergence of an official national discourse. Of all the local variations of the merengue, the one that has attained the status of national symbol is the version from El Cibao, a rural zone with the highest proportion of descendants of European immigrants (Austerlitz, 5).[3] The merengue from El Cibao became more prominent within the national discourse during the resistance to the American invasion of 1916. However, it was not until 1930, when it was adopted by the Trujillo regime to mobilize his political campaign, that the merengue consolidated its place as the representative rhythm of Dominicanness (Austerlitz, 52; Pacini Hernández, 35; Batista Matos, 36). At that moment, popular music became part of state discourse, abandoning the subversive role that had characterized many of the compositions dating from the proclamation of the republic and the American invasion. Since 1960 this musical genre has been transnationalized as a result of the massive emigration of Dominicans.

The study of the merengue poses a crucial question: to whom does this cultural practice belong? Given its mobility and commercialization, one could say that it belongs to more than one national tradition (see Austerlitz, and Aparicio). For the purpose of this essay, however, I analyze a sample of merengues that became "greatest hits" in Puerto Rico in the 1980s and 1990s, musical pieces that became favorites, not only on radio and television—where the strategies of marketing reflect and promote the public's "tastes"—but also in parties and private music collections that better represent the process of direct interpellation between the consuming public and the cultural product. I refer to widespread commercial hits such as "El africano" and "El venao" that made possible a direct interaction between Dominican artists and a Puerto Rican audience, an interaction quite different from the contacts encouraged by ethnic jokes, literature, "graffiti," and documentaries. Although some of these songs are not necessarily the work of Dominican composers, it is interesting to examine how they are incorporated into the Puerto Rican cultural arena as Dominican products through Dominican performers. My selection of five songs—"El barbarazo" (Ramón Díaz, Wilfrido Vargas); "El africano" (Calixto Ochoa, Wilfrido Vargas); "Los limones" (Conjunto Quisqueya); "Ojalá que llueva café en el campo" (Juan Luis Guerra, 440), and "El venao" (Cuco Valoy, Ramón Orlando)—responds mostly to the identification of songs widely acknowledged as musical hits in Puerto Rico during the last three decades of the twentieth century.

In 1976, "El barbarazo" (The barbarian) became the first merengue to reach best-selling status in Latin America (Batista Matos, 93). The song consists of a man's voice complaining because his wife has betrayed him: "Qué barbaridad / lo que tú me has hecho / entregarte a otro / en mi propio lecho." (What an outrage / you have done to me / to give yourself to another / in my own bed.)[4] Although this is a sensitive topic in Puerto Rican culture, the lyrics highlight some of the humorous aspects of this experience, precisely through the way in which infidelity is described: "Ese barbarazo / acabó con tó . . . / Qué descaro tuvo / el que fue tu amante / usar mi mujer / y mi desodorante. / Se afeitó la barba / en mi tocador / me dañó la radio / y la televisor." (That barbarian / used everything . . . / What insolence / that of your lover / to use my wife / and my deodorant / He shaved his beard / at my dresser / broke my radio / and my TV.)

The song's refrain gives a humoristic turn to the experience of infidelity (a popular theme in the merengue and *bachata*) through the way in which the song alternates stanzas that lament the loss of his wife—"Qué barbaridad /

qué tremenda herida / después de haber sido / tan grande en tu vida" (What an outrage / what a terrible wound / after having been / so important in your life)—with stanzas that identify his wife with domestic objects and comforts that the husband has lost as a result of her extramarital relationship. This alternation between lamenting the lover's betrayal and bewailing the loss of material possessions lightens the treatment of the theme of adultery through a parody of patriarchal discourse. The combination of the song's parodical register with the fact that the enunciating voice is a Dominican "macho" in disgrace is precisely what explains the great acceptance of this song by a Puerto Rican audience. This thematic register, so close to the wounding farce, makes the image of the male cuckold more palatable to a mass audience. Finally, the woman's lover is identified with a barbarian capable of outrageous acts, not only through his sexual relationship with another man's wife, but also through his uncontrolled use of the objects and food of a household not his own. The text associates the male lover with barbarity since he challenges both matrimony and good manners.

The social and cultural limits explored by "El africano" (The African) are different. This song was originally a Colombian *vallenato*, but Vargas adapts it to the rhythm of a merengue and makes it popular while living in Puerto Rico (Batista Matos, 96). The piece opens with a male voice speaking an unintelligible language. This opening could be a pejorative allusion to Haitian Creole or an exotic representation of the black subject as foreign, that is, literally an African. The brief lyrics of the song are thus:

> La Negrita llamaba a su madre / y así le decía: / Mami, el negro está rabioso, / quiere pelear conmigo, / decíselo a mi papa . . . / Mami, yo me acuesto tranquila, / me arropo 'e pie a cabeza / y el negro me destapa . . . / Mami, ¿qué será lo que quiere el negro? (The young black girl called to her mother: / Mami, the black guy is furious, / He wants to argue with me, / Tell daddy about it . . . / Mami, I go to bed quietly, / Cover myself from head to toe / And the black guy uncovers me . . . / Mami, what does the black guy want?)

These lyrics are repeated some four times and alternate with the intervention of the presumed "Negro," who emits a series of guttural sounds that the listener cannot understand. The young woman who asks for her mother's advice seems fearful of the evidently sexual advances of this man whom no one understands but everyone fears. The song explores, then, the racial and social limits of blackness and foreignness and confronts the audience with its own distancing from the black race and African culture, but again from a humorous perspective. The representation of "El africano" as a subject excluded from the Spanish language shared by performer and audience underscores the significance of race as an inassimilable element, represented as untranslatable and even unacceptable in the context of enunciation of this song, as in "El barbarazo." The text also dramatizes the stereotype of the black man as hypersexual and aggressive, identifying blackness with savagery and lack of "civilization." The song is transferred to a new context of signification through its local broadcasting in the form of a merengue. In the insular Caribbean, this song alludes to the shared prejudice of lighter-skinned Dominicans and Puerto Rican against blacks. However, this piece gains another level of reading when it is performed for a Puerto Rican public, since, if for Dominicans this song is seen as referring to a Haitian, for Puerto Ricans the "africano" is most likely a Dominican. This is a good example of how the transnational circulation of a cultural artifact cannot escape the regional readings that its narratives can mobilize. Local and global elements overlap in this case to produce regional interpretations.

On the other hand, "Los limones" (The lemons) returns to the use of the sexual referent to resignify an everyday narrative: a man on the market square meets a woman he finds attractive and helps her buy and taste some lemons.[5] In this case we have a Dominican song that became popular in Puerto Rico, the center of operations for Conjunto Quisqueya, the group that recorded it. The lyrics of the song play with the double-entendre—another common element in Dominican merengue—to produce a narrative that alludes surreptitiously to the prohibited sexual encounter between the two characters who hold a dialogue in the song:

> Estando yo en el Mercado / comprando limones, / pasó Mercedes, señores / la de Don Simón. / De pronto ella me dijo / "no me mires tanto / en vez de eso mejor / dame ese limón." / Ella me dijo, "muchacho, / ven párteme uno, / párteme uno, caramba, que quiero chupar." / Pónmelo ahí, que lo vo'a partir, / que lo vo'a partir . . . Saque esa mano / de ahí / que saque esa mano / de ahí. (As I was in the market buying lemons, gentlemen, / Mercedes, the wife of Don Simón, / passed by. / Suddenly she said to me, / "Don't stare at me like that; / instead, and better yet / give me that lemon." / She said to me, "My boy, / come and split it open for me, split it open for me, 'caramba,' / that I want to suck." /

Put it there, that I am going to split it open, / I am going to slice it ... / Take your hand / out of there / take your hand / out of there.)

The lemon is a metaphor for the female sexual organ, particularly when the man speaks to Mercedes about that fruit's positive characteristics: "Ya que esa fruta la gente / siempre la disfruta, / porque es tan buena, caramba, / que sirve pa' tó." (This fruit is always / enjoyed by all / since it is so good, oh my / that it's useful for everything.) It is through this dialogue that the song represents the couple's shared sexual desire and explores the social limits that regulate the physical contact between the potential lovers. In the representation of sexual desire, this song echoes a similar image of the Dominican as that depicted in "El barbarazo" and "El africano." The Dominican occupies a liminal space in the Puerto Rican imaginary, and his otherness is portrayed through excessive sexuality and inappropriate behavior that flaunt social norms of decency and intelligibility. Finally, Dominican masculinity is represented either as a failed performance of the patriarchal role—in the cases of husbands betrayed by their wives—or as a direct threat to the institution of marriage through the implication of an extramarital affair with Mercedes in "Los limones."

Like other songs written by Juan Luis Guerra, "Ojalá que llueva café ..." marks a significant change in the type of merengue Puerto Ricans listened to in the 1990s.[6] This song was included in Guerra's third CD, which carries the same title, and led the band 440 to international recognition (Batista Matos, 155). This singer/songwriter preserves the formal structure of the merengue—using an introductory *paseo*, a main section, and the final *jaleo*—but contrary to the predominant tradition, his songs blend well-crafted verses with social criticism (Duany 1994, 76). His music sets aside the register of the sexual double-entendre in order to incorporate the poetry of Pablo Neruda and Federico García Lorca, jazz, songs from the *nueva trova*, and the lyrical styles of Joan Manuel Serrat, Mercedes Sosa, and Facundo Cabral, as well as part of the oral tradition of the Dominican Republic (Duany 1994, 76; and Batista Matos, 149). The Puerto Rican middle class, finding that his lyrics presented love and economic misery from a more literary and poetic perspective, greeted his music with great enthusiasm. For many Guerra is "the Rubén Blades of merengue," since he is seen as having transformed merengue into a genre with higher aesthetic value.

"Ojalá que llueva café ..." develops in the space of desire, projecting an ideal society in the Dominican Republic. The song describes a productive agrarian society that signals the end of the country's social and economic misery:

Ojalá que llueva café en el campo / que caiga un aguacero de yuca y té, / del cielo una jarina de queso blanco / Y al sur una montaña de berro y miel / . . . / Ojalá el otoño en vez de hojas secas / vista mi cosecha piti salé. / Sembra' una llanura de batata y fresas / Ojalá que llueva café. (Let's hope it rains coffee in the countryside / a heavy shower of cassava and tea / a light rain of white cheese from the sky / And in the south a mountain of / watercress and honey / . . . / Let's hope that fall instead of dry leaves / dresses my harvest *piti salé* / planting the soil with sweet potato and strawberries / Let's hope it rains coffee.)[7]

The singer's voice alternates with a chorus of children's voices that celebrates a paradise of fruits that fall, literally, from heaven, as in a biblical setting. The song identifies the chorus of children singing happily with the desire for a space of abundance and richness invoked by the phrase "Let's hope" repeated over and over again by the voice of the performer who projects through his lyrics a space that does not yet exist. This musicalized "desire" culminates in the creation of a collectivity that receives and celebrates the gifts of the paradisiacal space: "Pa' que to's los niños canten en el campo: / Ojalá que llueva café en el campo. / Pa' que en La Romana oigan este canto: / Ojalá que llueva café en el campo." (So that all the children sing in the countryside: / Let's hope it rains coffee in the countryside. / So that in La Romana they can hear this song: / Let's hope it rains coffee in the countryside.") The song thus invokes the collectivity and the national geography of the Dominican Republic, both to be reinvigorated by the metaphoric rain of agricultural products (Duany 1994, 78).

In Puerto Rico, the success of this song by El Grupo 440 seemed to be a response more to the change in linguistic and thematic register than to the specifically Dominican referents in the lyrics. I disagree with those cultural critics who see the success of the merengue in Puerto Rico as a democratic incorporation of Dominican artistic manifestations into the cultural field, or those who idealize dancing as an experience of solidarity and sympathy. The fact is that the merengue burst into the Puerto Rican cultural space without necessarily increasing people's knowledge of the neighboring island.[8] The debut of this recording in 1989 marked a significant broadening of the Puerto Rican public that enjoys, collects, and consumes merengue music, especially that of El Grupo 440 and other artists who rearranged songs originally popular as ballads and which began to be translated (or *fusiladas*) more intensely into merengue rhythm in the 1990s. This consumption, however, is still marked by practices of exclusion, which explains the need to reclaim the genre by Puerto Rican artists who then validate the merengue as their own musical practice.

Finally, it is necessary to comment on one of the most massive hits in Puerto Rico's musical market, "El venao," which marked a return to the most popular linguistic register of the merengue and became one of the most played songs during the 1995 Christmas season.[9] "El venao" presents a situation similar to that of "El barbarazo": a man laments the possible infidelity of his wife. However, the man's suspicions are based on rumors and gossip about the behavior of his mate, who is living away from him:

> Y cuando fui a Puerto Rico / estabas llena de chichones / No hagas caso, son jugadas / son rumores, son rumores. / Vitincito a ti te vio / cantando en los callejones / No hagas caso, son jugadas / son rumores, son rumores. / Coro: Y que no me digan en la esquina / el venao, el venao / eso a mí me mortifica / el venao, el venao, / que no me voceen en la esquina / el venao, el venao, / que eso a mí me mortifica. (And when I went to Puerto Rico / you were covered with bruises / Don't pay attention, they're tricks / They are rumors, they are rumors. / Vitincito saw you / singing in the alleys / Don't pay attention, they're tricks / They are rumors, they are rumors. / Chorus: And let them not call me on the corners / the deer, the deer / it really mortifies me / the deer, the deer / don't let them yell at me at the corner / the deer, the deer / it really mortifies me. . . .)

The first thing that draws our attention is that the song represents a long-distance love affair, and this narrative is developed through the rumors about the wife's possible infidelity that torment the husband. The *venao* (stag) is an important metaphor of the song, since its horns were used as a direct reference to the cuckolded husband. In fact, one of the reasons for the song's popularity was that people would dance the chorus of the song mimicking a pair of imaginary horns to make fun of the husband's marital crisis. However, it is also significant that the song alludes specifically to Puerto Rico and New York City, two common spaces in the migratory circuit that articulates the Dominican community. Thus the text evokes a geographic imaginary where the experience of displacement of the Dominican community is already implicit.

This song also alludes to several important boundaries in the love relationship: it repeats the theme of infidelity and points to gossip and social reputation as key places in the public representation of masculinity and the institution of marriage. We are not dealing here with a case such as that of "El barbarazo"—in which the man himself narrates his experience when faced with his partner's infidelity—but with a song that addresses the suspicions that emerge from what others have seen and said about the wife who lives elsewhere. The lyrics, then, refer directly to a reconfiguration of the family nucleus and of the networks of social communication that is the result of a displacement that has disarticulated the traditional patterns of the Dominican family and society. Here gossip functions as a means of re-establishing and maintaining the coherence of a community that has apparently been diluted by the migratory process. In its implicit reference to the diaspora, this song explores an additional function of rumor, since the reconnection between the members of the dispersed family goes beyond what Gayatri Spivak describes as the repressive and/or liberating roles of gossip within a stable and enclosed community (Spivak, 23).

Why do these songs enjoy such overwhelming popularity in Puerto Rico? What themes or perspectives operate in them, making them so easy to consume by a hegemonic sector of that same Puerto Rican society that rejects the presence of the Dominican immigrant on the island? Or is it just that culture is more porous than the social environment in its acceptance of these "foreign" cultural manifestations? How can we relate the locality invoked by the genre of the merengue with the transnationality constructed by the commercialization of a musical genre that is listened to, for example, in New York City, Venezuela, San Juan, and the Dominican Republic? This intense commercialization of the merengue has lead to a significant growth in the number of Puerto Rican performers who have begun to appropriate the genre and to incorporate into it other types of narrative and styles to produce a music that is simultaneously Dominican, Puerto Rican, and Caribbean. The merengue thus becomes a malleable frontier in which Dominicans as well as Puerto Ricans negotiate the redefinition of common imaginaries and disparate identities, with their insistence on distancing themselves from the traditional content and/or structure of the genre to maintain their cultural and/or ethnic specificity. It is precisely at the center of that dialogue—complicated and problematic—where a new debate that transcends the limits of identity emerges to question the ways in which a national subjectivity inscribed in a global community defines itself. Let us review some of the key coordinates of these "local" interpretations of merengue.

The first thing we notice is that there are songs that explore the vulnerability of a Dominican identity located literally in the sexual, racial, and moral margins of contemporary Puerto Rican society. If it is indeed true that the merengue is accepted enthusiastically on the island as a catchy danceable rhythm, this type of cultural production continues to be linked with a Dominican subject that produces, performs, and is represented in many of the narratives elaborated in these songs. That is why, when a song speaks of "marital infidelity," of the savageness of the black or African man, or of unbridled sexual desire, these disparaging representations of the male subject are associated with the same Dominican identity rejected through other social and public cultural expressions such as the ethnic joke or "graffiti." The audience takes in these rather sensitive themes with a certain humor and distance, since the *bárbaro*, *cornudo* (cuckold), or even the *negro* is not necessarily a Puerto Rican but a Dominican. In the same way, humor contributes to the location of the subject-that-enunciates in a liminal place between the acceptable and the unacceptable, so that laughter opens a space in which to incorporate themes and identities that in any other way would remain excluded from more official registers of cultural representation. Therefore, I propose the hypothesis that the success of this type of merengue—excluding the case of Juan Luis Guerra and his band 440, and the pieces produced by local artists who reclaim merengue as a *boricua* cultural production—responds also to the acceptance of a type of linguistic and cultural register that is understood to be typical of Dominican culture. After the problematic arrival of merengue in Puerto Rico, it is not surprising to see the growing popularity of those songs whose humorous content and vulgarity become simultaneously part of the negative stereotype that Puerto Ricans have of Dominicans. It is a case, therefore, of a "success" that traces anew the problematic space occupied by Dominicans in Puerto Rican society, as if that acceptance of the cultural manifestation of the immigrant required at the same time the denigration of the subject that produces and enunciates the music.

However, "Ojalá que llueva café . . . ," like other hits by 440, falls outside the register occupied by the other songs discussed here. Its acceptance and popularization correspond, to a certain degree, to a rejection of the "vulgar" register that characterizes many of the other songs. The music of 440 interpellates a middle-class audience that expresses a preference for the "*buen* merengue" or a "refined" merengue that addresses topics related to social criticism or which deploys a more lyrical or literary register when referring to love or the attraction between two people. Likewise, many of these songs deal with social criticism or the representation of economic hardship, topics that could be appealing to a Puerto Rican public that can feel solidarity toward a migrant Dominican community given that community's marginal position in the economy of its country of origin, or in the local Puerto Rican economy. However, as we have already seen, often this massive consumption of merengue does not imply a better understanding of Dominican culture or history, as clearly evidenced in the decontextualized appropriation by Puerto Rican performers of this musical genre in order to rearrange or remix well-known ballads. Consequently, this success can be linked to the formulation of a cultural frontier that attempts to separate the Dominican manifestations—supposed to be of inferior quality because of their *vulgaridad*—from the massive reception by a Puerto Rican public that understands that it has a more refined taste than the average Dominican (Dávila, 238).

We have seen how a cultural artifact receives very local interpretations as it displaces itself between audiences belonging to two different Caribbean countries. Puerto Ricans appropriate the Dominican merengue and add to this genre a very specific reading that manifests the vital boundaries between these two national groups coexisting on the island of Puerto Rico and in the city of New York. However, this same experience is replicated in the circulation and appropriation of cultural materials within one single national community dispersed as a result of massive exile or migration. I would like, then, to use the Cuban situation as my second example, to discuss a series of songs in which the experience of exile is re-signified according to the location of the audience that interprets a particular performance. The central question in the following section is this: How is exile read inside the island of Cuba in contrast to the way it is understood by the Cuban community living in the United States?

Rereadings of Exile Inside and Outside Cuba

Behind all those years
behind the fear and the pain
we live in longing for something
something that never came back.

Behind those who did not leave
Behind those who are no longer here
There is a family photograph
in which we cry at the end.

Carlos Varela, "Foto de familia"

Carlos Varela's song, "Foto de familia" (Family photo, 1994), explores one of the predominant gestures in the representation of exile in the island of Cuba: the reticence and melancholy when faced with a definite separation from loved ones due to the intransigence of the migration policies of Cuba and the United States.[10] Exile is a recurrent theme in Varela's songs, but his texts explore the limits of the visibility of Cuban emigrants in the island through the use of silence, re-signification, and negativity. In the case of the song I just quoted, the photograph occupies the place of the absent ones, and the gaze reads the irreparable and useless gaps that are the result of emigration:

Tratando de mirar por el ojo de la aguja / tratando de vivir / dentro de una misma burbuja / solos, solos. / Detrás de toda la nostalgia, / de la mentira y la traición, / detrás de toda la distancia, / detrás de la separación, / detrás de todos los gobiernos, / de las fronteras y la religión / hay una foto de familia / hay una foto de los dos. / Detrás de todos esos años, / detrás del miedo y el dolor / vivimos añorando algo, / y descubrimos con desilusión / que no sirvió de nada, de nada, de nada / que no sirvió de nada, de nada, de nada, / que no sirvió de nada, de nada, de nada, / que no sirvió de nada o casi nada / que no es lo mismo, pero es igual. (Attempting to look through the eye of the needle / trying to live / inside the same soap bubble / alone, alone. / Behind all the nostalgia, / the lies and betrayal / behind all the distance, / behind the separation, / behind all the governments, / all the frontiers and religion, / there is a family photo / there is a photo of us both. / Behind all those years, / behind the fear and the pain / we live longing for something, / and we discover with disappointment / that it was useless, useless, useless, / that it was useless, useless, useless, / that it was useless, useless, useless, / that it was useless, or almost useless / which is not the same, but it makes / no difference.)

The first stanza, used as the epigraph to this part of my essay, signals that peculiar state of the melancholic subject that attempts to recover something lost. The lyrics refer to something not concretized as a specific object, but always invoked as a semantic excess. As Freud points out, the loss of melancholy is sometimes elusive since we "don't quite manage to discern with precision what was lost . . . [although sometimes we] know who was lost, but not what we lost in them" (Freud, 243). The photographs evoked by Varela serve as a visual pretext that marks the redundancy of a loss that is painful because it cannot be verbalized. The lyric voice speaks on behalf of an "us"—perhaps a reference to the nation as a whole—who keep family photos that still include those who are absent. The paradoxical visual presence of the absent ones made possible by the photograph initiates the melancholic gesture that does not end and is not contained throughout the song. At the same time, the chorus refers to the difficulty of transit, or even of the conceptualization of one space by another—"attempting to look / through the eye of a needle"—and the condition of isolation—"trying to live / within the same soap bubble"—in which those who have remained in Cuba live. Between immobility and isolation, the gesture of nostalgia becomes an infinite cycle, a solitary exercise.

The second stanza can be read as a reticent story of the Cuban migration experience. This narrative is constructed through words such as "nostalgia," "lies," "betrayal," "separation," "governments," "frontiers," and "religion." The nouns invoke two semantic fields, one linked to official discourse on migration—"lie," "betrayal," "governments," and "frontiers"—and the other to the intimate and personal experience of these displacements— "nostalgia," "distance," "separation," and "religion"—and concludes with the reunification of both communities and discourses when what is "behind" both narratives is revealed: "there is a family photo / there is a photo of us both." The song suggests, then, the articulation of an unuttered experience that implies the possibility of reunification and the existence of a series of hidden plots invoked by the constant repetition of the word *detrás* (behind). It is precisely in the reverse of these family images that Varela rescues and brings together the perspectives of those who have left and those who have remained; the redundancy of feeling produced by the photo becomes an alternative discourse joining those present and absent. The song articulates a search that fulfills itself in that photographic image of the family that remains despite the passage of time and the obstacles to a reunion.

The song's last stanza underscores the melancholic quality that enlivens this narrative—the lyrics speak of an "open wound" that cannot be healed

(Freud 250), claiming that what is to be found behind absence and longing is total or almost total uselessness: "and we discover with disappointment / . . . that it was useless or almost useless / which is not the same but it makes no difference." The song presents two parallel gestures. On the one hand, it substitutes the repetition of the word *detrás*, which is an invitation to a search, with the reiteration of the word *nada* (useless, although in Spanish it literally means "nothing"), which cancels out the possibility of a harmonious and satisfactory resolution of the pain brought by absence and longing. But, on the other hand, it opens the text to the polysemy of the intertext through its allusion to Silvio Rodríguez's "Pequeña serenata diurna" (Brief daytime serenade, 1974):

> Vivo en un país libre / cual solamente puede ser libre / en esta tierra, en este instante / y soy feliz porque soy gigante. / Amo a una mujer clara / que amo y me ama / *sin pedir nada /—o casi nada, / que no es lo mismo / pero es igual.* (I live in a free country / that can only be free / in this land, at this instant / and I'm happy because I'm a giant. / I love a straightforward woman / I love her and she loves me / *who asks for nothing /—or almost nothing / which is not the same thing / but makes no difference* [my emphasis].)

As it is readily apparent, Rodríguez's song conveys a completely different set of emotions than those suggested by Varela's lyrics. The voice in this song enumerates all the things that make him a satisfied and joyful individual. The song is a celebration of the fullness of life created by the satisfaction of the basic necessities: freedom, love, creativity, and vitality. However, Varela proposes a reinterpretation of Rodríguez's song from the perspective of exile, a reading in which the unnamable ache of the absent one predominates. The phrase borrowed—"o casi nada, que no es lo mismo, pero es igual"—invokes two paradoxical or inverse meanings. In Rodríguez's lyrics we are dealing with the expression of the fullness of life, here identified with the perfection of a love for a woman who makes no claims on him. In Varela's song, the same phrase points to emptiness and uselessness: the many years of searching for a hidden meaning behind the incomplete photographs, the separations, and the pain brought about by distance culminates in absolute, or almost absolute futility, which is not exactly the same, but has the same devastating effect on the enunciating subject. Therefore, Varela's text is constructed over the implicit negation of Rodríguez's narrative. At the same time, because of his intertextual engagement with Rodríguez's song, Varela's work rejects closure; the last stanza opens itself to that incomplete dialogue evoked by the very fragmented and tenuous quotation of Rodríguez's lyrics. Those who listen to Varela's song can recognize Rodríguez's verses, so that it could be said that this ending avails itself of a very intense but fluid resonance of the original text. In this way, the structure of the work itself resists the healing of its wounds in order to leave them open, exposed, without the promise of a future restoration. Openness, negativity, and polysemy are the simultaneous strategies with which Varela's song ends.

In Varela's "Círculo de tiza" (Chalk circle), included in *Monedas al aire* (1992), the reticence to address the topic of exile is supplemented by a play of semantic contiguities:

> Pintaba el asfalto con trozos de cal / en mi sucio barrio de la Habana oscura. / "Cuba declara la guerra en contra de"[11] / Mi religión no es de cruz, ni de altar, / pero voy a rezar porque un día / se acabe la niebla. / Yo perdí un amigo en la guerra de África / y a otro que escapando se lo tragó el mar. / "Cuba declara la guerra en contra de" / Mi religión no es de cruz, ni de altar, / pero voy a rezar porque un día / se acabe la niebla. (I painted the asphalt with pieces of chalk / in my dirty barrio of dark Havana. / "Cuba declares war on . . ." / My religion is not of the cross or the altar / but I will pray that one day / the fog will lift. / I lost a friend in the African war / and another was swallowed by the sea when he tried to escape. / "Cuba declares war on . . ." / My religion is not of the cross or the altar / but I will pray that one day / the fog will lift.)

In this song, Varela sets in motion a series of images of Cuba at the end of the twentieth century, while incorporating direct and indirect allusions to that massive migration that divided, literally, the contours of a community that thought of itself as an organic whole. The voice that enunciates in "Círculo de tiza" places itself in a Havana where uncertainty and hopelessness reign. In the midst of that city of losses, the singing voice identifies the soldier who leaves for Angola, sent there by the government, with the *balsero*, or the rafter who drowns in the sea.[12] Soldier and rafter occupy, discursively and semantically, the same place in the imaginary that invokes them: that of the loss of two friends who sally forth to struggle for what they believe in. The hero and the illegal emigrant are identified in the text, thus questioning the value of legality and illegality when they are both opposed to a very human sense of justice. In this way, for the subject who speaks there is no difference between one Cuban and another, between one loved one and another, between the two sides of that imaginary frontier that separates the Cuban community in the 1990s.

In this part of the song the reaction of the public becomes very significant, since it supplements the reticence of Varela's text. The version included in *Monedas al aire* is from a live concert at the Teatro Carlos Marx in Havana in 1991. When the lyric voice refers to the loss of the friend in Africa the audience grows excited, but when he mentions the Cuban who dies at sea the public applauds and cheers. The inclusion of the rafters, although reticent, interpellates intensely the Cuban audience, which proceeds to *dar voz* (give voice) to that discursive vacuum signaled by the singer, and which makes explicit the audience's identification and acceptance of that gesture of inclusion proposed in the lyrics. Since "Círculo de tiza" is the only live recording included in this CD, the desire to include this very local dimension of the musical "performance," usually lost in the studio recording of a song, becomes more significant. In this case, the participation of the public in Havana goes on to become part of the text that is disseminated through the CD, so that the context of the localized reception—insular in this case—underscores, albeit partially, the theme of exile in Cuba.

The rest of the song alludes to the isolation and crisis in which Cuba lives because of its delicate political impasse, so the singing voice has lost all hope for a political and individual future. Cuba's lonely struggle against the world traps it into a Brechtian *círculo de tiza* (chalk circle) that serves as a wall simultaneously unbreachable and fragile. As in Brecht's dramatic piece, *The Caucasian Chalk Circle* (1944), the chalk establishes an ephemeral and vulnerable limit that redefines the organic sense of belonging between the insular and the global. The island seems to occupy a liminal space paradoxically close to the rest of the countries of the world from which it lives so distanced. In this alternation between an unknown exterior and an interior in crisis, the emigrant is presented as a point of contact between both spaces who does not manage to insert himself altogether in the narrative the song proposes.

In contrast, in Varela's "La política no cabe en la azucarera" in *Como los peces* (1994), exile is re-signified through the transfer from the semantic contiguity explored in "Círculo de tiza" to the loss of the spatial contiguity proposed here:

Un amigo se compró un Chevrolet del 59, / no le quiso cambiar algunas piezas y ahora no se mueve, no. / Hace mucho calor en la vieja Habana / la gente espera algo pero aquí no pasa nada. / Un tipo gritó sálvese quien pueda, / cada día que pasa sube más la marea. / Felipito se fue a los Estados Unidos, / allí pasa frío y aquí estaba aburrido, / en la mesa del domingo hay dos sillas vacías / están a noventa millas de la mía... / pero entiéndelo bróder, tómalo como quieras, / la política no cabe en la azucarera. (A friend bought a 1959 Chevrolet, / he didn't want to replace some parts, and now it doesn't run, no. / It's very hot in old Havana / people are waiting but nothing is happening here. / A guy cried out "every man for himself," / the tide gets higher every day. / Felipito left for the United States, / there he is cold, but here he was bored, / there are two empty chairs at the Sunday table / they are ninety miles away from mine... / but understand this, brother, take it anyways you like, / politics don't fill / fit in the sugar bowl.)

This song begins with the very metaphor of displacement, since the Revolution is identified with a '59 Chevrolet that has stopped working because of a lack of parts. The lyrics also narrate the vicissitudes of the Cubans (in the island and the United States) as a result of the embargo, the economic crises, and the difficulties of emigration. In this context, migration is narrated from a highly critical gaze that favors neither the one who stays nor the one who leaves. The song refers to exile openly through the character of Felipito, but it also refers implicitly to illegal departures through the phrase: "the tide gets higher every day." At the same time, the irony of the splitting of a community that privileges nearness stands out, since the absent ones are a mere ninety miles away from the families that remain in Cuba. That unnamable thing that is emigration reappears in Varela's songs as an element that is very close to the contemporary Cuban identities who walk the streets of Havana, especially in that metaphor of the empty chairs at the "mesa del domingo."

Varela again uses Silvio Rodríguez's lyrics as an intertext by quoting two lines of "Llover sobre mojado" (1982): "Un obrero me ve, me llama artista / y muy noblemente me suma a su estatura." (A laborer sees me, calls me an artist / and very nobly adds me to his stature.) Rodríguez's song, included in *Tríptico* (1984), a collection of three CDs celebrating the first twenty-five years of the Cuban revolution, narrates one day in the life of an artist who describes his daily vicissitudes and tedium, and his desire for a historical moment more significant than the stagnant routine that is either a dissolution of a glorious past or a repetition of the same accomplishments and losses. In this case Varela's reference to Rodríguez is used to develop further the description of the boredom and emptiness of day-to-day Havana. Nonetheless, in Rodríguez's song the worker's recognition of the singing subject as an artist legitimates his position as a "visionary" of the collective's will or needs, while in Varela's song the same worker is now "trafficking with tourist money / he has four children and life is quite hard," so the worker himself becomes the focus, as another very specific example of the economic crisis faced by Cubans living on the island. Thus, Varela expands and updates Rodríguez's song by transforming this individual narrative into a collage of the many ways in which the embargo, exile, and the *Período especial* (Special period) have transformed the daily lives of the Cuban community.

This song retakes the counterpoint between what is legal and what is fair of "Círculo de tiza." It opposes legal practices—the 1959 constitution of the revolutionary state, the practice of "apartheid" in South Africa, and the U.S. economic embargo—to illegal practices such as the traffic in dollars at the beginning of the 1990s, prostitution, and emigration itself, in order to question which of them is more detrimental to Cubans. More than characterizing the communist state negatively or describing the marvels of life outside Havana, this voice represents the extreme deprivations that result from certain state practices, local as well as international. The problem is not, therefore, that metaphoric '59 Chevrolet, but the lack of new parts to maintain the revolutionary promise. At the same time, the benefits offered by the national state are not necessarily consonant with the needs of a community of citizens dedicated to a series of unnamable practices that in the song become part of their everyday lives. Politics become, then, a very limited practice, to the degree in which they cannot minimize the difficulties of a community that begins to imagine itself through certain continuity with its absences. And in that context the "unsayable" in official Cuban discourse becomes a very eloquent part of reality, manifested beyond words or the limited recognition of what is legal.

I would like to end this section with a discussion of Pablo Milanés' "Éxodo,"[13] one of the most explicit songs on Cuban exile:

¿Dónde están? / quiero verlos para saber / que soy humano / que vivo y siento por mis hermanos / y ellos por mí. / Donde estén, un saludo para / decir que los he amado / y he deseado más de una vez / verlos conmigo aquí . . . morir. (Where are they? / I want to see them, to know / that I am human / that I live and feel for my brothers / and they for me. / Wherever they are, a greeting to / say that I have loved them / and I have desired more than once / to see them here with me. . . . to die.

The theme is striking, because Milanés, a well-known figure in official Cuban music, expresses his desire to reunite the two sides of this national community. This song uses a classical topic, alluding to the opening words of a well-known motif of medieval Latin poetry: *Ubi sunt qui ante nos fuerunt?* However, Milanés turns the question to the longing produced by massive Cuban emigration among those who stayed on the island.

The first stanza of the song is a set of open questions about the uncertain location of beloved ones who are not physically close to the lyric voice. The second stanza plays with the use of proper names and deictics: "Pepe allí," "Juan acá," "Hildita allí," and "Vladimir y Tomás allá." The song proposes, then, a counterpoint between five Cubans and their absence and dispersion after the migratory experience. Milanés plays with the ambiguity of the lyrics, as the absence of these Cubans could be explained as a result of their literal "exodus" or their symbolic departure after death (see Martínez-San Miguel, chapter 4). The third stanza is the longest one, and in it the lyrical voice proposes a reappropriation of the five characters. This act of repossession of the absent ones is crucial, since each one of the characters is defined in terms of a profession that specifies his or her contribution to the Cuban nation and its culture before exile. Milanés includes all kinds of fields in this enumeration of professions: manual labor, scientific knowledge, financial expertise, and artistic sensibility. This gesture of the song is crucial, as Pepe, Juan, Hildita, Vladimir, and Tomás are remembered in the past tense, when they were present in the island, and before the dispersion represented in the second stanza. At the same time, the lyrical voice occupies a central role in the narrative, and the archetypical Cubans also represent the community and diversity of ideas within a single nation.

The fourth stanza transcends once more the individual referents to expose the need to re-establish a connection between the two sides of the Cuban community. Thus, the last stanza of the song breaks the silence between and about exiles, and the lyrical voice sends a greeting to all Cuban émigrés and expresses his wish of having them close and able to come back to the *patria* (fatherland) to die with the other Cubans who never left the island.

I would like to focus on the song's last stanza, as it uses a common motif in nationalistic discourse, and especially in the representations of the *patria* by exiles. A paradigmatic example of this discourse is included in the *Anuario de familias cubanas* of 1982, a yearbook published in Puerto Rico by the Cuban community in exile. In its preface, the yearbook is defined thus: "Every issue of the *Cuban Family Yearbooks* is a living piece of Cuba abroad, an affirmation of an indestructible Cubanness and a promise that we will return, dead or alive, . . . when Cuba is once again free and happy" (Posada, 5). Milanés revisits this discourse of homecoming by inviting Cuban exiles to return to die with the other Cubans who remained in the island. Therefore, this song acknowledges the other side of the "longing" for the *patria* as a desire to reunite with the absent ones to die together in their motherland. According to Milanés, this song "proposes to be a bridge of love between them and us" and in his text he mentions "people of different trades and professions who left Cuba and who, as he says, he hopes that they can come back to their country before they die" (*El Nuevo Herald* 2001).

Some members of the Cuban American community read this ending as an invitation to return to the island to validate their identities by sharing and surviving the difficulties of the *Período especial* in revolutionary Cuba. Achy Obejas, in contrast, proposes a very different reading of this song in relation to Milanés' artistic work in revolutionary Cuba, and in the specific context of the concert in which he included "Éxodo": "At his Chicago show, Milanés' adherence to Cuba's variable official policies came into bold relief with two of the evening's most well-received songs: the beautiful 'Éxodo,' a stunning call to reconciliation among Cubans from his new album, and the show finishing 'Amo esta isla,' a 20–year-old anthem that essentially condemned the wave of exiles who left the island in the 1980 Mariel boatlift" (Obejas). Once again, each side of the Cuban community reads the same song from a very different perspective, so that Milanés's inclusive gesture does not escape the effects of locality and contextualization, even within what could be considered a single national community. My contention is that both the insular and the diasporic interpretations become "original meanings" for this song, as they reflect what Haraway would define as a "situated knowledge" (Haraway, 188). In a certain way, to propose the same idea using some Cuban referents, this variable reception of Milanés's song illustrates what Cristina García denominates as "The Languages Lost" in *Dreaming in Cuban*, or what Jesús Díaz sees as the inevitable *Lejanía* between the Cubans living in the island and the Cubans living in exile (García; Díaz).

Conclusion: The Limits of Globalization

> When the movements of the margins are so profoundly threatened by the global forces of postmodernity, they can themselves retreat into their own exclusivist and defensive enclaves. And at that point, local ethnicities become as dangerous as national ones. We have seen that happen: the refusal of modernity, which takes the form of a return, a rediscovery of identity which constitutes a form of fundamentalism.
>
> Stuart Hall, "The Local and the Global: Globalization and Ethnicity"

I would like to conclude this essay by using Stuart Hall's correlation between the "global forces or postmodernity" and the "local ethnicities" that retreat to "their own exclusivist and defensive enclaves." In his reflection on globalization and ethnicity, Hall invites us to reconsider the political dimensions of the transnationalization of subjects, economies, and forms of identity. Culture, as a crucial space of symbolical imagination, does not escape the effects of these contradictory pulses of globalization: "But now the velocity of communication and of transnational movements, not to mention economic migration, is producing culturally and ethnically hybrid spaces where the self is always multiply located. This is one of the central contradictions of cosmopolitanism today, since modern constitutionalism was never designed to deal with the problem of cultural diversity" (Rodowick, 15).

The examples I have just discussed illustrate the ways in which cultural artifacts become sites of multiple signification and interpretation between members of a Hispanic Caribbean community sharing social spaces as a result of displacements and diasporas, or even between the members of the same national community that has become diversified after a prolonged and massive experience of relocation or exile. Translocation in the Caribbean produces an international culture that is both global and very regional. In his recent book *The Puerto Rican Nation on the Move*, Jorge Duany poses some similar questions focusing on massive emigration and circular migration in the case of Puerto Rico. In his introduction, Duany even proposes the existence of more than one Puerto Rican literature, based on crucial differences in central motives and strategies, and in the diversity in terms of place and context of production: "I would add that Puerto Rican literature on the Island has been primarily concerned with the assertion of a national identity, whereas Nuyorican literature is better understood as part of an ethnic minority canon, especially developed by African American and Chicano writers in the United States.... While both literatures provide significant insights into the Puerto Rican experience, they do so from different standpoints" (Duany 2002, 31). Thus, locality is still crucial in the production of cultural diversity. In the songs I have just analyzed, nonetheless, we have what could be considered as "fixed" linguistic and musical texts that attain different meanings according to their place of reception. Therefore, these musical pieces illustrate the clear limits to a "universal" or "global" public sphere: "As geography becomes less and less a barrier to communication and movement, cultures become more exposed to one another. This produces an intricate field of tensions, creolizing not only identity but also communities, whose active reception and use of global media become novel and unpredictable" (Rodowick, 16).

Many of these songs also remind us of the dynamic nature of language as a site for any identity. If in the case of Puerto Rican literature, English, Spanish, and Spanglish collide and interact in the production of a set of identities that are not the same but not completely different, in the Dominican and Cuban songs I have just discussed, we have a set of texts written in the same official language—Spanish—but we can still sense the characteristic "heteroglossia" of these brief verbal productions.[14] If an identity is constituted in language by the common referents that make communication and understanding possible, a diversity of referents within and between national and ethnic communities illustrates the negotiated nature of all individual and collective ontologies. Diaspora, migration, and exile just add another dimension to the polysemous nature of linguistic communication:

Language travels; its dense destiny lies in the promise of metaphor, in the supplement that transforms the inherited into the unexpected. If language provides us with a home, it simultaneously precedes and exceeds us; it sends us on our way. And if language is our home, it is also a home for others. This thought opens up an unstable perspective.... To insist, against the odds, that language is our home and at the same time a translated space, a site of transit and difference, is to suggest that a diverse sense of identity might begin to be acknowledged here. (Chambers, 30)

Music, as an instance of some of these traveling languages in the global-ized context of the Hispanic Caribbean, becomes a very clear example of those unequally shared spaces of knowledge and negotiation. These songs propose a narrative that is re-signified by the location and context of its reception, and their messages can follow or be transformed by the multiple members of a broad and fluid audience. Harmony, noise, and silence coex-ist in these musical compositions, and as such they sometimes function as those offbeat tunes that can become uncannily familiar in their disso-nance.

Notes

I would like to thank Catherine N. Duckett and Mark A. Trautman for reading and revising a previous version of this paper.

1. The Cuban migration began in 1959, after the triumph of the Cuban Revolution. A significant portion of that migrant population came to Puerto Rico, New York, and Miami between 1965 and 1973 and became active in the primary sector of the economy. The massive displacement of Dominicans began in 1961, after the assassination of Tru-jillo, but intensified in 1965 when civil war erupted and was followed, in that same year, by the U.S. occupation. Finally, the Puerto Rican migration began around 1945 as a by-product of the Popular Democratic Party's modernization project that used the U.S. labor market to alleviate the island's high levels of unemployment. See Portes and Grosfoguel.

2. This essay includes revisions of portions of chapters 3 and 4 of my book *Caribe Two Ways*. My thanks to Ediciones Callejón for permission to publish these sections of the book in translation.

3. There is, however, a long debate about the Hispanic, African, and Caribbean ori-gins of the merengue. For more details, see Batista Matos, especially the chapter titled "¿Qué sabe del merengue?"

4. The first two songs I analyze are performed by Wilfrido Vargas, originally a trum-pet player and the leader of Los Beduinos, a group that gained fame during the 1970s and 1980s. Vargas continued Johnny Ventura's tendency to speed up merengue's rhythm and introduced the use of the synthesizer, possibly as a result of Haitian influence. Var-gas lived in Puerto Rico for some time, beginning in 1977. For a more detailed discus-sion, see Austerlitz, 92–96; and Batista Matos, 85–96. The author of "El africano" is the Colombian Calixto Ochoa. In Puerto Rico the song was received as a Dominican product, since Vargas popularized it.

5. This song became a hit for Conjunto Quisqueya, a group of musicians living in Puerto Rico that gained great popularity during the Christmas seasons of the second half of the 1970s. "Los limones" became a musical hit in 1975, but given its highly sexual content the Dominican government prohibited its broadcast on either radio or televi-sion. For more details, see Batista Matos, 104.

6. Guerra was born in Santo Domingo and emerged as a prominent figure in Dominican merengue in the 1980s and 1990s. He studied at the Conservatorio Dominicano and the Berklee College of Music in Boston. In 1990 he received international recognition for his CD *Bachata rosa,* and in 1992 he won a U.S. Grammy Award. For more details, see Pacini Hernández, 185–217; Austerlitz, 106–7; and Batista Matos, 149–68.

7. I am following very closely Jorge Duany's translation of this song, which is included in his article "Ethnicity, Identity, and Music" (Duany 1994).

8. I discussed these songs with my students at the University of Puerto Rico (1995–97), and one of the points of greatest contention was that many of those who consumed the music of 440 did not understand the song's Dominican referents or had not even realized the tragic representation of the theme of migration in "Visa para un sueño." This is not limited to Puerto Rico, since my Hispanic students at U.S. universities also complain that I have "spoiled the song for them" because once they realize that this piece is about a failed migratory attempt they cannot dance to this tune without thinking about the difficulties of migration. Thus it is important to understanding the breach between cultural consumption and social and political incorporation, acceptance, or visibility.

9. The performer is Ramón Orlando, son of Cuco Valoy, founder of the orchestra La Tribu. Orlando gained considerable success as an arranger and composer, and "El venao" was the greatest hit of Los Cantantes, an orchestra he founded in 1995. His work has been recognized by the Asociación de Cronistas de Arte, which awarded him the 1992 Casandra prize. See Batista Matos, 248–50.

10. Carlos Varela is a singer/songwriter born in Havana in 1963. He started writing songs at the end of the 1970s, and his texts incorporate elements of Cuba's *nueva trova,* rock in Spanish, and pop music. His songs became well known in the 1980s, as part of the *novísima trova* (very new song). His work includes the following productions: *Nubes (2000), Jalisco Park* (1989), *Monedas al aire* (1992), *Como los peces* (1994), and *Siete* (2003), among others.

11. This phrase refers to a Cuban children's game called "Stop o Juegos de Guerra." See Varela's web page, http://www.cantautores.org/varela.htm.

12. Varela refers here to the troops sent by Cuba to Angola to fight for that country's independence from Portugal in 1975 by supporting the Popular Movement for the Liberation of Angola (MPLA) against the National Union for the Total Independence of Angola (UNITA) during the civil war preceding and following the declaration of independence. In Varela's song these soldiers who were sent as representatives of the Cuban government's support for Angola against South Africa and U.S. interests are equaled to the rafters who try to leave the country illegally.

13. "Éxodo" is included in Pablo Milanés's most recent CD, *Los días de Gloria* (2000). Milanés was born in Bayamo, Cuba in 1943. He began his career in the 1960s and is one of the most important singers and composers of "filin," a "hyperromantic evolution of bolero that surged at the end of the 40s." Milanés and Silvio Rodríguez are the major figures of the *nueva trova* in Cuba.

14. Bakhtin acknowledges the dynamic and mutable nature of language:

At any given moment of its evolution, language is stratified not only into linguistic dialects in the strict sense of the word (according to formal linguistic markers, especially phonetic), but also—and for us this is the essential point—into languages that are socio-ideological: languages of social groups, "professional" and "generic" languages, languages of generations and so forth.... Alongside the centripetal forces, the centrifugal forces of language carry on their uninterrupted work; alongside verbal-ideological centralization and unification, the uninterrupted process of decentralization and disunification go forward. (Bakhtin 1981, 271–72)

Here I consider ethnic identity and migration as two other socio-ideological components of language.

9

The New Atlantis

The Ultimate Caribbean Archipelago

ANTONIO BENÍTEZ ROJO
TRANSLATED BY JAMES E. MARANISS

In these times, when the maps of nations are continually remade and new delegations and flags shuffled in the United Nations, it is almost obligatory to think about political geography. What will the world be like in the twenty-first century? Surely it will differ from what it is today. Some states will pull apart, and others will join together. This is nothing new, but the principle by which borders are made and unmade may be different this time. To judge from current appearances, it will no longer be ideology and politics that give coherence to a state, but historical and cultural affinities within the economic unit. Everything indicates that the coming years will be characterized by the tendency of multinational states to separate into nation-states or to shape themselves as federated republics. In parallel fashion, as with the integrative process that one sees now mainly in Europe, the different regions of the globe will go on finding advanced forms of association and collaboration. And so the countries of the world will separate in one way and come together quickly in another.

This process has been dealt with abundantly in the press. But I want to concentrate on a certain part of the world that, because of its territorial smallness, is generally forgotten by futurologists and the great architects of globalization: the Antilles. In an era of quantification, it makes sense to look at the cluster of features that this region offers to present-day geography before we travel to the future. What demographic and territorial importance does the Antillean archipelago have? Its population occupies

218,708 square kilometers and is projected to number 36,449,000 by the year 2000. Politically, it is remarkably pluralistic: for example, Cuba defines itself as a "unitary and socialist" republic; Dominica as an island "commonwealth" governed by constitutional monarchy within the British Commonwealth; the Dominican Republic as a "multiparty republic"; Martinique as an "overseas department of France"; the Netherlands Antilles as a "nonmetropolitan territory of the Netherlands"; Puerto Rico as a "free associated state"; Saint Kitts-Nevis as a "federated republic"; and the Virgin Islands as a British dependency and a "nonincorporated territory of the United States." The region's linguistic pluralism is also notable: not only Dutch, English, French, and Spanish but also Chinese and Hindi are spoken there, as well as different Creole dialects, among them Haitian Creole, Jamaican, and Papiamento. This diversity bespeaks the archipelago's ethnic fragmentation, to which the peoples of four continents have contributed socially and culturally.

In spite of this fragmentation, there arose in the twentieth century a cultural discourse that broke the old colonial conception of the Antilles as a group of islands irreconcilably divided into linguistic blocs by recognizing certain patterns that repeated themselves within the archipelago. Advancing this discourse were, among others, Jean-Stéphen Alexis, Emilio Ballagas, Kamau Brathwaite, Lydia Cabrera, Alejo Carpentier, Aimé Césaire, Nicolás Guillén, C. L. R. James, Fernando Ortiz, Luis Palés Matos, Jean Price-Mars, and Jacques Roumain. In the beginning it centered on the important impact of the African diaspora on the different island cultures and societies, defining concepts such as *négritude,* transculturation, *mestizaje,* and magic realism. But more recently the referential base of this discourse has expanded to include continental territories with Caribbean coasts, as well as to study the entire sociocultural phenomenon of the area from the point of view of the Creole or creolization. This new notion refers not just to the meeting of African and European peoples in the region; it also embraces the contributions of others, primarily Native Americans and Asians. The idea of the Caribbean as an area with its own distinctive characteristics has not only become known throughout the world but has also given rise to many historical, economic, sociological, and literary works, among others those of Juan Bosch, Franklin W. Knight, Sidney Mintz, Arturo Morales Carrión, Manuel Moreno Fraginals, and Eric Williams. Initiatives have been undertaken to achieve economic cooperation, such as the Caribbean Free Trade Association and, later, the Caribbean Community and Common Market. To foster artistic expression, the Caribbean Festival of the Creative Arts was organized. In short, Antillean discourse has expanded to become Caribbean discourse, and it is widening still further to include points of connection to much of the rest of the world. This global perspective can be observed in such works of literary and cultural analysis, published between 1983 and 1998, as Jean Bernabé's, Patrick Chamoiseau's, and Raphaël Confiant's *In Praise of Creoleness*; J. Michael Dash's *The Other America*; Édouard Glissant's *Poétique de la relation*; Wilson Harris's *Womb of Space*; and my own *Repeating Island*.

From this all-too-rapid survey it is easy to conclude that Antillean cultural discourse, in spite of its relative newness, has shown a clear tendency to expand. But how will it develop in the twenty-first century? I want to address in particular the practical effects of regional collaboration within the ongoing process of globalization and to analyze the relationship that the Antilles will have to the other islands of the subtropical and tropical Atlantic. As all of these islands together have no collective name, I will call them the New Atlantis, the ultimate archipelago.

Much has been written about these islands, but I know of no work that has studied them in depth as a group, that is, from the perspective of the historical, socioeconomic, and cultural links within the vast territory that includes Anguilla, Antigua and Barbuda, Aruba, the Azores, the Bahamas, Barbados, Bermuda, Bioko (formerly Fernando Póo), the British Virgin Islands, the Canary Islands, the Cape Verde Islands, the Cayman Islands, Cuba, Dominica, the Dominican Republic, Grenada, Guadeloupe, Haiti, Jamaica, the Madeira Islands, Martinique, Montserrat, the Netherlands Antilles, Puerto Rico, Saint Helena and Ascension, Saint Kitts-Nevis, Saint Lucia, Saint Vincent and the Grenadines, San Andrés y Providencia, São Tomé and Príncipe, Trinidad and Tobago, the Turks and Caicos Islands, and the Virgin Islands of the United States. These islands together measure some 270,000 square kilometers, more or less the size of Italy; their population, some 44 million, exceeds that of Spain; and their population density, 163 people per square kilometer, is the same as Switzerland's. In short, the New Atlantis presents itself to us as a sizable archipelago.

Rather than try to define the similarities and differences among these islands, which could be done only through detailed comparative analysis, I want to propose a few general alignments to guide the development of a disciplinary discourse for a comprehensive study of this ocean territory. Once such a discourse has been established, it may not be strange to find that the different states and communities that coexist in this area of the Atlantic but hardly know one another should move toward some form of integration. The economic, political, and sociocultural advantages would be enormous, especially in the long run. The sources of energy that will succeed oil, gas, and nuclear fission are the sun and the sea, whose availability on these islands is as great as anywhere in the world. The islands of the Atlantic will be coveted again, not for their mercantile significance, as during the formation of empires, but for their energy. What were slave colonies in the past and are tourist resorts in the present may become power plants in high demand from all regions of the globe.

In any event, some kind of archipelagic association will be desirable. Why not begin with tourism, a major source of wealth on the great majority of the islands? Their mild winters, warm waters and breezes, and palm-lined beaches are common features of interest in and of themselves. Moreover, their fishing and agriculture, together with newer avenues of commercial export, such as undersea mining, could serve as the basis of economic integration. I have already mentioned the Caribbean Festival of the Creative Arts, from which starting point it would be easy to organize other music and dance festivals, art exhibitions, and meetings of artists and intellectuals. In September 1997 the Centro Atlántico de Arte Moderno, located in Las Palmas de Gran Canaria, held the international exposition "Islas," followed by a symposium on the theme of insularity. Why should similar symposia not be organized throughout the New Atlantis, for the benefit of all its constituent populations?

Yes, we New Atlanteans are distant from one another, but not so distant as New York is from Honolulu, where one and the same flag flies. Yes, we speak different languages, but in this age linguistic barriers are no longer insurmountable. Europe, for one, has overcome them. The Caribbean, which would round out the extreme southeast of the New Atlantis and among whose islands integration has already occurred, is another case in point. Caribbean studies, which seem to attract more and more interest both inside and outside the Antilles, began as a scholarly discipline only a couple of decades ago. Until then it was not widely recognized that places colonized by Danes, Dutchmen, Englishmen, Frenchmen, Portuguese, Spaniards, and Swedes might have much in common, and yet it is obvious today that they do. One may well conclude that the New Atlantis is not just a possible form of association but a probable one.

It is not by chance that I propose to call this island region the New Atlantis, for there is nothing like a founding myth to consolidate an identity, and Plato's myth of Atlantis fits like a glove. Whether or not the archipelago claims it in the future, it may still be ours. No other territorial myth outdoes it in prestige or in poetic resonance.

Of all the disciplinary discourses, those belonging to the natural sciences, archeology, and history contribute the most to the search for roots in a common past. If the governments of our islands have one fruitful enterprise before them, it is to provide funds for botanical and zoological studies, archeological excavations, and research on colonial documents in the world's archives. One must remember that our flora and fauna have enriched the world's diets and augmented its medical resources, and our native species, from the draco to the iguana, have enlarged its understanding of nature. When colonized by European powers, our aboriginal populations all had Neolithic cultures, and by studying these cultures comparatively, one might reach conclusions that hold for all such cultures: their contributions to contemporary humanity, for example, beginning with toponymy and ending with cornmeal and tobacco. Although these cultures no longer exist and have nothing to do ethnically with many of us, their genetic legacy is still alive in some of our populations. For the purposes of a genealogical-nationalist discourse, they are *we*, and to them we owe the legitimacy of our roots on the New Atlantis.

I turn now to history, and here I envision a magisterial book, still to be written, of course, and divisible into long thematic chapters. Parts of our islands were populated by aborigines, and parts were uninhabited at the time of their discovery by Europeans. In the first chapter of our common history, we would observe that conquest and colonization, throughout the fifteenth, sixteenth, and seventeenth centuries, were astonishingly similar regardless of the nations that carried them out. In the beginning, there was mutual incomprehension between conqueror and conquered. On certain islands the Europeans were taken to be gods, and on others the natives were thought to have no souls. Once these religious aspects had been addressed, the islanders fought the invaders tooth and nail until the cannon, the harquebus, the pike, and the sword prevailed. The conquered were enslaved or shared out or made vassals; many died from European punishments or sicknesses, and those who did not were baptized, given the names of saints, and made subjects of a foreign empire—second-class subjects, for although they survived the abrupt transition from the Stone Age to the Renaissance, a leap of seven thousand years in a single generation, they were never forgiven for not grasping Western lifestyles and ways of understanding.

The second chapter of the history of the New Atlantis would deal with the organization of colonial life, and it, too, would present surprising similarities: the exploitation of natural resources; the construction of towns with stone houses; the incursion of foreign institutions and colonists; the introduction of foreign livestock and crops; and the implanting of a colonial bureaucracy. The third chapter would describe the beginnings of Atlantic commerce: Iberian mercantile monopolies vis-à-vis Dutch, English, and French; the legal and illegal traffic in African slaves; and the development of the plantation. Then the different types of plantations would be taken up, particularly sugar plantations. Their spread would be followed from the year 1452, when they were brought, in succession, from Sicily to the Madeiras; to the Azores, the Cape Verde Islands, and the Canaries, whence Columbus introduced them to Hispaniola; to Puerto Rico, Jamaica, and Cuba; and, later, to Trinidad, Barbados, and the rest of the Lesser Antilles. Naturally, the fewer natives and the more plantations there were, the greater the importation of African slaves.

Eventually, the slave trade had vast sociocultural consequences, to be explored in the fifth chapter, because the fourth chapter would deal with maritime warfare, privateering, and piracy. From the Azores to Saint Helena and Ascension, our islands served as key military positions for the European powers and frequently as booty—and even as bases of operations—for corsairs and buccaneers. In their waters the most notable captains and admirals of the world fought: from Menéndez de Avilés and the Marqués de Santa Cruz to Drake, Hawkins, Hein, LeClerc, Morgan, Nelson, Rodney, and Surcouf. The islands' role in the military and commercial expansion of Europe was crucial. Our coasts and bays not only provided space for the development of the Atlantic economy but also provided for its protection. A list of the old castles, forts, and walls that still loom over our ports, from the Azores to Saint Helena, is enough to impress one with the military threats that surrounded us for four centuries. But another plague menaced us, too: piracy. If not for our islands, the history of privateering and piracy would not go beyond a twenty-page pamphlet, and *Treasure Island* and *Captain Blood* would never have been written. This chapter might end with Napoleon's last defeat and his exile on Saint Helena, although I myself would take it all the way to the so-called Spanish-American War, obviously a war of plunder, the kind of war that comes nearest to piracy.

The fifth chapter, as I said, would be dedicated to our peripheral societies, including the springing up of local cultures and smuggling as an economic alternative. This chapter could extend to the first quarter of the nineteenth century, by which time the majority of the islands had developed Creole cultures and dour local pride and a sense of belonging had spread among their populations. The chapter would speak of the great political, economic, technological, social, and ethnic differences that always separated the island societies from their metropolises or administrative centers. In themselves, these differences were neither good nor bad; for us, however, they were never good because of our status as second-class colonies and provinces. While mercantile accumulation and industrial revolution took place in the metropolises, our archipelago saw only sugar plantations, contraband, grapevines, tobacco, indigo, coffee, coconuts, bananas, and other fruit—the staples of an economy that continues today, albeit with the support of hotels and restaurants for tourists.

I now move on to the theme of culture. It is not imprudent to say that "French" culture does not exist, although I would not recommend that it be shouted in the Place de la Concorde or in the shadow of the Arc de Triomphe. What we call French or Spanish or English culture is not a homogeneous blend but a heterogeneous system of regional, national, and local cultures that differ among themselves so greatly that even in France, as in Spain and in the so-called United Kingdom, there are separatist movements. I say this to defend the heterogeneity that the cultural system of the New Atlantis must have. Nonetheless, I hasten to add that within the disorder of this heterogeneity differences will repeat themselves from one island to another, giving the archipelago a strange cultural coherence that will be understandable when we note that the culture brought to the island territory by the first colonizers, whoever they may have been, underwent changes that made it unique. These changes happened because of the meeting of cultural agents from different sources on each of the islands.

I take as an example Cuba, the island that I know best. If we say that Cuban culture is the product of the contributions of aborigines, Spaniards, and Africans, we are telling the truth, but only half of it, for there remain the peculiarities of Cuban culture vis-à-vis the cultures of Tenerife, the Dominican Republic, and Puerto Rico, where there were also aborigines, Spanish colonizers, and African slaves. On Cuba, unlike the other Greater Antilles, there were three aboriginal cultural systems, one from Central America and two from the Guianas. Furthermore, we say "Spaniards" without noting that there has never been a single Spanish nation but several, a fact recognized only recently by the central government. Cuba received a good sampling of its peoples: Andalusians, Aragonese, Asturians, Basques, Castilians, Extremadurans, Galicians, and also many Canarians; indeed, Cuban literature was founded not by a Cuban but by a native of Grand Canary, Silvestre de Balboa. In Cuba—and of course in Puerto Rico and the Dominican Republic—these nationalities were never separated by region, as they had been in Spain. Thus from the earliest days Cuba fostered an Iberian-based cultural syncretism that had never existed on the Peninsula.

Something similar can be said of the African contribution to Cuban culture. In present-day Cuba we recognize components of Bantu, Efik, and Yoruba cultures, which, on coming into contact with European ones, produced the habanera, the *danzón*, the *son*, the conga, the rumba, the *bolero cubano*, the mambo, the chacha, the salsa, and so-called Latin jazz, as well as the music of Amadeo Roldán and Alejandro García Caturla, the poetry of Guillén and Ballagas, and the pictorial art of Wilfredo Lam. In Puerto Rico, the number of slaves was not as great, and so the African influence there was smaller. But Puerto Rico witnessed a Corsican immigration that never happened in Cuba, while the latter, for its part, saw an appreciable influx of Chinese, Frenchmen, and Yucatecans. So Cuba, and every other archipelagic island, has its own cultural history to relate. Yet in spite of this fragmentation, all of the island cultural systems have one feature in common: their Atlantic complexity.

The next chapter of the history of the New Atlantis would deal with the archipelago's extremely complex political history and the struggle of its peoples to rise socially. It would depict all of the rebellions and revolutions; all of the interventions, occupations, and changes of flags; all of the acts of popular resistance to military and non-military dictatorships; and it would offer a critical vision of the incomplete process of decolonization that began after World War II, as well as touch on the appearance of a few forms of nationalism in our islands.

The penultimate chapter would show the old relations that exist among our peoples, as well as their sociocultural impact. Of particular interest are the Canarian emigration to the Caribbean and its contribution to the rural folk music of Cuba and Puerto Rico. Of great importance is the Cuban exile of refugees from the Haitian revolution. Musicians from the old Saint

Domingue brought to Santiago de Cuba the music that became known there—and still is known—as *tumba francesa* and *cocoyé*; they also introduced the rhythmic unit called the *cinquillo*, which influenced Cuban country dance as much as the habanera did. Later, of course, came the participation of Puerto Rican and Dominican patriots in Cuba's independence movement, from Eugenio María de Hostos and Ramón Emeterio Betances to Máximo Gómez, who was general-in-chief of the revolutionary forces.

I would devote the last chapter of the history of the New Atlantis to a description, on both a personal and an institutional level, of our connections with the rest of the world. The case of Simón Bolívar is instructive. In the first place, there is the so-called Jamaican Letter, a document written in the Caribbean, which is without a doubt the deepest and finest reflection on the struggle for independence. But on a practical level, there is the assistance offered by Haiti and, above all, the advice of its president, Alexandre Pétion, to the effect that the war could not be won without liberating the slaves.

Another interesting episode involved the schooner *Amistad*, commandeered in Cuban waters in 1839 by the slaves it was transporting. After many days the *Amistad* reached Long Island, where it was captured by the United States Coast Guard. The long and complicated trial that followed nearly ruptured diplomatic relations between Spain and the United States. Public opinion favored the removal of the slaves to their African homeland, which is what finally occurred. Thanks to this famous case, the first anti-slavery societies were organized in the United States, and American abolitionism began to take form. The *Amistad* case was so historically significant that in preparation for the U.S. bicentennial a replica of the ship was built to take its place alongside others of national importance.

The valuable contributions of Arthur Schomberg, Claude McKay, and Marcus Garvey to the African American movement in the United States also come to mind as topics for this chapter. Perhaps literary figures should be included with them, from Alonso Ramírez, whose misfortunes were edited by Sigüenza y Góngora, all the way to the Nobel laureate Derek Walcott. Now that I think about it, this chapter might be so extensive that it should be published independently—a sort of *Who's Who* dedicated to those who have contributed, through their discoveries, creativity, or celebrity, to the sciences, scholarship, politics, social betterment, the arts, literature, entertainment, and sports, from Dámaso Pérez Prado, the mambo king, to Daniel Santos, the restless *anacobero*; from Kid Gavilán, creator of the bolo punch, to Félix

B. Cañet, author of *El derecho de nacer* and founder of the Latin American soap opera.

Finally, I want to touch on an aspect that at once unifies us and differentiates us from other societies, that oscillates between the psychological and the anthropological: our condition as islanders. The eternal seascape has made us look outward, toward the horizon. It has turned us into an extrovert people, smiling and generous to the stranger. Surely this is nothing new; thousands of Englishmen, Frenchmen, and Germans have noted it in their travel books. But within us there is something more difficult to see: a secret sadness, shared rarely—the product, I believe, of our microcosmic isolation, of our solitude in the midst of so much sun and so many tourists. It is a shipwrecked impatience, in fact, which has always pushed us to abandon the islands for other, ampler, richer, more populous lands, for scientific and technological capitals where we think that things of capital importance happen. In time we become disenchanted, and our nostalgia for sea and breeze comes back, for modest cathedrals, for colonial facades and rusty cannons, for palm trees and *carnaval*. Sometimes, sadly, we die without going back. The fact is that, in order not to exile ourselves, we need the idea of belonging to a very large native land, the concept that we are not sailing alone. We need the certainty that our individuality has indeed produced part of a grand collective history and culture. We need to know that, as peoples of the sea, we are unique and our horizon reaches far beyond sight.

Works Cited

Printed Sources

Aching, Gerard. 1994. "On the Creation of Unsung National Heroes: Barnet's Esteban Montejo and Armas's Julián del Casal." *Latin American Literary Review* 22: 31–50.

Adorno, Theodor. 1997. *Aesthetic Theory*. Ed. Gretel Adorno and Rolf Tiedemann. Trans. Robert Hullot-Kentor. Minneapolis: University of Minnesota Press.

Agamben, Giorgio. 2005. *State of Exception*. Chicago: University of Chicago Press.

Agar, Michael H. 1996. *The Professional Stranger: An Informal Introduction to Ethnography*. San Diego: Academic.

Alleyne, Brian. 2002. *Radicals Against Race: Black Activism and Cultural Politics*. Oxford: Berg.

Amaral Ferlini, Vera Lucía. 1989. "Polémicas e Controversias sobre a Genese Do Escravismo." *Suplemento de Anuario de Estudios Americanos* (Escuela De Estudios Hispano-Americanos, Seville) 46 (1): 3–10.

Amin, Samir. 1991. "The Ancient World-Systems versus the Modern World-Systems." *Review* 14 (3) (summer): 354.

Anderson, Jack. 2006. "Katherine Dunham, Dance Icon, Dies at 96." *New York Times*, May 23: B7.

Angrosino, Michael V. 2002. *Doing Cultural Anthropology: Projects for Ethnographic Data Collection*. Prospect Heights, IL: Waveland.

Aparicio, Frances. 1998. *Listening to Salsa: Gender, Latin Popular Music, and Puerto Rican Cultures*. Hanover, NH: Wesleyan University Press.

Arrom, José Juan. 1980. "Mitos taínos en las letras de Cuba, Santo Domingo y México." In *Certidumbre de América: Estudios de letras, folklore y cultura*, 56–73. Havana: Letras Cubanas.

Arthur, Charles, and Michael Dash, eds. 1999. *Libété: A Haitian Anthology*. Kingston: Ian Randle.

Austerlitz, Paul. 1996. *Merengue: Dominican Music and Dominican Identity*. Philadelphia: Temple University Press.

Bakhtin, Mikhail M. 1981. *The Dialogic Imagination*. Austin: University of Texas Press.

Banks, Russell. 1985. *Continental Drift*. New York: Harper and Row.

Barnet, Miguel. [1968]. *The Autobiography of a Runaway Slave*. Trans. Jocasta Innes. New York: Pantheon.

———. 1968. *Biografía de un cimarrón*. Barcelona: Ediciones Ariel.

———. 1979. *La canción de Rachel*. Barcelona: Editorial Laia.

———. 1979. *The Documentary Novel*. Trans. Paul Bundy. Amherst: Council on International Studies, State University of New York at Buffalo.

———. 1991 [1969]. *Rachel's Song: A Novel*. Trans. W. Nick Hill. Willimantic, Conn.: Curbstone Press.

Barreiro, José. 1989. "Indians in Cuba." *Cultural Survival Quarterly* 13 (3): 56–60.

Barthes, Roland. 1977. "Introduction to the Structural Analysis of Narratives." In *Image-Music-Text,* ed. Stephen Heath. New York: Hill and Wang.

Batista Matos, Carlos. 1999. *Historia y evolución del merengue*. Santo Domingo: Editora Cañabrava.

Benítez Rojo, Antonio. 1996. *The Repeating Island: The Caribbean and the Postmodern Perspective*. Durham, N.C.: Duke University Press.

Bennett, Jill. 2005. *Emphatic Vision: Affect, Trauma, and Contemporary Art*. Stanford, Calif.: Stanford University Press.

Benson, LeGrace. 2005. "A Long Bilingual Conversation about Paradise Lost: Landscapes in Haitian Art." In *Caribbean Literature and the Environment: Between Nature and Culture*, ed. Elizabeth M. DeLoughrey, Renée K. Gosson, and George B. Handley, 99–109. Charlottesville: University Press of Virginia.

Bernard, H. Russell. 1994. *Research Methods in Anthropology: Qualitative and Quantitative Methods*. Thousand Oaks, Calif.: Sage.

Bernstein, J. M. 1994. "Self-knowledge as Praxis: Narrative and Narration in Psychoanalysis." In *Narrative in Culture: The Uses of Storytelling in the Sciences, Philosophy, and Literature,* ed. Christopher Nash. London: Routledge.

Beverley, John. 2001. "The Im/possibility of Politics: Subalternity, Modernity, Hegemony." In *The Latin American Subaltern Studies Reader*, ed. Ileana Rodríguez, 47–63. Durham, N.C.: Duke University Press.

Blake, John W. 1937. *European Beginnings in West Africa, 1454–1578*. Westport, Conn.: Greenwood.

Blanchot, Maurice. 1986. *The Writing of Disaster*. Trans. Ann Smock. Lincoln: University of Nebraska Press.

Blanco, Gladys. 1989. "Indians of Cuba." *Granma Weekly Review* (international edition) 25 (June 18): 4.

Boggs, Grace Lee. 1993. "Thinking and Acting Dialectically." *Monthly Review* 45 (5) (October): 38–46.

———. 1995. "C.L.R. James: Organizing in the U.S.A., 1938–1953." In *C.L.R. James: His Intellectual Legacies*, ed. Selwyn R. Cudjoe and William E. Cain, 163–72. Amherst: University of Massachusetts Press.

———. 1998. *Living for Change*. Minneapolis: University of Minnesota Press.

Bogues, Anthony. 1997. *Caliban's Freedom*. London: Pluto.

———. 2000. "Afterword to *The Black Jacobins*." *Small Axe* 8 (September): 113–17.

———. 2003. *Africana Heretics and Prophets: Radical Political Intellectuals*. London: Routledge.

Boyle, Sheila Tully, and Andrew Bunie. 2001. *Paul Robeson: The Years of Promise and Achievement*. Amherst: University of Massachusetts Press.

Bradford, James C., ed. 1993. *Crucible of Empire: The Spanish-American War and Its Aftermath*. Annapolis, Md.: Naval Institute Press.

Bradford, Richard H. 1980. *The Virginius Affair*. Boulder: Colorado Associated University Press.

Brantlinger, Patrick. 1995. "'Dying Races': Rationalizing Genocide in the Nineteenth Century." In *The Decolonization of Imagination: Culture, Knowledge, and Power*, ed. Jan Nederveen Pieterse and Bhikhu Parekh, 43–56. London: Zed.

Brathwaite, Edward Kamau. 1999. "Dream Haiti." In *The Oxford Book of Caribbean Short Stories*. New York: Oxford University Press.

———. 2005. "Keynote Address." 6th International Conference on Caribbean Literature, November 1–5, St. Croix, U.S. Virgin Islands.

Braudel, Fernand. 1984. *Civilización material, economía y capitalismo: Siglos XV–XVIII*. Vol. 3. Madrid: Alianza Editorial.

Braziel, Jana Evans. 2006. "Haiti, Guantánamo, and the 'One Indispensable Nation': U.S. Imperialism, 'Apparent States', and Postcolonial Problematics of Sovereignty." *Cultural Critique* 64: 127–60.

"Brazil to Supply Organization of Eastern Caribbean States with Antiretroviral Drugs." 2006. *Medical News Today*. www.medicalnewstoday.com.medicalnews.php?newsid=42457.

Brecht, Bertolt. 1944, rpt. 1976. *The Caucasian Chalk Circle*. In *Collected Plays*, 7: 135–229. New York: Vintage Books.

Brinton, Daniel G. 1898. "The Archaeology of Cuba." *American Archaeologist* 2 (10) (October): 253–56.

Brown, Karen McCarthy. 1991. *Mama Lola: A Vodou Priestess in Brooklyn*. Berkeley: University of California Press.

———. 1996. "Art and Resistance: Haiti's Political Murals, October 1994." *African Arts* (spring): 47–57, 102.

Buhle, Paul. 1988. *C.L.R. James: The Artist as Revolutionary*. London: Verso.

———. 1992. "The Making of a Literary Life: C.L.R. James Interviewed by Paul Buhle." In *C.L.R. James's Caribbean*, ed. Paget Henry and Paul Buhle, 56–62. Durham, N.C.: Duke University Press.

Campbell, W. Joseph. 2002. "Not a Hoax: New Evidence in the *New York Journal's* Rescue of Evangelina Cisneros." *American Journalism* 19 (4) (fall).

Carby, Hazel. 1988. "Proletarian or Revolutionary Literature? C.L.R. James and the Politics of the Trinidadian Renaissance." *South Atlantic Quarterly* 87 (1) (winter): 41–52.

Carpentier, Alejo. 1980. "La cultura de los pueblos que habitan en las tierras del mar Caribe." *Casa de las Américas* 118: 2–8.

Chauvet, Marie. 1968. *Amour, Colère et Folie*. Paris: Gallimard.

Chambers, Iain. 2002. "Citizenship, Language, and Modernity." *PMLA* 117 (1) (January): 24–31.

Clark, William J. 1898. *Commercial Cuba: A Book for Business Men.* New York: Charles Scribner's Sons.

Cliff, Michelle. 1978. "Obsolete Geographies." *Conditions: Three* 1:3 (1978): 44–49.

Coll y Juliá, N. 1950. "Vicente Yáñez Pinzón, descubridor del Brasil, corsario en Cataluña." *Hispania* 10: 594–597..

Collado Villalta, Pedro. 1985. "La nación genovesa en la Sevilla de la Carrera de Indias." In *Presencia italiana en Andalucía, siglos XIV–XVII.* Seville: Escuela de Estudios Hispano-Americanos.

Columbus, Christopher. 1893. *The Spanish Letter of Columbus to Luis de Sant' Angel.* London: Bernard Quaritch.

Conner, Floyd. 1993. *Lupe Vélez and Her Lovers.* New York: Barricade Books.

Coronil, Fernando. 1995. Introduction to Fernando Ortiz's *Cuban Counterpoint: Tobacco and Sugar*, trans. Harriet de Onís, ix–lvi. Durham. N.C.: Duke University Press.

Cortés, Vicente. 1963. "La trata de esclavos durante los primeros descubrimientos, 1489–1516." *Anuario de Estudios Atlánticos* 9: 23–50..

Cosío y Cisneros, Evangelina. 1898. *The Story of Evangelina Cisneros, Told by Herself.* New York: Continental Publishing Company.

Cosmas, Graham A. 1971. *An Army for Empire: The United States Army in the Spanish-American War.* Columbia: University of Missouri Press.

Costa Lima, Luiz. 1988. *Control of the Imaginary: Reason and Imagination in Modern Times.* Trans. Ronald W. Sousa. Minneapolis: University of Minnesota Press.

Cruz-Malavé, Arnaldo. 1995. "Towards an Art of Transvestism: Colonialism and Homosexuality in Puerto Rican Literature." In *¿Entiendes? Queer Readings, Hispanic Writings*, ed. Emily L. Bergmann and Paul Julian Smith, 137–67. Durham, N.C.: Duke University Press.

Cudjoe, Selwyn. 1983–87. "A Conversation with C.L.R. James" (videotape interview). Ithaca: Cornell University Media Services

———. 1992. "The Audacity of It All: C.L.R. James's Trinidadian Background." In *C.L.R. James's Caribbean*, ed. Paget Henry and Paul Buhle, 39–55. Durham, N.C.: Duke University Press.

———. 2003. *Beyond Boundaries: The Intellectual Tradition of Trinidad and Tobago in the Nineteenth Century.* Wellesley, Mass.: Calaloux.

Culin, Stewart. 1902. "The Indians of Cuba." *Bulletin of the Free Museum of Science and Arts, University of Pennsylvania, Philadelphia* 3 (4): 185–226.

———. n.d. "Cuba—Correspondence." Expedition Records, Central America: Caribbean (Cuba and Puerto Rico), Box 1. University Museum Archives, University of Pennsylvania.

Cunningham, Ineke. "Reflections about a Latino Agenda for Behavioral and Social Science HIV/AIDS Research." http://clnet.sscnet.ucla.edu/research/aids/conf/reflectl.htm.

Dacal Moure, Ramón, and Manuel Rivero de la Calle. 1984. *Arqueología aborigen de Cuba*. Havana: Editorial Gente Nueva.

Danticat, Edwidge. 1994. *Breath, Eyes, Memory*. New York: Vintage Books.

———. 1996. *Krik? Krak!* New York: Vintage Contemporaries.

———. 2005. "Not Your Homeland." *The Nation* (Digital Edition). September 26.

Dash, J. Michael. 1997. *Haiti and the United States: National Stereotypes and the Literary Imagination*. 2nd ed. New York: St. Martin's Press.

Dávila, Arlene M. 1997. "Contending Nationalisms: Culture, Politics, and Corporate Sponsorship in Puerto Rico." In *Puerto Rican Jam: Rethinking Colonialism and Nationalism*, ed. Frances Negrón-Muntaner and Ramón Grosfoguel, 231–42. Minneapolis: University of Minnesota Press.

Davis, Dave D. 1996. "Revolutionary Archaeology in Cuba." *Journal of Archaeological Method and Theory* 3 (3): 159–88.

Davis, Dave, and Christopher Goodwin. 1990. "The Island Carib Origins: Evidence and Nonevidence." *American Antiquity* 55 (1): 37–48.

Davis, Richard Harding. 1897. *Cuba in War Time*. Illustrated by Frederic Remington. New York: R. H. Russell.

———. 1898. *The Cuban and Porto Rican Campaigns*. New York: Charles Scribner's Sons.

———. 1914. "Breaking into the Movies." *Scribner's Magazine* 55 (3) (March): 275–93.

———. 1916 [1897]. *Soldiers of Fortune*. New York: Charles Scribner's Sons.

———. 1918. *Adventures and Letters of Richard Harding Davis*. Ed. Charles Belmont Davis. New York: Charles Scribner's Sons.

Dayan, Joan. 2004. "A Few Stories about Haiti, or, Stigma Revisited." *Research in African Literatures* 35 (2) (summer): 157–172.

De la Campa, Román. 1999. *Latin Americanism*. Minneapolis: University of Minnesota Press.

Deming, Mark. "Review of Bruce Springsteen's *The Ghost of Tom Joad*." All Music Guide. http://www.mp3.com/albums/179364/reviews.html.

Derrida, Jacques. 1992. "Faxitexture." In *Anywhere*, ed. Cynthia Davidson, trans. Laura Bourland, 18–33. New York: Rizzoli.

Diamond, Jared. 2005. *Collapse: How Societies Choose to Fail or Succeed*. New York: Viking.

Díaz, Jesús. 1985. *Lejanía*. Havana: ICAIC.

Dippie, Brian W. 1982. *The Vanishing American: White Attitudes and U.S. Indian Policy*. Lawrence: University Press of Kansas.

"Does Our Flag Shield Women? . . . Refined Young Women Stripped and Searched by Brutal Spaniards While Under Our Flag on the Olivette." 1897. *New York Journal*, February 12.

Dow, Mark. 2004. *American Gulag: Inside U.S. Immigration Prisons*. Berkeley: University of California Press.

Draper, Andrew S. 1899. *The Rescue of Cuba: An Episode in the Growth of Free Government*. Boston: Silver, Burdett.

Duany, Jorge. 1994. "Ethnicity, Identity, and Music: An Anthropological Analysis of the Dominican Merengue." In *Music and Black Ethnicity: The Caribbean and South America*, ed. Gerard H. Béhague, 65–90. Miami: North-South Center, University of Miami.

———. 1998. "'Lo tengo dominao': El boom de las merengueras en Puerto Rico." *Diálogo* (October): 28–29.

———. 2002. *The Puerto Rican Nation on the Move: Identities on the Island and in the United States*. Chapel Hill: University of North Carolina Press.

Duberman, Martin. 1988. *Paul Robeson*. New York: Knopf.

Dumain, Ralph. n.d. Commentary on "The Negro Question." C.L.R. James Institute Document 4493.

Dyer, Thomas G. 1980. *Theodore Roosevelt and the Idea of Race*. Baton Rouge: Louisiana State University Press.

El Nuevo Herald. 2001. "La Isla." Noticias de Cuba. April 9. http:// www.cubanet.org/ CNews/y01/apr01/0901.htm.

Enhancing Care Initiative (Harvard AIDS Institute). "Team Puerto Rico, Western Region." http://www.eci.harvard.edu/teams/pr/index.html.

Fan, Hung, Ross F. Conner, and Luis P. Villareal. 1994. *The Biology of AIDS*. 3rd ed. Boston: Jones and Bartlett.

Farmer, Paul. 1992. *AIDS and Accusation: Haiti and the Geography of Blame*. Berkeley: University of California Press.

Fernández-Armesto, Felipe. 1987. *Before Columbus: Exploration and Colonization from the Mediterranean to the Atlantic, 1229–1492*. London: Macmillan Education.

Ferré, Rosario. 1988. *Sweet Diamond Dust*. New York: Ballantine.

Fewkes, J. Walter. 1902. "Prehistoric Puerto Rico." *Proceedings of the American Association for the Advancement of Science* 51: 487–512.

———. 1904. "Prehistoric Culture of Cuba." *American Anthropologist* 6 (4): 535–38.

Foley, Barbara. 1986. *Telling the Truth: The Theory and Practice of Documentary Fiction*. Ithaca, N.Y.: Cornell University Press.

Foner, Philip S. 1972. *The Spanish-Cuban-American War and the Birth of American Imperialism, 1895–1902*. 2 vols. New York: Monthly Review Press.

Foot, Michael. 1995. "C.L.R. James." In *C.L.R. James: His Intellectual Legacies*, ed. Selwyn R. Cudjoe and William E. Cain, 98–105. Amherst: University of Massachusetts Press.

Foucault, Michel. 1973. *The Order of Things: An Archaeology of the Human Sciences*. New York: Vintage Books.

Freud, Sigmund. 1976 [1914–16]. "Duelo y melancolía." In *Obras completas,* 14: 235–55. Buenos Aires: Amorrortu Editores.

Freytes, Teo. 1991. *El gobierno tiene las manos llenas de sangre*. San Juan: n. p.

Fritz, Sonia, dir. 1994. *Un retrato de Carlos Collazo*. San Juan. Instituto de Cultura Puertorriqueña.

Frus, Phyllis. 1994. *The Politics and Poetics of Journalistic Narrative: The Timely and the Timeless*. New York: Cambridge University Press.

Gaither, Larvester. 2000. "C.L.R. James" (interview). *Gaither Reporter* 4 (7) (31 December): 8–13.

Galeano, Eduardo. 1973. *Open Veins of Latin America: Five Centuries of the Pillage of a Continent.* Trans. Cedric Belfrage. New York: Monthly Review Press.

García, Cristina. 1992. *Dreaming in Cuban.* New York: Ballantine Books.

García Arévalo, Manuel A. 1988. *Indigenismo, arqueología e identidad nacional.* Santo Domingo: Fundación García Arévalo.

García Ramis, Magali. 1986. *Felices días, tío Sergio.* Río Piedras, P.R.: Editorial Cultural.

Gasyon, Jan-Franns. 2006. *Hamlet, Amlèt: Trajedi youn nèg ki pa ka deside.* Bloomington: AuthorHouse.

Gates, R. Ruggles. 1954. "Studies in Race Crossing: VI. The Indians of Eastern Cuba." *Genetica* 27: 65–96.

Gatewood, Willard B., Jr. 1975. *Black Americans and the White Man's Burden, 1898–1903.* Urbana: University of Illinois Press.

Gautier Benítez, José. 1880. *A Puerto Rico.* San Juan: Ateneo Puertorriqueño.

Geggus, David. 1982. "British Opinion and the Emergence of Haiti." In *Slavery and British Society 1776–1846*, ed. James Walvin, 123–49. London: Macmillan.

———. 1997. "The Naming of Haiti." *New West Indian Guide* 71 (1–2): 43–68.

Géricault, Théodore. Web Gallery of Art. http://www.wga.hu/frames-e.html?/html/g/gericaul/1/105geric.html.

Gil, Juan. 1989. *Mitos y utopías del descubrimiento: Colón y su tiempo.* Madrid: Alianza Universidad.

Gil, Juan, and Consuelo Varela. 1984. *Cartas de particulares a Colón y relaciones coetáneas.* Madrid: Alianza Universidad.

Giménez Fernández, Manuel. 1953, 1960. *Bartolomé de las Casas.* 2 vols. Seville: Escuela de Estudios Hispano-Americanos.

Glaberman, Martin. 1994. "C.L.R. James: A Recollection." In *C.L.R. James and Revolutionary Marxism: Selected Writings of C.L.R. James, 1939–1949*, ed. Scott McLemee and Paul LeBlanc, 45–52. Atlantic Highlands, N.J.: Humanities.

Glissant, Edouard. 1999. *Caribbean Discourse: Selected Essays.* Trans. J. Michael Dash. Charlottesville: University Press of Virginia.

Goldstein, Brandt. 2005. "Clinton's Guantánamo: How the Democratic President Set the Stage for a Land without Law." *Slate Magazine*, December 21. http://www.slate.com.

Gomes, Albert. 1978. "Black Man." In *From Trinidad: An Anthology of Early West Indian Writing*, ed. Reinhard Sander, 223–26. New York: Africana Publishing.

Gómez, María A., Diana M. Fernández, José F. Otero, et al. 2000. "The Shape of the HIV/AIDS Epidemic in Puerto Rico." *Revista Panamericana de Salud Pública* 7 (6) (June): 377–83.

González Echevarría, Roberto. 1985. *The Voice of Masters: Writing and Authority in Modern Latin American Literature.* Austin: University of Texas Press.

Gosson, Renée, and Eric Faden, dir. 2003. *Landscape and Memory: Martinican Land-People-History* (videocassette). Third World Reel.

Gove, Philip Babcock, ed. 2002. *Webster's Third New International Dictionary*. Springfield, Ill.: Merriam-Webster.

Gradente, William. 1980. "Merengue." In *The New Grove Dictionary of Music and Musicians*, ed. Stanley Sadie, 12: 180. Washington, D.C.: Macmillan Publishers Limited.

Green, David and Peter Seddon. 2000. *History Painting Reassessed: The Representation of History in Contemporary Art*. Manchester and New York: Manchester University Press.

Grimshaw, Anna. 1991. *Popular Democracy and the Creative Imagination: The Writings of C.L.R. James, 1950–1963*. New York: C.L.R. James Institute.

Grove, Richard H. 1995. *Green Imperialism: Colonial Expansion, Tropical Island Edens, and the Origins of Environmentalism, 1600–1860*. Cambridge: Cambridge University Press.

Gutiérrez, Pedro Juan. 1987. "Have Cuban Aborigines Really Disappeared?" *Granma Weekly Review* (international edition) 20 (May 24): 12.

Hall, Stuart. 1987. "Minimal Selves." In *Identity: The Real Me; Post-Modernism and the Question of Identity*, ed. L. Appignanesi, 44–46. London: ICA Documents.

———. 1997a. "The Local and the Global: Globalization and Ethnicity." In *Culture, Globalization, and the World-System*, ed. Anthony King, 19–39. Minneapolis: University of Minnesota Press.

———. 1997b. "Old and New Identities, Old and New Ethnicities." In *Culture, Globalization, and the World-System*, ed. Anthony King, 41–68. Minneapolis: University of Minnesota Press.

Handley, George B. 2005. "The Argument of the Outboard Motor: An Interview with Derek Walcott." In *Caribbean Literature and the Environment: Between Nature and Culture*, ed. Elizabeth M. DeLoughrey, Renée K. Gosson, and George B. Handley, 127–42. Charlottesville: University Press of Virginia.

Haraway, Donna. 1991. *Simians, Cyborgs, and Women*. New York: Routledge.

Harrington, Mark Raymond. 1921. *Cuba before Columbus*. 2 vols. New York: Museum of the American Indian, Heye Foundation.

Haut, Woody, and Paul Buhle. 1989. "Interview with C.L.R. James, February 15, 1989." Annotation by Ralph Dumain. C.L.R. James Institute Document 1614.

Heers, Jacques. 1989. *Esclavos y sirvientes en las sociedades mediterráneas durante la Edad Media*. Valencia: Institucio Valenciana D'Estudios I Investigacio.

Hill, Robert A. 1993. "Literary Executor's Afterword." In Bill Schwarz, *C. L. R James: American Civilization*, 293–376. Cambridge: Blackwell.

Hill, Robert T. 1898. "Cuba." *National Geographic* 9 (5) (May): 193–242.

Hillegas, Jan. 1986a. "Conversation with C.L.R. James, June 21, 1985" (interview). and In *1985 Conversations*, ed. Jan Hillegas, 21–46. Jackson: New Mississippi.

Hinsley, Curtis M., Jr. 1981. *Savages and Scientists: The Smithsonian Institution and the Development of American Anthropology 1846–1910*. Washington, D.C.: Smithsonian Institution Press.

———. 1990. "The World as Marketplace: Commodification of the Exotic at the World's Columbian Exposition, Chicago, 1893." In *Exhibiting Cultures: The Poetics and Politics of Museum Display,* ed. Ivan Karp and Steven D. Lavine, 344–65. Washington, D.C.: Smithsonian Institution Press.

Hulme, Peter. 1986. *Colonial Encounters: Europe and the Native Caribbean, 1492–1797.* London: Methuen.

———. 1996. *Rescuing Cuba: Adventure and Masculinity in the 1890s.* College Park, Md.: Latin American Studies Center.

———. 1997. "El encuentro con Anacaona: Frederick Albion Ober y el Caribe autóctono." *Op. Cit.: Revista del Centro de Investigaciones Históricas* 9: 75–109.

———. 2000. *Remnants of Conquest: The Caribs and Their Visitors, 1877–1998.* Oxford: Oxford University Press.

Iglesias, Fe. 1975. "La explotación del hierro en el sur de Oriente y la Spanish American Iron Company." *Santiago* 12 (March): 59–106.

Jaggi, Maya. 2004. "Island Memories." *Guardian* (London). Digital Edition. , November 20.

James, C.L.R. 1939. "The Negro Question." Typescript April 12, 1939. C.L.R. James Institute Document 4493.

———. 1969a. "Black Struggle in the Caribbean" (transcript of speech delivered September 7, 1969). C.L.R. James Institute Document 777.

———. 1969b [1938]. *A History of Negro Revolt.* New York: Haskell House.

———. 1977. "Down with Starvation Wages in South-East Missouri." In *The Future in the Present.* Vol. 1 of *Selected Writings,* 89–94. London: Allison and Busby.

———. 1978. "The Intelligence of the Negro." *From Trinidad: An Anthology of Early West Indian Writing,* ed. Reinhard Sander, 227–37. New York: Africana Publishing.

———. 1980a. "Discovering Literature in Trinidad: The 1930s." In *Spheres of Existence.* Vol. 2 of *Selected Writings,* 237–44. London: Allison and Busby.

———. 1980b. *Notes on Dialectics.* London: Allison and Busby.

———. 1984a. "Black Sansculottes." In *At the Rendezvous of Victory.* Vol. 3 of *Selected Writings,* 159–62. London: Allison and Busby.

———. 1984b. "Discussions with Trotsky." In *At the Rendezvous of Victory.* Vol. 3 of *Selected Writings,* 33–64. London: Allison and Busby.

———. 1984c. "George Padmore: Black Marxist Revolutionary." In *At the Rendezvous of Victory.* Vol. 3 of *Selected Writings,* 247–54. London: Allison and Busby.

———. 1989. *The Black Jacobins: Toussaint L'Ouverture and the San Domingo Revolution.* New York: Vintage.

———. 1993. *Beyond a Boundary.* Durham, N.C.: Duke University Press.

———. 1996a. "Paul Robeson: Black Star." In *C.L.R. James on the "The Negro Question,"* ed. Scott McLemee, 255–62. Jackson: University Press of Mississippi.

———. 1996b. "Preliminary Notes." In *C.L.R. James on the "The Negro Question,"* ed. Scott McLemee, 3–16. Jackson: University Press of Mississippi.

———. 1996c. "The Revolutionary Answer to the Negro Problem in the United States." In *C.L.R. James on the "Negro Question,"* ed. Scott McLemee, 138–47. Jackson: University Press of Mississippi.

———. 1996d. *Special Delivery: The Letters of C.L.R. James to Constance Webb, 1939–1948*. Ed. Anna Grimshaw. Cambridge: Blackwell.

———. 1996e. "With the Sharecroppers." In *C.L.R. James on the "The Negro Question,"* ed. Scott McLemee, 17–51. Jackson: University Press of Mississippi, 1996.

———. n.d. Unpublished Autobiography. C.L.R. James Institute Documents 770, 797, 805, 1020.

James, C.L.R., and Martin Glaberman. 1999. *Marxism for Our Times*. Jackson: University Press of Mississippi.

James, C.L.R., Grace C. Lee, and Pierre Chaulieu. 1974. *Facing Reality*. Detroit: Bewick.

Johnson, James Weldon. 1995. *The Autobiography of an Ex-Colored Man*. Mineola, N.Y.: Dover.

Kaplan, Amy. 1993. "Black and Blue on San Juan Hill." In *Cultures of United States Imperialism*, ed. Amy Kaplan and Donald E. Pease, 219–36. Durham, N.C.: Duke University Press.

———. 2004. "Violent Belongings and the Question of Empire Today." Presidential address to the American Studies Association, October 17, 2003. *American Quarterly* 56 (1): 1–18.

Kaplan, Caren. 2002. "Transporting the Subject: Technologies of Mobility and Location in an Era of Globalization." *PMLA* 117 (1) (January): 32–42.

Kelley, Robin D. G. 1996. "The World the Diaspora Made: C.L.R. James and the Politics of History." In *Rethinking C.L.R. James,* ed. Grant Farred, 103–30. Cambridge: Blackwell.

Kincaid, Jamaica. 1988. *A Small Place*. New York: Farrar, Straus, Giroux.

———. 1985. *Annie John*. New York: Farrar, Straus and Giroux.

———. 1990. *Lucy*. New York: Farrar, Straus and Giroux.

———. 1999. *My Brother*. New York: Farrar, Straus and Giroux.

King, Nicole. 2001. *C.L.R. James and Creolization: Circles of Influence*. Jackson: University Press of Mississippi.

Kristeva, Julia. 1982. *Powers of Horror: An Essay on Abjection*. Trans. Leon S. Roudiez. New York: Columbia University Press.

Küchler, Suzanne, and Walter Melion, eds. 1991. *Images of Memory: On Remembering and Representation*. Washington, D.C.: Smithsonian Institution Press.

Larsen, Neil. 1996. "Negativities of the Popular: C.L.R. James and Limits of 'Cultural Studies.'" In *Rethinking C.L.R. James,* ed. Grant Farred, 85–102. Cambridge: Blackwell.

Las Casas, Bartolomé. 1995. *Historia de las Indias*. Vol. 1. Mexico City: Fondo de Cultura Económica.

Lasserre, Guy. 1961. *La Guadeloupe: Etude géographique*. 2 vols. Bordeaux: Union Française d'Impression.

Lavaud, Michel. 2005. "Haïti: Fils de trois races et de combine de cultures." *Loxias* 9 (June 15). http://revel.unice.fr/loxias/sommaire.html?id=160.

Lawless, Robert, Vinson Sutlife Jr., and Mario D. Zamora, eds. 1983. *Fieldwork: The Human Experience*. New York: Gordon and Breach.

Lazarus, Emma. 1889. *The Poems of Emma Lazarus*. Boston: Houghton, Mifflin.

Lehman, Daniel W. 1997. *Matters of Fact: Reading Nonfiction over the Edge*. Columbus: Ohio State University Press.

Lehmann, Paul. 1979. "8,000 Haitians Need Political Asylum Now." *New York Times*, October 25, A19.

Lemebel, Pedro. 1997. *Loco afán: Crónicas de Sidario*. Santiago: LOM Ediciones.

Leys, Rejin. 2002. *Wherever There's Someone Fighting . . . 2002 Social Justice Calendar*. New York: Bread and Roses Cultural Project.

López, Consuelo. 1983. "C.L.R. James: The Rhetoric of a Defiant Warrior." Ph.D. diss., Indiana University.

López Torregrosa, Luisita. 2001. "Puerto Rican Art Moves Outward, and More Inward." *New York Times*, March 11.

Lubow, Arthur. 1992. *The Reporter Who Would Be King: A Biography of Richard Harding Davis*. New York: Charles Scribner's Sons.

Lucena, Manuel. 1988. *Descubrimiento de América, novus mundus*. Madrid: Grupo Anaya, S.A..

Lugo-Ortiz, Agnes I. 1995. "Community at Its Limits: Orality, Law, Silence, and the Homosexual Body in Luis Rafael Sánchez's '¡Jum!'" In *¿Entiendes? Queer Readings, Hispanic Writings*, ed. Emily L. Bergmann and Paul Julian Smith, 115–36. Durham, N.C.: Duke University Press.

Luis, William. 1989. "The Politics of Memory and Miguel Barnet's *The Autobiography of a Run Away Slave*." *Modern Language Notes* 104 (2) (March): 475–91.

Lynch, Barbara Deutsch. 1993. "The Garden and the Sea: U.S. Latino Environmental Discourses and Mainstream Environmentalism." *Social Problems* 40 (1): 108–24.

Mahan, Capt. A. T. 1897. *The Interest of America in Sea Power, Present and Future*. London: Sampson Low, Marston. .

Malabou, Catherine, and Jacques Derrida. 2004. *Counterpath: Traveling with Jacques Derrida*. Stanford, Calif.: Stanford University Press.

Marrero, Edna, Maritza Cruz, and Sandra Miranda de León. 2005. "Perfil epidemiológico para la prevención del VIH en Puerto Rico." *El Nuevo Día*, November 6. http://avert.org/aidslatinamerica.htm.

Martí, José. 1977. *Our America: Writings on Latin America and the Struggle for Cuban Independence*. Ed. Philip S. Foner. Trans. Elinor Randall. New York: Monthly Review Press.

———. 1992. *Obras Escogidas*. 3 vols. Havana: Editorial de Ciencias Sociales.

Martínez-San Miguel, Yolanda. 2003. *Caribe Two Ways: Cultura de la migración en el Caribe insular hispánico*. Río Piedras, P.R.: Ediciones Callejón.

Martorell, Antonio. 1997. "Artist's Statement." In *Memory and Mourning: Shared Cultural Experience* (group exhibition). http://www.albany.edu/museum/wwwmuseum/death/index.html.

McElvaine, Robert S., ed. 1983. *Down and Out in the Great Depression: Letters from the Forgotten Man*. Chapel Hill: University of North Carolina.

McLeod, Judi. 2005. "Bill Clinton's Affair with Voodoo." *Canada Free Press*, June 28.

Mederas, Octavio de. 1945. *Antología.* Madrid: n.p.

Melville, Elinor G. K. 1994. *A Plague of Sheep: Environmental Consequences of the Conquest of Mexico.* Cambridge: Cambridge University Press.

Mignolo, Walter. 2000. *Local Histories/Global Designs: Coloniality, Subaltern Knowledges, and Border Thinking.* Princeton, N.J.: Princeton University Press.

Migrants contre le SIDA. 1997. "Report: Puerto Rico 3rd in U.S. AIDS cases." http://www.hivnet.ch/migrants/news/1997/971018.html.

Mizejewski, Linda. 1999. *Ziegfeld Girl: Image and Icon in Culture and Cinema.* Durham, N.C.: Duke University Press.

Monsiváis, Carlos. 1988. *Escenas de pudor y liviandad.* Mexico City: Grijalbo.

Moore, Henrietta. 1999. "Anthropological Theory at the Turn of the Century." In *Anthropological Theory Today,* ed. Henrietta Moore, 1–23. Cambridge: Blackwell.

Moore, John H. 1994. "Putting Anthropology Back Together Again: The Ethnogenetic Critique of Cladistic Theory." *American Anthropologist* 96: 925–48.

Moreiras, Alberto. 1996. "The Aura of Testimonio." In *The Real Thing: Testimonial Discourse and Latin America,* ed. George M. Gugelberger, 192–24. Durham, N.C.: Duke University Press.

Morote Creus, Luis. 1908. *Sagasta. Melilla. Cuba.* Paris: Sociedad de Ediciones Literarias y Artísticas.

Morrisseau-Leroy, Felix. 1999. "Boat People." In *Libété: A Haitian Anthology.* Ed. Charles Arthur and Michael Dash. Kingston: Ian Randle.

Moscoso, Francisco. 1987. *Tribu y clase en el Caribe antiguo.* San Pedro de Macorís: Ediciones de la Universidad Central del Este.

Murray, Jim. 1996. "The Boy at the Window." In *Rethinking C.L.R. James,* ed. Grant Farred, 203–18. Cambridge: Blackwell.

———. n.d. Annotation of "Down with Starvation Wages in Southeastern Missouri." C.L.R. James Institute Document 2103.

Myers, Robert. 1986. "Island Carib Cannibalism." *New West Indian Guide* 60 (3–4).

Nary, Gordon. 1998. "Truth and Art in the New Age of AIDS." *Journal of the International Association of Physicians in AIDS Care* http://www.thebody.com/iapac/art.html.

Negrón-Muntaner, Frances. 2004. *Boricua Pop: Puerto Ricans and the Latinization of American Culture.* New York: New York University Press.

New Chronicle (Dominica). 1993. "Carib Council Puts Genome Programme on Hold." July 23.

North, Douglass C., and Robert P. Thomas. 1978. *El nacimiento del mundo occidental: Una nueva historia económica, 900–1700.* Madrid: Siglo XXI.

N'Zengo-Tayo, Marie-José. 1998. "Children in Haitian Popular Migration as Seen by Maryse Condé and Edwidge Danticat." In *Winds of Change: The Transforming Voices of Caribbean Women Writers and Scholars,* ed. Adele Newson and Linda Strong-Leek, 93–100. New York: Peter Lang.

Obejas, Achy. 2001. "Revolution Grown Old." *Chicago Tribune,* April 19.

Ober, Frederick A. 1879a. *Camps in the Caribbees: The Adventures of a Naturalist in the Lesser Antilles.* Boston: Lee and Shephard.

————. 1879b. "Ornithological Exploration of the Caribbee Islands." In *Annual Report of the Smithsonian Institution for 1878,* 446–51. Washington, D.C.: Government Printing Office.

————. 1893. *In the Wake of Columbus: Adventures of a Special Commissioner Sent by World's Columbian Exposition to the West Indies.* Boston: D. Lothrop Company.

————. 1897. *Under the Cuban Flag, or The Cacique's Treasure.* Boston: Estes and Lauriat.

————. 1901. *The Last of the Arawaks: A Story of Adventure on the Island of San Domingo.* Boston: W. A. Wilde.

Olivares, José de. 1899. *Our Islands and Their People as Seen with Camera and Pencil.* Ed. William S. Bryan. 2 vols. St. Louis: N. D. Thompson.

Olivart, Marquis de. 1898. "Le différend entre l'Espagne et les Etats-Unis au sujet de la question cubaine." *Revue Générale de Droit International Public* 5: 358–422.

Ortiz Fernández, Fernando. 1922. *Historia de arqueología indocubana.* Havana: Imprenta "El Siglo XX."

————. 1978 [1940]. *Contrapunteo del tabaco y del azúcar.* Caracas: Biblioteca Ayacucho.

————. 1993. *Etnia y sociedad.* Ed. Isaac Barreal. Havana: Editorial de Ciencias Sociales.

————. 1995. *Cuban Counterpoint: Tobacco and Sugar.* Trans. Harriet de Onís. Durham, N.C.: Duke University Press.

Pacini Hernández, Deborah. 1995. *Bachata: A Social History of a Dominican Popular Music.* Philadelphia: Temple University Press.

Paravisini-Gebert, Lizabeth. 2004. "Caribbean Literature in Spanish." In *The Cambridge History of African and Caribbean Literature,* ed. Abiola Irele and Simon Gikandi, 370–410. Cambridge: Cambridge University Press.

————. 2005a. "Enrique Laguerre: Obituary." *The Guardian* (London), July 1.

————. 2005b. "He of the Trees: Nature, Environment, and Creole Religiosities in Caribbean Literature." In *Caribbean Literature and the Environment,* ed. Elizabeth M. DeLoughrey, Renée K. Gosson, and George B. Handley, 182–98. Charlottesville: University Press of Virginia.

Parker, John H. 1898. *History of the Gatling Gun Detachment Fifth Army Corps, at Santiago.* Kansas City: Hudson-Kimberly Publishing Co.

Patterson, Thomas C. 1995. *Toward a Social History of Archaeology in the United States.* Fort Worth: Harcourt Brace College Publishers.

Pattullo, Polly. 2004. *Last Resorts: The Cost of Tourism in the Caribbean.* 2nd ed. New York: Monthly Review Press.

Peña Vargas, Ana C. 1987. *Lenguas indígenas e indigenismos: Italia e Iberoamérica.* Caracas: n.p.

Pérez, Lisandro. 1982. "Iron Mining and Socio-Demographic Change in Eastern Cuba, 1884–1940." *Journal of Latin American Studies* 14: 381–406.

Pérez, Louis A., Jr. 1983. *Cuba between Empires, 1878–1902.* Pittsburgh: University of Pittsburgh Press.

Pérez Fernández O. P., Isacio, ed. 1989. *Brevísima relación de la destrucción de África.* Salamanca: Editorial San Esteban, Instituto Bartolomé de las Casas.

Pérez Firmat, Gustavo. 1989. *The Cuban Condition: Translation and Identity in Modern Cuban Literature.* Cambridge: Cambridge University Press.

Phillips, William D. 1991. "The Old World Background of Slavery in the Americas." In *Slavery and the Rise of the Atlantic System,* ed. Barbara L. Solow, 43–61. Cambridge: Cambridge University Press.

Pichardo Moya, Felipe. 1945. *Los indios de Cuba en sus tiempos históricos.* Havana: Imprenta "El Siglo XX."

Porter, Robert P. 1899. *Industrial Cuba.* New York: G. P. Putnam's Sons.

Portes, Alejandro, and Ramón Grosfoguel. 1994. "Caribbean Diasporas: Migration and Ethnic Communities." *Annals of the American Academy of Political and Social Science* 533 (May): 48–69.

Posada, Joaquín de, ed. 1982. *Anuario de familias cubanas.* San Juan: Graficart.

Pospíšil, M. F. 1971. "Physical Anthropological Research on Indian Remnants in Eastern Cuba." *Current Anthropology* 12 (2): 229.

Poupeye, Veerle. 1998. *Caribbean Art.* London: Thames and Hudson.

Powell, Patricia. 1994. *A Small Gathering of Bones.* Boston: Beacon Press.

Prados-Torreira, Teresa. 2005. *Mambisas: Rebel Women in Nineteenth-Century Cuba.* Gainesville: University Press of Florida.

Prieto, Eric. 2005. "The Uses of Landscape: Ecocriticism and Martinican Cultural Theory." In *Caribbean Literature and the Environment: Between Nature and Culture,* ed. Elizabeth M. DeLoughrey, Renée K. Gosson, and George B. Handley, 236–46. Charlottesville: University Press of Virginia.

Pyne-Timothy, Helen. 1995. "Identity, Society, and Meaning: A Study of the Early Stories." In *C.L.R. James: His Intellectual Legacies,* ed. Selwyn R. Cudjoe and William E. Cain, 51–60. Amherst: University of Massachusetts Press.

Quintero Herencia, Juan Carlos. 1996. "La superioridad del isleño." *Diálogo* (September): 24.

Ramón y Rivera, Luis Felipe. 1980. "Dominican Republic." In *The New Grove Dictionary of Music and Musicians,* ed. Stanley Sadie, 5: 535–38. Washington, D.C.: Macmillan.

Ramos Pérez, D. 1982. *El conflicto de los lanzas jinetas.* Santo Domingo: Ediciones Fundación García-Arevalo, Inc.

Reutter, Mark. 2004. *Making Steel: Sparrows Point and the Rise and Ruin of American Industrial Might.* Urbana: University of Illinois Press.

Richards, Glen. 1995. "C.L.R. James on Black Self-Determination in the United States and the Caribbean." In *C.L.R. James: His Intellectual Legacies,* ed. Selwyn R. Cudjoe and William E. Cain, 317–27. Amherst: University of Massachusetts Press.

Richardson, Al, Clarence Chrysostom, and Anna Grimshaw. "C.L.R. James and British Trotskyism." Revolutionary History web site, http://www.revolutionary-history.co.uk.

Rivera-Pagán, Luis N. 1990. *Evangelización y violencia: La conquista de América.* San Juan: Ediciones Cemí.

Rivero de la Calle, Manuel. 1973. "Los indios cubanos de Yateras." *Santiago* 10: 151–74.

———. 1978. *Cuba arqueológica.* Santiago: Editorial Oriente.

Roach, Joseph. 2006. *Cities of the Dead: Circum-Atlantic Performance.* New York: Columbia University Press.

Robinson, Cedric J. 1983. *Black Marxism: The Making of the Black Radical Tradition.* London: Zed.

Roderick, Rick. 1995. "Further Adventures in the Dialectic." In *C.L.R. James: His Intellectual Legacies,* ed. Selwyn R. Cudjoe and William E. Cain, 205–11. Amherst: University of Massachusetts Press.

Rodowick, D. N. 2002. "Introduction: Mobile Citizens, Media States." *PMLA* 117 (1) (January): 13–23.

Rodríguez Juliá, Edgardo. 2005. *San Juan, ciudad soñada.* Madison: University of Wisconsin Press.

Roosevelt, Theodore. 1900. *The Winning of the West.* 6 vols. New York: G. P. Putnam's Sons.

———. 1951. *The Letters of Theodore Roosevelt.* Ed. Elting E. Morison. Cambridge, Mass.: Harvard University Press.

———. 1990 [1902]. *The Rough Riders.* New York: Da Capo Press.

Ross, Andrew. 1996. "Civilization in One Country? The American James." In *Rethinking C.L.R. James,* ed. Grant Farred, 75–84. Oxford: Basil Blackwell.

Roumain, Jacques. 1997. *Masters of the Dew.* Trans. Langston Hughes and Mercer Cook. Oxford: Heinemann.

Rouse, Irving. 1942. *Archaeology of the Maniabón Hills, Cuba.* Yale University Publications in Anthropology 26. New Haven, Conn.: Yale University Press.

———. Forthcoming. "History of Archaeology in the Caribbean Area." In *The History of Archaeology: An Encyclopedia,* ed. Tim Murray. New York: Garland.

Ruth, Joel A. 1998. "Voodoo and Clinton's Fate: Haitian Sorcerers Claim Credit for His Victories and Defeats." WorldNetDaily.com, December 14.

Rutherford, Blair. 2003. Review of *Africanizing Anthropology: Fieldwork, Networks, and the Making of Cultural Knowledge in Central Africa* by Lyn Schumaker. *Canadian Review of Sociology and Anthropology* 40 (3) (August): 370–73.

Ryan, Lyndall. 1981. *The Aboriginal Tasmanians.* St. Lucia: University of Queensland Press.

Saco, José Antonio. 1974. *Historia de la esclavitud.* Gijón: Ediciones Júcar.

Sander, Reinhard. 1978. *From Trinidad: An Anthology of Early West Indian Writing.* New York: Africana Publishing.

Saxton, Alexander. 1990. *The Rise and Fall of the White Republic: Class Politics and Mass Culture in Nineteenth-Century America.* London: Verso.

Scarry, Elaine. 1985. *The Body in Pain: The Making and Unmaking of the World.* London: Oxford University Press.

Schulman, Ivan A. 1992. "Social Exorcisms: Cuba's (Post)Colonial (Counter)Discourses." *Hispania* 75: 941–49.

Schwartz, Stuart B. 1985. *Sugar Plantations in the Formation of Brazilian Society, 1550–1835.* Cambridge: Cambridge University Press.

Sklodowska, Elzbieta. 1977. "Uncharted Territories: Space and Memory in *Rachel's Song* by Miguel Barnet." *Journal of Narrative Technique* 27 (1): 113–27.

———. 2002. "Author-(dys)function: Rereading *I, Riboberta Menchú.*" In *Foucault and Latin America: Appropriations and Deployments of Discoursive Analysis,* ed. Benigno Trigo, 197–207. New York: Routledge.

Slotkin, Richard. 1994. "Buffalo Bill's 'Wild West' and the Mythologization of the American Empire." In *Cultures of United States Imperialism,* ed. Amy Kaplan and Donald E. Pease, 164–84. Durham, N.C.: Duke University Press.

Spivak, Gayatri Chakravorty. 1988. "Subaltern Studies: Deconstructing Historiography." In *Selected Subaltern Studies,* ed. Ranajit Guha and Gayatri Chakravorty Spivak, 3–32. New York: Oxford University Press.

St. Louis, Brett. 1998. "Mapping Spontaneity: C.L.R. James in America." Paper delivered at the American Studies Association meeting. Seattle. November 19–22.

Stafford, Fiona J. 1994. *The Last of the Race: The Growth of a Myth from Milton to Darwin.* Oxford: Clarendon Press.

Sued Badillo, Jalil. 1978. *Los Caribes: Realidad o fábula.* Río Piedras: Editorial Antillana.

———. 1992. "Facing up to Caribbean History." *American Antiquity* 57 (44): 599–607.

———. 1995. "The Theme of the Indigenous in the National Projects of the Hispanic Caribbean." In *Making Alternative Histories: The Practice of Archaeology and History in Non-Western Settings,* ed. Peter R. Schmidt and Thomas C. Patterson, 25–46. Santa Fe: School of American Research Press.

Sweig, Julia. 2006. "The Dark Stain of Guantanamo." *Baltimore Sun,* June 8.

Tabío, Ernesto, and Estrella Rey. 1985. *Prehistoria de Cuba.* Havana: Editorial de Ciencias Sociales.

Taibo I, Paco Ignacio. 1985. *María Félix: 47 pasos por el cine.* Mexico City: Joaquín Mortiz/Planeta.

Thomas, Hugh. 1971. *Cuba: The Pursuit of Freedom.* New York: Harper and Row.

Thomas, Nicholas. 1994. *Colonialism's Culture: Anthropology, Travel, and Government.* Princeton, N.J.: Princeton University Press.

Trask, David F. 1981. *The War with Spain in 1898.* New York: Macmillan.

Turner, Lou. 1995. "Epistemology, Absolutes, and the Party: Critical Examination of Philosophic Divergences within the Johnson-Forrest Tendency, 1948–1953." In *C.L.R. James: His Intellectual Legacies,* ed. Selwyn R. Cudjoe and William E. Cain, 193–204. Amherst: University of Massachusetts Press.

Tylor, E. B. 1871. *Primitive Culture: Researches into the Development of Mythology, Philosophy, Religion, Language, Art, and Custom.* London: John Murray.

"Ubi Sunt." 2003. Encyclopædia Britannica Premium Service. http://www.britannica.com/needmore.

UN/AIDS Epidemic Update. 2005. http://www.unaids.org/epi/2005/doc/EPIupdate2005_htmlen/epi05_08_en.htm.

United States Adjutant-General's Office. 1993. *Correspondence Relating to the War with*

Spain, April 15, 1898, to July 30, 1902. Washington, D.C.: Center of Military History United States Army.

United States Army, Department of Santiago and Puerto Príncipe. 1899. *Special Report on Insular Affairs of the Provinces of Santiago and Puerto Príncipe, Cuba.* Submitted by Brigadier-General Leonard Wood, U.S.V. Washington, D.C.: Government Printing Office.

Utley, Robert M. 1962. *Custer and the Great Controversy: The Origin and Development of a Legend.* Los Angeles: Westernlore Press.

Varela, Consuelo. 1982. *Cristóbal Colón: Textos y documentos completos.* Madrid: Alianza Universidad.

———. 1988. *Colón y los florentinos.* Madrid: Alianza América.

Vargas-Irenas, Iraida. 1996. "La arqueología social: Un paradigma alternativo al angloamericano." *El Caribe Arqueológico* 1: 3–7.

Vázquez, Víctor. 1991. *El reino de la espera.* San Juan: Galería Latino Americana.

Vega, Ana Lydia. 1982. "La alambrada." In *Encancaranublado y otros cuentos de naufragios,* 49–51. Havana: Casa de las Américas.

———. 1989. "Cloud Cover Caribbean." In *Her True-True Name,* ed. Pamela Mordecai and Betty Wilson, 105–11. London: Heinemann.

Viglucci, Andres. 1993. "500 March, Call for Haitian Equality." *Miami Herald,* February 5:2B.

Vitier, Cintio. 1970. *Lo cubano en la poesía.* Havana: Instituto del Libro.

Walcott, Derek. 1998. "The Antilles: Fragments of Epic Memory." In *What the Twilight Says: Essays.* New York: Farrar, Straus and Giroux.

———. 2005. *The Prodigal.* London: Faber and Faber.

Wall, Angela. 1997. "Conflicts in AIDS Discourse: Foucault, Surgeon Generals, and the [Gay Men's] Healthcare Crisis." In *Bodily Discursions: Genders, Representations, Technologies,* ed. Deborah S. Wilson and Christine Moneera Laennec, 221–39. Albany: State University of New York Press, 1997.

Walter, Monica. 2000. "Testimonio y melodrama: En torno a un debate actual sobre *Biografía de un cimarrón* y sus consecuencias posibles." In *Todas las islas la isla: Nuevas y novísimas tendencies en la literatura y cultura de Cuba,* ed. Janett Reinstadler and Ette Omar, 25–38. Frankfurt: Vervuet-Iberoamericana.

White, Hayden. 1973. *Metahistory: The Historical Imagination in Nineteenth-Century Europe.* Baltimore: Johns Hopkins University Press.

White, Richard. 1999. "The Nationalization of Nature." *Journal of American History* 86 (3): 976–86.

Whitehead, Neil L. 1984. "Carib Cannibalism: The Historical Evidence." *Journal de la société des américanistes* (Paris) 70 (1): 69–88.

———, ed. 1995. *Wolves from the Sea: Readings in the Anthropology of the Native Caribbean.* Leiden: KITLV Press.

Wilkie, Tom. 1993. *Perilous Knowledge: The Human Genome Project and Its Implications.* Berkeley: University of California Press.

Wilson, Deborah S., and Christine Moneera Laennec, eds. 1997. *Bodily Discursions: Genders, Representations, Technologies.* Albany: State University of New York Press.

Wisan, Joseph E. 1965 [1934]. *The Cuban Crisis as Reflected in the New York Press.* New York: Octagon Books.

Wright, Irene A. 1910. *Cuba.* New York: Macmillan.

Worcester, Kent. 1996. *C.L.R. James: A Political Biography.* Albany: State University of New York Press.

Wynter, Silvia. 1971. "Novel and History, Plot and Plantation." *Savacou* 5: 95–102.

Yaremko, Jason M. 2006. "*Gente bárbara*: Indigenous Rebellion, Resistance, and Persistence in Colonial Cuba, c. 1500–1800." *KACIKE: The Journal of Caribbean Amerindian History and Anthropology* (on-line journal). Available at http://www.kacike.org/Yaremko.html [17.1.2007].

Zahareas, Anthony N. 1988. "The Historical Function of Picaresque Biographies: Toward a History of Social Offenders." In *Autobiography in Early Modern Spain,* ed. Nicholas Spadaccini and Jenaro Talens, 129–72. Minneapolis: Prisma Institute.

Sound Recordings

Conjunto Quisqueya. 1994. "Los limones." In *Super Éxitos del Conjunto Quisqueya.* Aponte (Santurce).

Díaz, Ramón. 1985. "El barbarazo." In *Los años dorados.* Karen Publishing Company (Miami).

Guerra, Juan Luis, et al. 1990a. "Ojalá que llueva café en el campo." In *Ojalá que llueva café en el campo.* Distribuidora de Discos Karen (Santo Domingo).

———. 1990b. "Visa para un sueño." In *Ojalá que llueva café en el campo.* Distribuidora de Discos Karen (Santo Domingo).

Milanés, Pablo. 2000. "Éxodo." In *Los días de Gloria.* Universal Music (Mexico).

Ochoa, Calixto. 1985. "El africano." In *Los años dorados.* Karen Publishing Company (Miami).

Rodríguez, Felipe. 1996. "La cama vacía." In *La cama vacía.* Spanoramic Records (New York).

Rodríguez, Silvio. 1974. "Pequeña serenata diurna." In *Días y flores.* EGREM (Havana).

———. 1984. "Llover sobre mojado." In *Tríptico.* Discos Fuentes (Colombia).

Valoy, Cuco. 1996. "El venao." In *Los grandes del merengue super mix.* Karen Publishing Company (Miami).

Varela, Carlos. 1992. "Círculo de tiza." In *Monedas al aire.* MSI Music (Miami Lakes, Florida).

———. 1994a. "Foto de familia." In *Como los peces.* RCA Internacional (New York).

———. 1994b. "La política no cabe en la azucarera." In *Como los peces.* RCA Internacional (New York).

Contributors

Michael Aronna is an associate professor of Hispanic studies and Latin American and Latino(a) studies at Vassar College. He is the coeditor of *The Postmodernism Debate in Latin America* (1995) and the author of *"Pueblos Enfermos": The Discourse of Illness in the Turn-of-the-Century Spanish and Latin American Essay* (1999).

Antonio Benítez Rojo (1931–2005) was the Thomas B. Walton, Jr. Memorial Professor of Spanish at Amherst College. Although he is best known for his critical study *The Repeating Island: The Caribbean and the Postmodern Perspective* (1989), he published numerous works of critical scholarship and fiction, including the short story collection *Tute de reyes* (King's flush) for which he won Cuba's major literary award, the Casa de las Américas Prize, in 1967. Among his works that have been translated into English are *Sea of Lentils* (1985), *The Magic Dog and Other Stories* (1990), and *A View from the Mangrove* (1998).

Peter Hulme is professor of literature at the University of Essex. He is one of the central figures in postcolonial studies, whose book *Colonial Encounters* helped define the field. His most recent books are *Remnants of Conquest: The Caribs and Their Visitors, 1877–1998, The Cambridge Companion to Travel Writing* (ed. with Tim Youngs), and the *Norton Critical Edition of "The Tempest"* (ed. with William H. Sherman). His current research focuses on travel writing, Caribbean literature, and postcolonial studies.

Martha Kelehan, who received her master's in library science from the University of California at Los Angeles, is a research librarian at Binghamton University. She also has an M.A. degree in Latin American and Caribbean studies from Tulane University; her thesis compared the nationalist art movements of Haiti, Cuba, and Trinidad and Tobago between the two world wars.

Yolanda Martínez San Miguel is an associate professor of romance languages and literatures at the University of Pennsylvania. Her research focuses on Latin(o) American literature, particularly in colonial, Hispanic Caribbean, and Latino narrative and poetry. She has published two books, *Saberes americanos: Subalternidad y epistemología en los escritos de Sor Juana* (1999) and *Caribe Two Ways: Cultura de la migración en el Caribe insular hispánico* (2003) as well as a compilation of essays, coedited with Mabel Moraña, *Nictimene . . . sacrílega: Estudios coloniales en homenaje a Georgina Sabat-Rivers* (2003).

Kevin Meehan is an associate professor of English at the University of Central Florida. His research focuses on African American and Caribbean cultural studies, multiethnic U.S. literature, and the links between literature and educational development. He has published numerous reviews, scholarly essays, and book chapters, including "Decolonizing Ethnography: Zora Neale Hurston in the Caribbean" in *Women at Sea: Travel Writing and the Margins of Caribbean Discourse* (2001) and "'Titid ak pép-la se marasa': Jean-Bertrand Aristide and the New National Romance in Haiti" in *Caribbean Romances: The Politics of Regional Representation* (1999).

Lizabeth Paravisini-Gebert is the Randolph Distinguished Professor of Caribbean studies at Vassar College. She is the author of *Phyllis Shand Allfrey: A Caribbean Life* (1996), *Jamaica Kincaid: A Critical Companion* (1999), and *Creole Religions of the Caribbean: An Introduction* (with Margarite Fernández Olmos, 2003), among other books. Her coedited volumes include *Green Cane and Juicy Flotsam: Short Stories by Caribbean Women* (1991), *Sacred Possessions: Vodou, Santería, Obeah, and the Caribbean* (1997), and *Healing Cultures: Art and Religion as Curative Practices in the Caribbean* (2001). She has published numerous articles and book chapters.

Ivette Romero-Cesareo is an associate professor of modern languages and cultures at Marist College. She is the coeditor of *Women at Sea: Travel Writing and the Margins of Caribbean Discourse* (2001). Her numerous essays on Caribbean women, art, and literature have appeared in various journals and edited volumes. She is completing a book, *AIDS and Representation in Caribbean Literature and Art,* and is at work on *The Beauty of the Guajana: An Eco-Critical History of Puerto Rican Literature* (with Lizabeth Paravisini-Gebert).

Jalil Sued-Badillo is a professor and the chairperson of the General Social Sciences Department (Interdisciplinary Studies) at the University of Puerto Rico in Río Piedras. He is a leading ethnohistorian whose scholarship and teaching focus on early Puerto Rican and Caribbean history. His numerous books include *La mujer indígena y su sociedad* (1975), now in its fourth edition, *La pena de muerte en Puerto Rico* (2000), and *El Dorado Borincano* (2001), as well as edited works such as *General History of the Caribbean, Volume 1: Autochthonous Societies* (2003).

Index